D0350020

658 S 2010
Sobel, Milo.
MBA In A Nutshell /

VICTORVILLE CITY LIBRARY
15011 Circle Dr
Victorville, CA 92395
760-245-4222

MBA IN A NUTSHELL®

DR. MILO SOBEL

New York   Chicago   San Francisco   Lisbon   London
Madrid   Mexico City   Milan   New Delhi   San Juan
Seoul   Singapore   Sydney   Toronto

The *McGraw·Hill* Companies

1 2 3 4 5 6 7 8 9 0   WFR/WFR   1 5 4 3 2 1 0

ISBN   978-0-07-170172-3
MHID   0-07-170172-9

McGraw-Hill books are available at special quantity discounts to use as premiums and sales promotions, or for use in corporate training programs. To contact a representative, please e-mail us at bulksales@mcgraw-hill.com.

This book is printed on acid-free paper.

Library of Congress Cataloging-in-Publication Data

Sobel, Milo.
    MBA in a nutshell : master the key concepts taught at top business schools / Milo Sobel.
        p. cm.
    Includes bibliographical references and index.
    ISBN-13: 978-0-07-170172-3 (alk. paper)
    ISBN-10: 0-07-170172-9 (alk. paper)
1. Industrial management.   2. Management.   I. Title.
    HD30.3.S633 2010
    658—dc22

                                                            2009034196

This book is dedicated to my parents,

Fay and Henry L. Sobel, MBAs

(My Beloved Allies)

CONTENTS

ACKNOWLEDGMENTS

I wish to express my deep gratitude to the following individuals for their sage counsel and their contributions to this book:

From Academia:

Dr. Robert L. Cram, Professor of Education, Columbia University (Teachers College); Dr. I. Robert Parket, Professor of Marketing, City University of New York (Baruch College); and Dr. Howard N. Ross, Professor of Economics and Finance and Academic Director of the Executive MBA Program, City University of New York (Baruch College).

From Industry:

Ms. Ayda Akbelen, Vice President of Career Services, Citicorp; Ms. Gloria Gordon, Vice President of Technology Management, Xerox Corporation; Dr. Howard S. Mase, Vice President of Human Resources, Metropolitan Life Insurance Company; and Mr. Gary M. Zelamsky, Vice President of Operations, Viacom Cable.

From McGraw-Hill:

Philip Ruppel for his vision and commitment; my editor, Michele Wells, for her invaluable insights; and my developmental editor, Fiona Sarne.

From the New York Institute of Finance:

Mr. Robert W. Gulick, President; Mr. William A. Rini, Senior Vice President; and Ms. Eunice Salton, Vice President, for their encouragement and cooperation.

From the Securities Operations Forum:

Ms. Susan Solomon, Vice President, for championing my cause in the early hours.

From My Personal Support Team:

M. William Krasilovsky, Esq., legal eagle, for his advice, ethical and jurisprudential. But most important ... Judith Joseph Sobel, my beloved wife, for always being there for me, through thick and thin.

PROLOGUE: ORIENTATION TO THE PROGRAM

In 1986, I created *MBA in a Nutshell*, an educational program designed to impart the distilled essence of the MBA curriculum in just two days. The program has since been presented for major corporations and in public seminars from coast to coast throughout the United States and Canada. The course was inspired by two seemingly unrelated influences: the accelerated pace of learning employed by the U.S. military's Officer Candidate School (which was created to transform enlisted personnel into officers within a 90-day time frame, rather than the four years required by West Point and Annapolis) and by the anecdotal reports of MBA alumni that less than 10 percent of their graduate business school curriculum is actually necessary and useful in their careers. *MBA in a Nutshell* promises to deliver what you really need to know, in as little of your valuable time as possible. This book is the direct result of that program.

MBA in a Nutshell proximately mirrors a "real" MBA course of study. It covers pretty much the same functional disciplines and objectives. (Some B-schools regard "entrepreneurship" as a separate discipline. I regard the topic as an amalgam of all other disciplines.)

Marketing and Product Management	Develop new products and manage their growth.
Accounting	Understand key accounting principles and tax reduction methods.
Finance	Interpret financial statements and make savvy decisions.
Human Resources Management	Motivate your subordinates and peers, thereby increasing productivity.

Operations Management	Use decision-making formulas for optimization of resources.
Statistics	Grasp and use quantitative data to your full advantage.
Economics	Apply economic theory to everyday business situations.
Technology Management	Learn sophisticated applications of old and new technologies.
Business Policy and Ethics	Gain the framework from which to formulate ethical decisions.
Strategic Planning	Establish objectives, strategies, and plans for the future.

As you can see, the major concepts and techniques taught in B-schools are taught here as well. Of course, you will learn the "textbook stuff" that you would otherwise be exposed to in an academic setting. However, you will not have to suffer through complicated formulas. They are presented to you in a step-by-step manner that is very easy to understand. You will not even need to use a calculator. Just follow the instructions.

MBA in a Nutshell may not seem as thorough as the credential alternative. For example, the inherent time constraint precludes the use of in-depth case studies. It does, however, deliver three major benefits that few MBA programs offer:

1. The emphasis in this book is on practical and utilitarian applications rather than on the abstruse matter that a student may learn in order to pass an exam and soon forget because it has little or no meaning in everyday business life. In configuring this program, I asked myself: "What are the 'special tips' and 'guerrilla tactics' that I would share with a younger brother or sister?" Such otherwise "off-the-record" advice is included in this book.

2. The chapter on education and career pathing (not an academic subject in the MBA curriculum) can serve as a guide to help you ascertain whether you really need the MBA degree or whether

other degreed or nondegreed alternatives would be viable for your purposes.

3. There is a hidden "psychological agenda." Upon completion of reading *MBA in a Nutshell*, you will have a solid grounding in key concepts, techniques, and the terminology or jargon used by MBAs. Equally important, though, will be your sense of greatly increased confidence in your own new capabilities and enhanced ability to thrive in the business world, whether your goal is to function more effectively in an organizational environment and to climb the corporate ladder, or to launch and operate a business enterprise of your own successfully. Since you will be operating on a level of competence and sophistication that is roughly equivalent in functional terms to that of MBAs, you certainly will have no cause to be intimidated by them.

The MBA "Secrets of Life"

Over the past 15 years, I have experimented with modifications in the curriculum and fine-tuned the program accordingly. To obtain the greatest possible benefit from this book, the following ground rules are strongly suggested:

1. Sit on a firm upright chair and use a desktop. Be sure there is adequate lighting. If possible, avoid telephone calls and similar interruptions.

2. Read the book in sequence and in its entirety. Do not skim or even glance ahead. The content is *gestalt* in nature. In other words, the whole is greater than the sum of its parts. (In fact, my students often report a residual effect or delayed reaction to this learning experience, such that certain ideas become clear or hit them after completion of the curriculum.)

3. Take a 5- or 10-minute break on the hour. Research in the adult learning process indicates that many students suffer loss of concentration without brief rest periods. Try to complete at least one chapter per study session.

4. At the end of each chapter, reflect and ask yourself:
   a. How might I apply what I have just learned to my job or to my business?
   b. How might this relate to what I learned in the other chapters?
   c. What have I learned about how much I really know or don't know about the subject?
5. Be confident about your ability to turn the reading of this book into a rich learning experience. *No previous business knowledge is required.* The ability to read and to understand basic arithmetic functions will suffice.
6. Relax and enjoy.

Many MBAs would like you to believe that the study of business is extremely complex and difficult, almost surely beyond the comprehension of mere mortals. Although I very much appreciate all that I learned while studying for my MBA, I find this attitude arrogant, offensive, and totally unwarranted. In fact, some of the best and most successful businesspeople I have come to know over the years lack higher education and an MBA. These executives ... and millionaires ... seem to have learned intuitively what others are taught in business school. And that can be boiled down to the following verities:

The successful operation of a business enterprise requires a *triple focus*, involving constant attentiveness to *the customer, the product,* and *the employee* (see Figure P.1). After all, without the satisfied customer, there is no sale and, ultimately, no business. Similarly, we need the product (or service) to be of high quality or fair value to satisfy the customer's needs. And, of course, we need the employee who is well-trained and properly motivated to facilitate delivery of the product in order to satisfy the customer's needs.

Figure P.1 Triple focus of the successful business enterprise

Toward this end, it can be said that the most sophisticated and prosperous organizations are those that are marketing driven, that is, dedicated to customer satisfaction; financially oriented, that is, geared toward positive cash flow, creative and flexible in their funding and profitability; information and technology friendly, that is, embracing the state of the art in information resources and technology, telecommunications, and other areas; and human resources sensitive, that is, hiring properly, developing and motivating employees (see Figure P.2). Of course, the functional disciplines must be integrated. After all, marketing, finance, information and technology management, and human resources management should not operate in a vacuum, independent of one another. They must be strategically planned and managed, as well, not unlike the role of an orchestra's conductor.

Figure.P.2 Multidisciplinary and interdepartmental approach of the successful business enterprise

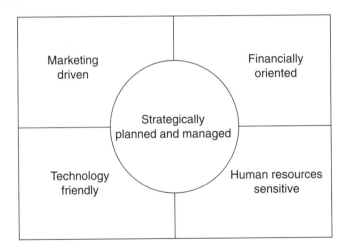

The aim of the MBA curriculum is to develop the skills necessary to plan and manage the various business disciplines. These different sets of skills fall into three categories: hard skills, soft skills, and what I refer to as "quali-quant" skills:

1. *Hard skills* involve quantitative or mathematical formulas. These enable us to succeed in a range of activities, including analyzing

financial statements, improving cash flow, reducing tax liability, evaluating investment options, forecasting profits as well as the time horizons and completion dates of projects, utilizing material and human resources efficiently, pricing, and employing statistical data to arrive at the best possible decisions—and for political advantage.

2. *Soft skills* are qualitative or conceptual. These enable us to succeed in understanding and satisfying the customer in terms of developing the product, advertising and otherwise promoting the product efficiently, and (ultimately) facilitating its purchase. Drawing heavily upon the social sciences, soft skills also help us to succeed in understanding and satisfying the employee in terms of motivation, as well as management style and personality differences.

3. *Quali-quant skills* (sometimes referred to as "Bayesian methods") are an amalgam of formulas and concepts designed to transform soft or subjective information (i.e., estimates) into a harder, more objective, and, ostensibly, more reliable, form. Applications span the functional areas of the business environment.

The program has been instructionally designed so that the reader will be alternating between hard and soft skills throughout the program, with most of the quali-quant skills incorporated into Chapters 3 and 8.

MBAs don't want you to know what I am about to share with you. They prefer that you think that the stuff that MBAs learn is so complex and so difficult to understand that only brain surgeons and rocket scientists ... and MBAs ... can comprehend it.

Well, that is just not so. The simple truth that governs all business, no matter what kind, ultimately boils down to this easy formula:

Revenues (all monies and items of value received by the organization, generally through sales)

minus

Costs (all money and items of value paid by the organization in order to run the organization)

equals

Operating income (the profit your organization earns, before taxes and interest on loans).

Operating income

minus

Taxes and interest expenses

equals

Net income (the profit your organization gets to keep, commonly known as "the bottom line").

Business becomes more profitable by:

- Increasing revenues
- Reducing costs (A funny Samuel Goldwyn quote: "Spare no expense ... to save money.")
- A combination of both

Off the top of my head, just to illustrate the point: A restaurant manager might increase revenues by training her waiters and waitresses to:

1. Gently coax patrons to have a glass of wine or a cocktail with their meal. "It aids digestion." (Keep in mind that alcoholic beverages offer high profit margins.)
2. For dessert, ask: "Will that be apple or cherry pie, sir?" rather than "Would you care for dessert, sir?" (The latter question is less likely to produce an order for dessert, because it makes "No" a more likely response.)
3. "Remind" the customer that, having just asked for coffee to accompany the pie dessert he just ordered, "freshly brewed" cappuccino is also available. "Would you prefer that instead, sir?" (Cappuccino offers much higher profit margins than regular coffee.)

The same restaurant manager might reduce costs by:

1. Serving soft drinks from the fountain or beverages that are self-mixed (i.e., iced tea) rather than by the bottle or can, which are usually rather more expensive.
2. Reconfiguring the menu to lean more toward items that are less expensive, less perishable, and associated with high profit margins (i.e., pasta dishes and omelets), rather than items that are not.
3. Minimizing waste by, for example, serving fewer rolls in each basket of bread, requiring customers to request a refill, which would (of course) be gladly served.

Growth is further accomplished by:

- Selling more of our established and existing (old) products to current (old) customers.
- Selling more of our established and existing (new) products to current (old) customers.
- Introducing (new) products to prospective (new) customers.
- Introducing (old) products to prospective (new) customers.

The single caveat regarding ways to increase revenues and reduce costs is that the manager must be mindful not to let quality slip in the process. The questionable story is told of the man in the sausage business who decides that he would cut costs by adding 10-percent grain "filler" to what had previously been an all-beef sausage. He got away with that, so he grew bolder and increased the filler amount to 20 percent. And before he truly realized it, his greed caused him to make a sausage that was mostly filler and had little beef in it. As a result, his business suffered irreparably. In today's unforgiving business environment, I doubt that a manufacturer could get away with even a 5-percent filler strategy. Probably not in the short run, and certainly not in the long run.

You don't need an MBA degree to understand this simple stuff. What an MBA curriculum can do, however, is sensitize you to the cardinal importance of it and introduce you to various sophisticated techniques and methods to orient your decision making toward more effective generation of revenues and reduction of costs.

And, in all fairness, if MBA programs were the panacea that some people think they are, wouldn't *everybody* who has an MBA be fabulously rich and successful? Well, as I think you will come to realize, even the best of MBA programs can do only so much. Business is so many parts science and so many parts art.

Some people learn what they know in business schools, while others learn from real life experience. In fact, some of my former students were quite familiar with most of the MBA material that was presented in the program, but they didn't know the names of the various concepts and techniques, and they hadn't integrated the material so that important interrelationships didn't even occur to them in the past.

As you proceed through *MBA in a Nutshell*, I suggest that you periodically ask yourself: How much of this stuff is art and how much is science? How much of this stuff did I "sort of" know, but didn't have the business vocabulary "lingua franca" (common language) to describe? How many *seemingly unrelated* things are actually *very much related* to each other?

I suspect that, by the time you complete *MBA in a Nutshell*, your perspective may change quite a bit.

1   MARKETING AND PRODUCT MANAGEMENT

Marketing involves those activities necessary for the planning and delivery of products or services from the producer (or performer) to the customer, to satisfy the customer and to meet the organization's objectives. These activities ultimately support the sales function (and profitability) and include:

- Product development
- Market research (including forecasting)
- Advertising
- Public relations (product publicity)
- Sales promotion
- Customer service

Differing Schools of Thought

Certainly, there may be ideological differences between departments within an organization and often between members of the same department as well. In fact, some individuals may claim to subscribe to a particular school of thought without truly understanding the implications of their positions. As this pertains to the marketing discipline, there are basically four ideological "camps": the product concept, the selling concept, the marketing concept, and the societal marketing concept.

The Product Concept

Ralph Waldo Emerson wrote, "Build a better mousetrap and the world will beat a path to your door." This concept—the *product concept*—suggests that the integrity of the product supersedes all other considerations and that quality alone determines the fate of the product. Therefore, no substantive marketing effort is required. A critical flaw in this approach is that potential customers may not even be aware of the product's existence, much less be able to evaluate it for purchase.

Another shortcoming is that "quality" may be subjective, differing from one individual to the next. (Surely, you've heard the saying, "One man's meat is another man's poison.") Those who subscribe to the product concept are often of the "techie" persuasion, with a background (or responsibility) in engineering, production, and operations management or a similar area.

The Selling Concept

The *selling concept* is predicated upon the notion that consumers will not make purchases in the absence of strong selling and promotional efforts. The negative stereotype of the automobile salesperson comes to mind in this regard. This individual has little concern for the consumer's well-being once the sale has been made. As a result, purchasers tend not to return. Surprisingly (or perhaps not), this doesn't bother the salesperson, since there are "a lot of fish in the sea." A major limitation of this position is that it greatly underestimates the cost of losing a customer and wrongly assumes that there is an infinite universe of potential customers from which to draw.

"Shirtsleeves" salespeople with little exposure to other influences within the marketing function may be prone to this mindset.

The financial people within their organizations, those who set or at least influence the setting of sales quotas, may also embrace the selling concept, in that they may, intentionally or otherwise, directly or indirectly, be pressuring the sales force to generate short-term profits at the expense of longer-term customer satisfaction.

The Marketing Concept

The *marketing concept* reflects the so-called "classical training" that MBAs receive. It is based upon the premise that the company must conduct research to learn what the customer wants. Having done so, the *marketing mix* or four Ps—*product, price, place* (channels of distribution), and *promotion*—are adjusted so that the customer will buy the product and use it with a high level of satisfaction. This approach complements the product concept, communicating the attributes of "the better mousetrap," and rather than assume that "the world will automatically beat a path to your door," makes that path to the company's door as attractive and easy to reach as possible. The marketing concept also tends to emphasize relationship-building, since (as we will learn later on) a company's future and long-term profitability ultimately depend upon satisfying the customer, not only initially, but repeatedly over time.

Marketing-oriented organizations such as Procter & Gamble (P&G) liberally employ "800" toll-free telephone numbers to address any concerns that customers might have. This is not as altruistic as it might seem. After all, the information that the company receives from the resulting telephone calls is, essentially, valuable and free market research.

If, for example, a sizable number of customers were to call and complain that they had found the corners of the Ivory soap bars they had purchased to be chipped, the company's product management team would almost certainly remedy the problem, perhaps by repackaging the product for greater protection. Moreover, P&G also unconditionally guarantees its products and offers refunds or exchanges, generally at the customer's option.

The Societal Marketing Concept

The *societal marketing concept* is actually a version of the marketing concept that includes the long-term welfare of the consumer and that of the general public as well. A notable success story in this category includes biodegradable laundry detergents in an age of ecological consciousness. However, the motorcycle manufacturing company that created a vehicle which reduced the loud, high-rpm sound typically associated with motorcycles to a quiet purr did very poorly with the product and was forced to abandon it. Apparently, the company's research and planning effort did not reveal what most of us probably suspect to be the cause: motorcycle enthusiasts actually *want* that noise.

In an organizational environment, policy decisions are often made by committee. The parties bring their various orientations to the table with them so that even an organization which, on the whole, embraces the marketing concept may have "pockets" of countervailing forces. Therefore, the various influences we have just discussed rarely exist in pure form within the organization. (One might seriously question the desirability of an organization in which everybody shared the same influences and agreed on everything.)

Customer Service and Customer Focus

In marketing warfare, it is the customer service effort that supports the sales function, before and after the fact. This includes providing information to prospective and existing customers, resolving (or, better yet, avoiding) grievances, passively taking orders, and even (as in the more sophisticated marketing-oriented organizations) actively making sales. These activities are performed by the "foot soldiers" or "troops" who implement the policies established by "the brass," the organization's senior management. The nature of any customer service effort is determined to a large extent by the degree to which the organization's senior management truly values the customer. We refer to this orientation as *customer focus*.

Several Common Customer-Focus Issues

Does management dictate that the telephones be answered, "Thank you for calling XYZ Company. How may I serve you?" or is it okay merely to say, "XYZ Company"? It costs nothing to be courteous if not actually gracious and sets the tone for the conversation to follow.

Should the telephones be answered promptly (by no later than the third ring) even if this would incur additional cost, or is it okay to let the telephones ring longer on the (totally incorrect) grounds that, "If they want what we have, they'll wait"? Customers may wait this time if circumstances are pressing, but you can bet they'll take their business elsewhere in the future when they are no longer desperate.

If the customer is unhappy with a product and claims that it is defective, does the organization put the onus on the customer to make his case before a refund or credit is granted or does it immediately apologize for any inconvenience that may have been suffered and then immediately please the customer?

Nordstrom, one of the most successful retail chains, is well-known for its customer-focused approach. As one of the Nordstrom executives put it, "I don't care if they roll a Goodyear tire into the store. If they say they paid $200, give them the $200 (refund.)"[1]

Is Nordstrom out of its mind?

Not at all.

First, research reveals that the vast majority of people are basically decent and honest. One study involved sending researchers to pose as foreigners at airports, to hail taxicabs, and to see whether the drivers would earn their fares honestly or take the supposedly ignorant and hapless "foreigners" in circles for a much-inflated fare. It was found that only 2 of the 39 rides involved dishonest "joy rides." In fact, one driver actually warned his passenger to beware of people who would try to take advantage. So, if approximately 5 percent of all customers are dishonest and try to get away with something, Nordstrom might decide to build a 5 percent increment or "cushion" into its selling price and absorb its anticipated losses in order to avoid alienating an otherwise good customer. (By the way, it is not uncommon, with the passage of time, for customers to forget where they purchased items. To inform an ostensibly decent and honest customer that he or she purchased an item elsewhere, however tactfully it may be communicated, runs the risk of causing him or her embarrassment such that the individual might find it difficult to return as a patron.)

Second, research reveals that it costs approximately five times more to gain a new customer than to keep and continue to serve an existing customer. Think about it for a moment. Consider what it costs in time and financial investment. This includes, but is certainly not limited to, sales appointments, written correspondence, telephone calls, advertising and promotion, travel and entertainment, and … I think you get the idea.

Research by the Xerox Corporation goes a step further. Findings suggest that the respondents who rate their satisfaction as "4" on a scale of "5" are six times more likely not to return as customers than those who rate their satisfaction as "5." In a similar vein, the folks at General Electric found that approximately 10 percent of the dissatisfied customers will not actually complain and, of that group, only 10 percent will buy again from that seller. Such information underscores not only *the importance* of customer focus but the *sensitivity* of customer satisfaction. Organizations have responded by keeping a tab on their "churn" rates (i.e., percentage of customers who do not return) and often do so by establishing a so-called "retention marketing" function.

An interesting phenomenon originating from the world of online marketing is that of *permission marketing.* Popularized by Seth Godin, this approach suggests that astute marketers should "barter" for the consumer's attention, offering something of value in return for the consumer's time. This is often in sharp contrast to conventional or "interruption" marketing. As an example, Godin allowed prospective buyers of his new book to read several chapters on the Internet *free of charge.* And as every serious marketer should know, *free* is an absolutely *magical* word.

(Abracadabra!)

Essentially, the challenge for marketers is to have the consumer perceive switching to a competitor's offering as an unattractive alternative. Frequent user programs (such as the "Frequent Flyer" programs popularized by many airlines) immediately come to mind. Similarly, the "universality" or widespread and convenient use of a particular technological format has served Microsoft rather well, as in the case of its Windows operating systems. Prospective buyers may be inclined to stick with the PC format (that is, the Windows-compatible PC format) rather than switch to Apple's Macintosh format, because Windows-compatible software is abundant and easily available, whereas Mac-compatible software is less so. (Interestingly, I am told by experts in the field that Mac is often technologically superior, particularly for so-called "creative" applications, such as with art and music.) Not to belabor the point, but might Microsoft have achieved such market dominance, at least in part, by employing its own special version of "FUD" (fear, uncertainty, doubt)? Food for thought.

Idiosyncratic Credit

The concept of *idiosyncratic credit* comes from the domain of educational sociology. Researchers have observed that a schoolteacher is generally able to get his or her students to comply with what might be regarded as unreasonable requests or instructions, so long as these students perceived that the teacher is genuinely committed to their well-being.[2]

Abstracting this notion to the realm of commerce, I suggest that customers will be willing to bear with a panoply of your shortcomings (or those of your products), as long as they perceive that you (personally) and your organization (collectively) are genuinely committed to their well-being. One way to accumulate idiosyncratic credit is to list your home telephone number on your business card, to be called after-hours in the event of an emergency or crisis. You might initially be thinking: "No way will I let my business life intrude on my family or private life!" But consider the following:

The odds of a client having the legitimate need to call you after hours is very small. If the need is any greater, then perhaps you need to improve your product or your performance and should welcome the call as an opportunity for product development or your continued on-the-job training. And, as corny or idealistic as it may sound, shouldn't you genuinely *want* to receive your clients' calls if they are actually in need? Consider, if you will, that their patronage pays for the food on your table. Moreover, they are people who have relied upon your claims and, just maybe, people whom you have come to know and like—and care about. And, if you really care about them, building idiosyncratic credit really isn't so idiosyncratic, after all.

Consider this *impressive* "idiosyncratic credit" story:

During an emergency, H. Ross Perot, when he was chairman of Electronic Data Systems, purportedly took all his available vice presidents away from their desks and flew them, at great cost, to a warehouse located in a remote part of Texas in order to count by hand the inventory levels of a small client whose computer-generated inventory reports would not otherwise be available on time. Now, if you were that client and you knew that the company you patronize was willing to go to such great lengths on your behalf, wouldn't you be inclined to remain loyal to that company and perhaps even expand your business relationship?

Consider this *cute* "idiosyncratic credit" story:

A shoemaker was asked to fix a pair of shoes that, as it turned out, were beyond repair. He returned the pair to the customer with a chocolate chip cookie wrapped in waxed paper inside each shoe, along with a note that said: *"Anything not worth doing is worth not doing well."*[3]

The Macroenvironment

Marketers are affected by *exogenous variables*, those beyond our control. These include social, cultural, political, legal, technological, scientific, economic, and competitive factors. Although marketers may not be able to prevent certain events or scenarios from taking place, they are nonetheless potentially able to anticipate such occurrences and can make contingency plans to address these changes. The key point here is to be proactive rather than reactive, to be an initiator rather than a victim of circumstances otherwise beyond your control.

For example, assume that you are the marketer of ready-to-eat packaged food products. Your research indicates that the percentage of the population consisting of well-paid, unmarried, urban professionals is large and increasing at a rapid pace. What might you do? Perhaps it would be a good idea to introduce a higher-priced line of single-portion gourmet meals.

Dimensions of Buyer Perception

The reasons that people decide to make a purchase or decline to do so can be boiled down to two primary dimensions and seven secondary dimensions that are corollaries of the primary ones. As you consider these (see Figure 1.1), you may wish to assign a value, let's say from 1 to 10, for each of the dimensions relating to the product or service that you offer as an entrepreneur or manager. In a similar vein, you may wish to do much the same as it would pertain to your competitors' products or services. If you sell something business-to-business (e.g., from wholesaler to retailer or from raw materials to processing into another type of product), you may additionally wish to do this in terms of your customers to better understand their needs, latent or overt. In these ways, you may reach valuable insights about your offerings and perhaps become better able to identify strengths and weaknesses which you can then act upon. Keep in mind that the cost of losing a preexisting customer lies somewhere between the ratio of 5 or 6 to 1 (5:1,6:1).

Primary Dimensions

Perceived Risk
Potential customers ask themselves, "How can this product harm me"? The greater the marketer's success in diminishing this perception of risk, the greater the likelihood of the purchase.

Some companies regard this element as the veritable cornerstone of their sales model. It is commonly known that IBM sales representatives were (at least in the past) encouraged to employ the so-called FUD (fear, uncertainty, doubt) approach in the face of resistance from a prospective buyer. If the buyer were to suggest that the purchase decision was leaning toward a competitor, the IBM rep might "innocently" ask how many years remained before the buyer would be fully vested in his or her pension and retirement plan. When the surprised prospect would respond "Why do you ask?," the rep would matter-of-factly explain that (I paraphrase), "It would be a real shame to lose your job so close to retirement/being fully vested ...

just because you didn't buy IBM. As I'm sure you know: Nobody ever gets fired for buying IBM." In this example, FUD is keyed to the self-interest of the buyer as a person, rather than to the best interest of the employer.

FUD strategies have been successfully utilized in many other situations. The marketing of life insurance, for example, may prey upon a breadwinner's fear of leaving his or her family destitute in the event of death. I have even seen FUD used in the sale of high-ticket (i.e., expensive, luxury) items to wealthy individuals, who may be subtly (or not-so-subtly) reminded that "the Joneses" already purchased one. Do you want to be left behind (socially)?" One of my clients, whose net worth is in billions of dollars, is usually brilliant in his business decisions. I am really extremely impressed by him and have actually learned a great deal from him. However, he is rigid about certain matters. When I try to influence him to change his mind pertaining to these matters, I sometimes resort to a FUD approach: "Wouldn't it be a real shame if your arch competitor, XYZ Company, does this before your company does? I know you'll be kicking yourself if you allow that to happen." In this instance, I appeal to my client's (personal) strong competitive nature and extraordinary drive to excel and achieve.

Relative Advantage

Potential customers also ask, "How is this product better for me than my other alternatives?" The greater the marketer's success in increasing the perception of relative advantage associated with your product, the greater the likelihood of the purchase.

Secondary Dimensions

Observability

"Can the product's benefits be seen?" The more observable the benefits, the less the perceived risk and the greater the relative advantage. This might help to explain why it is often more difficult to sell services (which are not tangible) than it is to sell products (which are tangible). Astute marketers *add value* (or the perception of it) by

Figure 1.1 Dimensions of buyer perception

Perceived Risk
How can this product harm me?

Relative Advantage
How is this product better for me than others?

Primary dimensions

Observability
Can the product's benefits be seen?

Immediacy
How soon will I see these benefits?

Complexity
Is the product difficult to understand and use?

Compatibility
Is the product's usage congruent with my attitudes, opinions, and belief systems?

Trialability
Can I use the product without making a permanent commitment?

Divisibility
Can I buy the product in a smaller quantity or size or otherwise limit my purchase?

Availability
Are the product and its related accessories or services be available to me?

Secondary dimensions

including easy-to-use owner's manuals and by remaining in close touch with their customers, calling to their attention positive benchmarks or milestones. For example, an automobile dealer might call customers on the annual anniversary of a purchase to congratulate them and (not coincidentally) to inform or remind them that one year has passed without the need for any more than routine maintenance.

Immediacy

"How soon will I see these benefits?" The more immediate the benefits, the less the perceived risk and the greater the relative advantage. (See the section "Postpurchase Dissonance" later in this chapter.)

Complexity

"Is the product difficult to understand and use?" The more complex the product is perceived to be, the less the relative advantage and the greater the perceived risk.

Compatibility

"Is product's usage congruent with my attitudes, opinions, and belief systems?" The more compatible the product is with one's belief system, the less the perceived risk and the greater the relative advantage.

In the early days of mass marketing food products following World War II, the manufacturers of Duncan Hines cake mixes found that housewives were reluctant to buy their product despite the fact that the product's flavor, price, and other features were appealing. Ultimately, research indicated that housewives felt guilty about "making" a tasty cake that required very little effort. Given the gender stereotypes of the day, they believed that they should be working hard in their homes, since their husbands worked hard in their role as "breadwinners." So, what did the Duncan Hines folks do to overcome the resistance? They reconfigured the products so that the housewives would have to add an egg to the batter or recipe mixture, a nominal yet important symbolic effort—and the rest is history. Both Duncan Hines and the housewives (and their hungry families) were able to have their cake and eat it too.

Trialability

"Can I use the product without making a permanent commitment?" The greater the opportunity to try the product, the less the perceived risk and the greater the relative advantage. Options can include refunds and exchanges, and, in the case of lease arrangements, upgrades. Ultimately, customer-focused marketers must assume risks relating to trialability. If the product has merit and delivers on its claims, the issue is merely academic. If, however, customers are displeased with the product and choose to exercise their right of redress, marketers should view this as a cost of doing business, albeit potentially substantial.

Divisibility

"Can I buy the product in a smaller quantity or size or otherwise limit my purchase?" The smaller the quantity the customer can buy at one time, the less the perceived risk and the greater the relative advantage. While this is not physically possible for certain types of transactions (i.e., one can't buy one-half of a car), minimum quantity requirements can be waived so that initial orders can be regarded, in effect, as "samples" for which the customer pays.

Availability

"Are the product and its related accessories or services available to me?" The more available the product, the less the perceived risk and the greater the relative advantage. Increasingly, the focus is shifting from the "core" product to accessories, on the part of the consumer as well as the marketer. For example, anyone who has bought video game hardware (e.g., Nintendo) will probably have ended up spending more for the software accessories (e.g., additional programs for games) than they originally spent for the primary video game product.

Similarly, many marketers of cellular telephones offer the cell phones *free*—if the consumer agrees to use or be billed for a minimum number of hours at a certain rate. Obviously, the revenues "lost" by "giving away" the phones are more than made up for by the revenues associated with billing for monthly usage.

For this reason, manufacturers of razor blades will make the hand razor apparatus (i.e., the item with a handle that holds the sharp blade in place) available to the consumer at low cost or perhaps even free of charge.

Participants in the Buying Process

While a single individual may be the one to authorize a purchase formally and perhaps even write a check, those who influence the purchase decision are often not readily apparent to the marketer. In organizations, it is often the executive's assistant who recommends that a particular brand of word processing software be purchased, although the marketer may wrongly assume that it is this individual's

boss who unilaterally makes the decision. Similarly, automobile dealers trying to make a sale to a married couple may, based upon sexist
assumptions, take the liberty of focusing on the male spouse as the
decision maker. Even if the wife were to have said something like,
"Oh, Bob makes all the technical decisions about cars. Men know
more about that kind of stuff," she may subtly—or not so subtly—be
exerting her influence on "Bob's decision." She may, for example,
lean toward an automobile or brand that is more or less stylish,
expensive, status-oriented, practical, safer, comfortable, and so on.
The dealer who does not identify and acknowledge her as an influ-
encer, and perhaps as the ultimate decision maker, is likely to fail.

The definitive textbook case on this subject, the *gatekeeper effect*,
involved observing mother and child shopping for breakfast cereal in
supermarkets. The child was told by the mother to "choose" a cereal
that he or she liked and wanted. But when the child actually "chose"
a particular brand, the typical mother "vetoed" the choice (perhaps
because the product contained too much sugar) and invited the child
to make another choice or other choices until she approved.[4] Who,
then, truly made these decisions? Needless to say, marketers of children's breakfast cereals typically seek Mom's approval.

The Rational Buyer Vis-à-Vis the Emotional Buyer

Conventional wisdom has it that people who buy for their organizations are driven by a set of motives different from those of individuals
who buy as consumers for their own personal needs.

The former has generally been regarded as *rational*, focusing
on such objective considerations as price, quality specifications,
promptness of delivery, and reliability; the latter, on the other hand,
has generally been regarded as *emotional*, focusing instead on such
subjective considerations as pride, guilt, sociability, and sensory satisfaction. Astute marketers understand that the dichotomy is not that
clear and simple, that buyers for organizations respond to emotional
appeals and that consumers in the general public respond to rational
appeals, as well. This would help to explain the increased acceptance
of such approaches as unit pricing (i.e., rational) for the general

public of consumers (i.e., emotional) and celebrity endorsements (i.e., emotional) for business-to-business marketing (i.e., rational).

Cognitive Dissonance

Cognitive dissonance is the condition in which an individual is faced with conflicting emotions, attitudes, and actions. For example, an individual may know that cigarette smoking causes cancer but will smoke anyway.[5] Obviously, marketers should be concerned about any aspects of their products that bring cognitive dissonance to the fore. They should strive to minimize it as much as possible. Let us say that we are the marketers of a delicious dessert product. It is high in fat and cholesterol, both of which, we are told by authoritative sources, contribute to heart disease and other maladies. We might overcome these health concerns on the basis of any number of rationales, including moderation ("Everything is okay in moderation"), reward ("You worked hard, and you deserve it" or, in a similar yet more familiar vein, "You deserve a break today"), and unbridled hedonism and inevitable mortality ("You only live once").

I'm not in any way suggesting that marketers abandon their ethical responsibilities to consumers, promoting the use of a product that would ultimately harm them. (In the face of immediate threat, the product should be withdrawn from the marketplace without equivocation. When the threat is less immediate or indirect, accurate representation and full disclosure of risk are absolutely required.)

Postpurchase Dissonance (Also Known as Buyer's Remorse)

Studies dealing with high-ticket purchases, in general, and automobile purchases, in particular, often characterize the buyer as second-guessing or regretting his or her purchase decision. (This might be triggered by a casual comment from a friend or relative such as, "Oh, your choice of Brand X is okay, but I've heard that Brand Y is a better value because ....") Marketers should anticipate this and can minimize or perhaps totally avert the problem by establishing an 800 toll-free telephone number to address questions and comments (particularly appropriate for technically oriented products, including computers and assemble-it-yourself items).

This is certainly not in lieu of having the salesperson and/or customer service representative follow up on the transaction with telephone calls (the first one within one week and the others three to four weeks apart for the first couple of months) to thank the individual for his or her order and to make sure that the individual is totally satisfied with the product. If for any reason the customer is less than totally satisfied, the salesperson or customer service representative will have the timely opportunity to remedy the situation. Moreover, the salesperson may seize this moment as an excellent opportunity to sell the satisfied customer an upgrade on the original purchase or accessories or to obtain referrals among the individual's family, friends, and business associates.

Dimensions of Market Segmentation

When marketers are able to identify characteristics that people share and there is a substantial enough number of such people in this group that would seem likely to want to purchase their products, it can be said that the marketers would ostensibly target these groups—or segments. We call these processes *market segmentation* and *target marketing*, respectively. The most widely accepted and used criteria or dimensions for market segmentation include the following:

- *Demographic*: Those based upon such factors as age, gender, sexual preference, race, ethnicity, education, marital status, number of children or other dependents, income, and so on.
- *Geographic*: Those based upon such factors as neighborhood (typically identified by ZIP code), city, state, region, and so on.
- *Psychographic*: Those based upon attitudes, interests, and opinions (AIO). These may be sociocultural, religious/spiritual, philosophical, aesthetic, ethical/moral, political, economic, technological/scientific, curricular or extracurricular/occupational or personal, and so on.
- *Usage related*: Those based upon how the product is actually used.

Quantity is one such element. Marketers of beer know that their strategies and tactics must be different for appealing to heavy users (e.g., the stereotype of construction workers) rather than moderate users (e.g., upscale connoisseurs, the stereotype of "yuppies"). *Timing* is another element. Operators of movie theaters know that customers who attend on weekday afternoons may be a different breed from those who attend on weekend evenings, and they must adapt their strategies and tactics to address this. *Application* or specific purpose of usage is critical. Purveyors of baking soda know that, while most customers use their product to prepare baked food items, these same individuals and other individuals may use the product as an odor absorbent (in refrigerators and in open spaces), a toothpaste, a poultice (for burns), a stain remover, and so on.

For business-to-business applications, you might also want to think in terms of:

- *Sector* (e.g., for-profit entities, not-for-profit entities)
- *Industry* (e.g., entertainment and media, financial services, petrochemical, biomedical, cyber-related and computer-based/high technology)
- *Size* (e.g., regarding annual sales volume, asset base; small, midsized, big business)
- *Territory* (e.g., by neighborhood, city, state, country, region/continent)

Marketing Strategies

Having identified market segments, marketers must then choose from *strategies* that best suit their objectives and limitations, as follows:

- *Concentrated marketing:* Involves introducing a single version of a product that is designed to appeal to a single, particular market segment. This approach is well suited to organizations that have limited financial resources and/or enjoy an expertise specific to a particular type of customer base. Weight Watchers is an organization that employs this strategy, for the latter reason. It concentrates on serving those who are overweight or weight conscious.

- *Differentiated marketing:* Involves introducing a number of different versions of a product, each designed to appeal to a different market segment. Generally, this strategy is adopted by organizations with substantial financial resources. They may have started out using a concentrated or undifferentiated marketing strategy and, as success and growth ensued, elected to develop, in effect, a concentrated marketing strategy for each of two or more market segments.

  General Motors and Ford Motor Company are organizations that employ this strategy. They both sell cars designed to appeal to many different types of consumers and/or to satisfy many different needs in the form of economy cars, sports cars, luxury cars, station wagons, vans, trucks, and so on.

- *Undifferentiated marketing:* Involves introducing only a single version of the product in the hope that it will appeal to an entire universe of consumers, an appeal to the lowest common denominator. Once upon a time, when life was simpler, when the world wasn't quite so fragmented and market segments didn't exist or perhaps, more accurately, were not readily identifiable or even thought of as significant, this approach was the norm. Prior to the days of Classic Coke, Diet Coke, Caffeine-free Diet Coke, Cherry Coke, and the myriad other versions of Coke, there was plain old Coke or Coca-Cola. And, in contrast to the previous example for the differentiated marketing strategy, Ford Motor Company limited its original product offering, the Model T, not only to a single version but to a single color. ("You can have any color you like, so long as it's black.")

Product Positioning

Using the technique of *product mapping* to graphically depict market segments relative to product attributes, we may endeavor to "match" market segments to product options. (To be precise, we should actually be referring to "brands" or competing versions within a product class.) In Figure 1.2, we have divided our universe of potential customers into quadrants, established by a vertical HI-LO axis for price and horizontal HI-LO axis for a particular product attribute. In this instance, the attribute relates to the degree to which the product is high or low in fat and calories. Quadrant I is characterized by a brand high in fat and cholesterol and in price as well. The square icons are indicative of the potential number of customers in this quadrant or market segment. Assuming that each of these icons represents many potential customers and that they are configured in a cluster formation, this would indicate that there very well may be a market for high-priced and rich (i.e., high-in-fat) food products. Similarly, the circles in quadrant II indicate that there may also be a market for high-priced diet (i.e., low-in-fat) food products. However, the triangle and diamonds in quadrants III and IV, respectively, suggest that the markets for low-priced rich food products as well as low-priced diet food products may not be sufficient to justify the investment and marketing effort.

Figure 1.2 Product positioning

Marketing Research

How do marketers obtain information about product positioning and other information necessary to make informed decisions? (See "Conducting a Research Project" in Chapter 4, "Statistics.")

The Marketing Mix

Whatever it is that you are marketing, it has four dimensions. These four *Ps* are *product, price, place* (i.e., channels of distribution), and *promotion*. It has been my personal experience that in Asia, particularly Singapore and Hong Kong, the four *Ps* are commonly referred to as the six *Ps*, the additional two being "people selling" (i.e., the salesperson's product knowledge) and "physical evidence" (i.e., packaging of the product).

Product

A *product* is an item or service that is offered to the consumer to satisfy his or her needs and to realize organizational goals.

Product Differentiation
Aside from customer focus, no concept is more important for marketers than that of *product differentiation*, that is, the effort to distinguish favorably one's brand from all other brands within its product class. Some brands are intrinsically differentiated. For example, when Häagen-Dazs ice cream was introduced a generation ago, its creator, Reuben Mattus, had as his intention the establishment of a new category of ice cream: *premium* ice cream. As such, Mattus put considerably more butterfat into the product than his competitors had in the past. In addition, he pumped less air into the product than his competitors did, making it thicker. From a purely objective standpoint, it can be said that the "formula" for the Häagen-Dazs brand was substantially different from that of competing brands. The product was *intrinsically* differentiated. But, of course, not all differences are intrinsic or in the product itself. The name Häagen-Dazs suggests a

product that is made in and imported from Scandinavia or Germany or the Alps, a part of the world that enjoys a fine reputation for quality dairy products. Most people don't know that Reuben Mattus completely made up the name Häagen-Dazs! They might be even more surprised to find that the product was originally manufactured in a borough of New York City known as the Bronx, which is (forgive me, fellow New Yorkers) not exactly one of the garden spots of the world. So it can also be said that Mattus succeeded in *extrinsically* differentiating his product by creating an appealing brand image.

At around the same time that Mattus was launching Häagen-Dazs, the Swiss, who had previously dominated the market for watches and timepieces, in general, woke up one day to find that the Japanese (specifically, the Seiko company) had succeeded in taking away much of their market share via the introduction of quartz technology. (Prior to the introduction of Seiko's quartz technology, the Swiss jewel movement was the standard.) A creative and outstanding response to this threat was to *redefine* what a watch really is (i.e., *differentiate* a particular type or brand of watch from all others within the same product category). The marketers reasoned that in "the old days," a watch was generally perceived to be something of moderate to great value that was often handed down from generation to generation and given as a gift on special occasions (e.g., school graduations, job retirements). But did it have to be? These folks reasoned that their (brand of) watch could be a more casual item, to be fun and perhaps to make a fashion statement. Different styles for different times of day and for different occasions. And what if you accidentally lost it? No problem, since it was relatively inexpensive (compared to the watch of "the old days"). I am referring, of course, to that great comeback story and textbook marketing case known as Swatch (SWiss wATCH).

Now we enter the bonus round. How does one differentiate a product that, by its very nature, is a commodity and (arguably, as such) cannot really be differentiated? For example, one might think "milk is milk," "steel is steel." The astute marketer would answer that *anything* can be differentiated. In the case of commodity products (e.g., eggs, steel, or lumber), one might focus on enhancing service quality or offering more favorable financing terms (i.e., *extrinsically* differentiating the product).

Food for thought: In the world of OEM (original equipment manufacturer) or "private label" marketing, wherein a manufacturer produces an item for another company so that company can put its label on the product, on what basis (other than price) can the manufacturer differentiate?

More food for thought: Between 1993 and 2000, the recording artist/musician Prince not only renounced his former name, he went so far as to render his official name as a "glyph" or visual symbol, rather than in an alphabetical format. In fact, Prince's office staff purportedly used Windows-compatible computers that graphically printed the glyph where the name would otherwise appear. Now, is that product differentiation, or what?!

What are the tools available to marketers to differentiate their brands and to protect their valuable interests?

Trademarks and Service Marks

Legal claims, such as trademarks and service marks, are designed to protect the goodwill that your brand name, corporate name, slogan, or logo succeeded in establishing. Trademarks are granted for an initial period of 10 years, but can be renewed. Consider, if you will, how terrible it would be for McDonald's if other hamburger marketers could get away with calling their offerings Big Macs. In some instances, a trade name is so powerful that it is virtually synonymous, in the mind of consumers, with the name of the product class in which it competes. In referring to those little sticks with cotton on the end that we use for personal hygiene and cleaning in crevices, many of us (and I'm guilty of this) ask for Q-tips rather than *cotton swabs*. If I were about to sneeze, I might ask if someone could spare a Kleenex rather than facial tissues.

The strongest form of protection is the *registered trademark* (for products or tangibles) or *registered service mark* (for services or intangibles). This is typically denoted by the symbol ® or the words "Registered Trademark." It is required that the applicant formally file a claim with the Patent and Trademark Office. Once this has been done, a reasonable period is allowed to transpire in which any parties who wish to challenge the claim may do so. If no such challenges are made or if challenges are ruled to be lacking in merit, then the claim is granted. Trademarks can be renewed indefinitely every 10 years.[6] (However, a trademark may be considered abandoned if it is not used for two years once the claim has been made.)

Another option is the *common law trademark* or *service mark*. Marketers may affix "TM" (for products) or "SM" (for services) under common law without formally filing a federal claim. It is recommended that TM or SM be used until application for a federally registered mark is approved. While neither affords the degree of protection that the registered trademark affords and may necessitate a greater burden of proof if the mark is challenged, each does provide public notice of claim. Also, each can be used immediately, whereas the registered mark can be used only after the claim has been approved. (Prior usage is in violation of federal law and subjects the offender to penalties.)

When a brand or trademark is particularly strong, it can be referred to as a *virtual synonym* for the entire product class in which it belongs. For example, a doctor who tells his nurse to, "Get me a Q-tip" may really be asking for a cotton swab (product class) made by a manufacturer other than Johnson & Johnson, the maker of Q-tips. Similarly, a trademark may also come to be improperly used, as a verb rather than only as a noun. For example, it is all too common to hear people say "Can you xerox this page for me?" when they are really asking for a photocopy (product class) made by a manufacturer other than Xerox (trademark). Of the names presented on the following list, can you identify which ones are trademarks and which are generic terms indicating product class?[7]

Ace Bandage	Clorox
Ant Farm	Colorization
Band-aid	Day-Glo
Brillo	Dictaphone
Cliffs Notes	Dixie Cup

Drivers Wanted	Novocain
Dumpster	Parcheesi
Express Mail	Photostat
Fiberglas	Ping-Pong
501 jeans	Plexiglas
Formica	Popsicle
Fudgsicle	Rollerblade
Got Milk?	Sanforized
Happy Meal	Scotch Tape
Heimlich Maneuver	Seeing Eye Dog
Hey, You Never Know	747 Aircraft
Hula-Hoop	Sheetrock
Jaws of Life	Styrofoam
Jeep	Swiss Army Knife
Jell-O	Tabasco Sauce
Kitty Litter	Technicolor
Krazy Glue	V8 Juice
Lava Lamp	Velcro
Lucite	Walkman
Mace	Windbreaker
Magic Marker	World Series
Naugahyde	

Which of the above are trademarked names? All of them.

Dos and Don'ts of Naming[8]

When you think about name branding, there are many considerations to think about. Here's a list of dos and don'ts:

1. Conduct a brainstorming exercise, conjuring and listing words or names that describe what the company or product does and how it is differentiated from the rest of the pack.
2. Ponder the image and mood you want to convey (e.g., fast and efficient, friendly and personal).

3. Look at the names of your main competitors. Yours should be "similar in tone," so that you will more likely be perceived to "belong" in the same industry, unless, of course, you want to be perceived as a renegade or revolutionary company that is bent on turning the industry upside down.
4. Avoid even the hint of negative connotations, particularly in foreign languages and other cultures.
5. Avoid choosing a name that is so narrow or specific that it would eventually have to be changed when the company grows or changes.
6. Avoid acronyms. With notable exceptions (e.g., IBM), they tend to be hard to remember.

Copyrights

Copyrights are legal claims designed to protect intellectual properties against unauthorized usage. They must be presented in fixed form rather than just as "ideas" and may include but are not necessarily limited to fiction and nonfiction texts, musical compositions, works of art, dramatic works, photographs, and computer software programs. *Ownership of copyright* exists when the work is completed in any fixed form regardless of the date of registration with the Copyright Office. However, the ability to defend a challenge to one's claim would certainly be enhanced by formally filing a claim with the Copyright Office. The duration of a copyright in the United States initiated in or after 1978 is 50 years after death of the author. However, each country has its own applicable copyright laws, such that duration of the copyright may extend to as much as 70 years after the author's death.

Notice is generally characterized by the word "Copyright" or the symbol © followed by the year in which the work was actually completed in fixed form and the copyright owner's name. If the work is presented in audio format (e.g., phonograph, audiocassette, compact disc), notice for the work in fixed form for this type of medium is generally characterized by the letter P with a circle around it, followed by the year in which the work was produced in that medium and the copyright owner's name. If the entity is, say, an audio version (i.e., recorded spoken word performance) of a book or collection of poems, it would be appropriate to include two copyright notices: one for the intellectual property (© for the book or collection of poems) and the other for the audio version (℗ for the spoken word performance).[9] (In fact, the very book you are now reading is protected by copyright law.)

In some instances, lack of copyright can have catastrophic consequences. The computer software developer who creates an absolutely brilliant program but neglects to copyright the work may find that his or her work is being misappropriated (or ripped off) and that he or she may have no remedy after a certain period of time, after which the work enters public domain. As a matter of policy, marketers should place copyright notices on virtually *all* marketing communications materials such as brochures, proposals, audiovisual presentations, advertisements, sales promotion items, and more. It costs nothing and establishes a claim for exclusive use of the properties in fixed form, discouraging competitors from bearing the fruits of your labors. (By the way, the greater importance of copyright is further underscored and gravely dramatized by the contention that Adolf Hitler might never have been able to commence hostilities against England were it not for his control of the copyright on his book, *Mein Kampf.* By restricting publication in England and other soon-to-be-allied nations to the original German language version, he was able to distort public opinion in those countries by concealing his evil intentions and delaying earlier and timely mobilization against his armed forces.)[10]

Patents

Patents are legal claims designed to protect a mechanical or scientific process, instrument, method, or design. Common law patents do not exist as such. The single meaningful option is formally filing a claim with the Patent and Trademark Office. Patents are characterized by display of the "Patent # XXXX" notice once the period for challenges is over and the claim has been granted. Until the patent is granted, the "Patent Pending" notice is affixed.

Patents are granted for a nonrenewable period of 17 years. They then expire, and other parties cannot be prevented from using them.

The sound quality of your favorite music recordings may have been enhanced by means of the Dolby noise reduction system, a patented method. Your apparel will not shrink by more than a minute percentage when you launder it if it was Sanforized or treated with the once-patented Sanforization process. An almost endless list of products is currently or previously has been protected by patents, from dynamite to the zipper, the electric guitar to the refrigerator. Recently, ethical controversy has erupted over legal rulings enabling entrepreneurs to patent medical innovations (e.g., gene therapy materials) and even business methods (e.g., the "reverse auction" bidding/buying system introduced over the Internet by Priceline).

Product Life Cycle

Just like human beings, *products have a life cycle*, too. They are *conceived* (i.e., via research and development), *born* (i.e., launched), *grow*, *mature*, *decline*, and eventually, *die*. There are particular characteristics of each stage and corresponding marketing implications. Astute marketers manage the product life cycle to greatest advantage, elongating the product's life cycle and/or its generation of cash. Figure 1.3 shows the stages of a product life cycle: introduction, growth, maturity, saturation, decline, and abandonment. The stages are discussed in the following:

Figure 1.3 Product life cycle

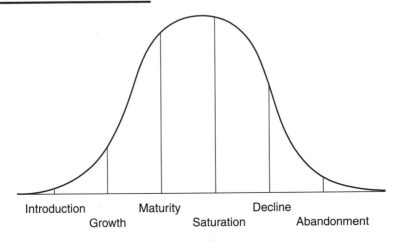

Introduction　　Maturity　　Decline
Growth　　Saturation　　Abandonment

1. *Introduction:* This stage is characterized by research and development. Sales and profits are usually very low, although costs may be substantial. This underscores the importance of adequately budgeting for or funding the project. (This point is worthy of greater discussion and is addressed in Chapter 2, "Accounting and Finance.")
2. *Growth:* This stage is characterized by increased sales and profits. Heavy promotional costs are often incurred.
3. *Maturity:* This stage is characterized by "peaking" and attempted maintenance of sales levels. It is possible to increase sales, but this would almost surely incur substantial costs. Profits may already have begun to diminish, and this may be related to a very high level of competition.
4. *Saturation:* This stage is characterized by decreased profitability linked to costs. Competition increases even more. The goal, at this juncture, is to maintain market share. However, this is often not possible.
5. *Decline:* This stage is characterized by perceived futility in the attempt to maintain market share. Typically, this is accompanied by cost cutting.
6. *Abandonment:* At this stage the product's performance no longer merits inclusion in the organization's product line.

The Boston Consulting Group (BCG) Growth-Share Matrix

In conjunction with the product life cycle, the *BCG model* provides a valuable framework that enables us to identify and evaluate our products relative to market share and the extent to which the market, as a whole, is expanding or contracting (as shown in Figure 1.4).

Products may be categorized as follows:[11]

- *Star:* Product with high market share in a high-growth market—every mother's dream.
- *Problem child:* Product with low market share in a high-growth market; mother is concerned because her child is not growing as anticipated. Another perspective is that mother shouldn't be quite so concerned if the child has carved out a little niche that is impervious to the competition; maybe slow yet consistent growth isn't so bad.

- *Cash cow:* Product with high market share in a low-growth market. Since the cow is generating milk (i.e., cash), the marketer may elect to "milk the cow dry," so to speak, accelerating cash flow and, not coincidentally, the product life cycle.
- *Dog:* Product with low market share in a low-growth market. In this sense, "dog" is certainly not "man's best friend." Rather, it is analogous to "bomb" (i.e., something that fails miserably) or to "lemon" (i.e., something that is defective or undesirable). So it would seem that we would want to drop the dog from our product line.

Figure 1.4 The Boston Consulting Group Growth-Share Matrix*

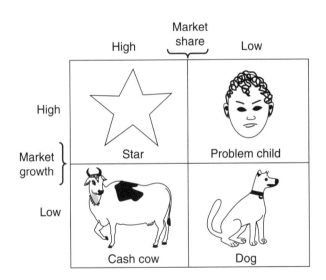

*The Experience Curve: The Growth-Share Matrix or the Product Portfolio. (Boston Consulting Group, 1973).

Product Line Inclusion or Exclusion

There may be circumstances under which excluding a product may ultimately have deleterious consequences for the entire product line, for example, the dog just happens to be the "flagship" brand or that which people readily identify with the company's product line. (Do you remember the uproar that ensued when Coca-Cola withdrew the original or "old" Coke from the marketplace, replacing it with the "new" Coke?) Another instance in which abandonment may be damaging might relate to the company's identity or image as a full-service resource. By dropping the product from its line, the company can no longer accurately claim to be a full-service entity. What, then, are some of the practical options?

Bundling

We may choose to package or bundle the product with other offerings in our product line. Cable TV system operators commonly use this approach, offering, say, five pay TV channels for the price of four in the hope that cable viewers will subscribe to more channels than they otherwise would if they were able to buy "a la carte" (i.e., each channel separately). By doing so, both parties may be perceived to have succeeded. The entrepreneurs gain by increasing their absolute sales volume. Moreover, they increase profitability by taking advantage of the economies of scale they enjoy from purchasing their programming in larger quantities. (See Chapter 3, "Human Resources and Operations Management," for greater elaboration on this point.)

Raising the Price

By increasing the selling price sufficiently, we may be able to keep the product in our line, since the profit margin may be acceptable even though sales volume in absolute dollars may leave something to be desired. This option would allow the entrepreneur to maintain the image of being a full-service entity without having to lose money on the product offering.

Product Development and Management

What are the key determinants of success or failure?[12]

1. *Does the product offer a technological innovation that satisfies a need?* 3M's Thinsulate fabric was a breakthrough in apparel, given its warmth yet ultra light weight.
2. *Is it a better version of a preexisting product?* Coca-Cola's introduction of New Coke was not perceived by the vast majority of

Coke drinkers as an improvement over the original version. In fact, it is interesting that Coca-Cola actually gained market share despite the poor showing of New Coke. Because of all of the massive advertising that worked at the time by Coke and Pepsi in the spirit of their arch rivalry, many of the smaller beverage brands (e.g., Hire's, Crush, Dr. Pepper) who could not keep pace in ad spending, were eclipsed in the process. Therefore, consumer attention was focused on Coke and Pepsi (both of whom gained in market share that was forfeited by the other brands).

3. *Is it perceived as a good value?* Toyota is not nearly the precision luxury automobile that the Rolls Royce is. But isn't it a "better deal," pound for pound, dollar for dollar, in utility?

4. *Does the product leverage the company's strength(s)?* It made sense for Dunkin' Donuts to introduce bagels to its product line, in light of the company's demonstrated strengths in baked goods and a breakfast-oriented and snack-oriented customer base. Conversely, Boston Market saw its profits shrink as a result of introducing a line of less expensive sandwiches, which "cannibalized" the sales of its chicken dinners.

5. *Has demand vis-à-vis supply been accurately estimated?* What can be worse than not having your product in stock when customers want to buy it? Perhaps having too much of your product in stock with virtually no buyers in sight. Personally, in my own experience as a consultant, this is a common scenario.

6. *Is your organization sufficiently financed to support a product launch and subsequent maintenance?* More capital and resources may be needed than originally calculated. It is wise to build a well-padded "cushion" into your budget and to have at the ready contingency plans in the event of unanticipated events or changes in the marketplace.

Price

Price, one of the four *P*s of the marketing mix, is what the customer pays for the product or service. Pricing options include the following.

Premium Pricing

Also known as "skimming the cream," *premium pricing* involves charging a high price relative to other brands within the product class. This can be an effective approach if it succeeds in, or at least lends support to, creating the perception of high quality. In other words, a product can be differentiated on the basis of price. (In my personal experience as an educator and consultant, I have found that consumers are generally far more reluctant to pay a price that is perceived as "too low" than one that is "too high.") The product category of cosmetics is one in which brand image (i.e., extrinsic differentiation) rather than objective and substantive product attributes tends to determine how well a product will fare. The contention is supported by the fact that cosmetics have one of the highest advertising-to-sales ratios of any industry or product class.

Let's discuss Clinique, a respected marketer of high-end cosmetics. One of its products, an astringent, consists almost entirely of alcohol. If we were to pay a visit to our local drug store, we would find that a similar bottle of alcohol would cost perhaps only 10 percent of what we would pay for Clinique astringent. Even if Clinique were to add other chemicals or substances to its astringent, the percentage of the product's cost that this would represent would be very small indeed and, I suggest, might not objectively justify a price that is so high.

So, how does Clinique, which I view as an excellent product line of high quality, justify its price? For one thing, it appears to position itself as a "medically approved" product, and this is in no way contradicted by the company's policy of dressing the sales representatives who staff their retail counters in "operating room" green or white laboratory-type coats.

Fair Pricing

Fair pricing involves charging a price that is objectively regarded as reasonable based upon market research. Ivory soap and Miller beer are examples of brands that successfully employ this approach.

Penetration Pricing

Penetration pricing involves charging a low price on the assumption of selling the brand in enormous quantities. This is based upon a strategy of profit through volume. McDonald's does it with burgers, and Bic does it with disposable pens, lighters, and razors.

Parity Pricing

Parity pricing involves setting a price that roughly matches the prices of competing brands within the product class. This approach may suggest that the marketer is not attuned to the importance of differentiation.

Cost-Plus Pricing

Cost-plus pricing involves setting a price that factors in a given profit margin (e.g., cost plus 25 percent). This approach may indicate a preoccupation with investment return and can be particularly unfortunate in the absence of a proper customer-focus orientation. The marketer may be oblivious to price sensitivity in the marketplace and competitors' pricing tactics.

Keep in mind that whatever option is chosen, it must be congruent or consistent with the other components of the marketing mix. If, for example, the product is of extremely high quality and of an "exclusive" nature, a high or premium price would seem to be appropriate.

Idiosyncratic Pricing

Before H. Ross Perot went on to greater success with Control Data, EDS, and Perot Systems, he was one of IBM's most successful sales executives. So much so, in fact, that he is legendary for having met his annual sales quota on January 17 (that's right, only 17 days into the year!). How did he do it? Perot listened carefully to identify the needs of the client and, essentially, asked the client: "If I can meet your needs, what is that worth to you?" Often, the figure given by the client *exceeded* what might otherwise be regarded as the "going rate."

Apples and Oranges Pricing

In 1959, Haloid Xerox (the company you know today as Xerox) introduced its Model 914 copier. The price was $27,500 (actually, about half a million dollars in today's currency). In absolute dollars, the price was so expensive that purchase of the product was ruled out by most firms. So, Haloid Xerox devised an alternative plan: to also make the copiers available via *leasing* arrangements, at a rate of $75 per month and approximately 5 cents per copy for all copies in excess of 2,000. (By doing so, it has been suggested that Haloid Xerox was able to drive down the level of decision making regarding the purchase to lower-level managers who had limited purchasing authority but were much more accessible.) This strategy proved to be extremely successful.[13]

Preemptive Pricing

How did the Dynamite Cartel manage to retain market share even after its patent on the explosive expired? The organization publicly announced a 10-percent price reduction whenever a company threatened to enter the market. This pricing strategy was designed to make the market less attractive to would-be competitors.

Push-versus-Pull Pricing

Push-versus-pull pricing addresses the balance that must be struck between the competing interests of buyers and sellers; provide enough profit for the selling entities (e.g., your sales force, wholesalers, retailers) and sufficient satisfaction (i.e., perception of value) for the buyers.

Threshold Pricing

Does it really make a difference whether you charge $99.99 or $100.00? Yes. It does if that one penny of difference can cause the prospective buyer to back off. For some people, $100 represents a psychological threshold they do not, consciously or otherwise, wish to cross. Marketers may address this by lowering the price by just a penny or by making the product available for sale for let's say, "four payments of just $25!"

Place

Place, another of the four *P*s of the marketing mix, is the component that deals with the product's channels of distribution or how it is conveyed from the producer to the end user. Its functions include manufacturing, transportation, warehousing, wholesaling, and retailing. The more of these functions that the company is willing to assume, the greater the percentage of selling price it can command. If an organization controls all the channels of distribution for its product, we say that it is "vertically integrated." The manufacturer acquiring a company in order to have access to the raw materials it wishes to use in its own products is integrating backward (i.e., toward the source of supply or seller), whereas the wholesaler acquiring retail outlets to expand distribution is integrating forward (i.e., toward the source of demand or buyer).

There are essentially three distribution options, as follows:

- *Intensive Distribution:* Aims for maximum exposure. The product is sold through any responsible wholesaler or retailer who will stock it. This pertains especially to convenience goods and so-called impulse or point-of-purchase items, such as razor blades or candy.
- *Elective Distribution:* Aims for moderate exposure. The product is sold through "better" retailers. This pertains especially to shopping goods or high-ticket items, such as home entertainment centers or appliances.
- *Selective Distribution:* Aims for limited exposure. The product is sold by a single dealer within each trading region. This pertains to specialty goods, those that are highly differentiated or luxury items.

Direct Response Marketing

When companies endeavor to "vertically integrate" (i.e., cut out intermediaries or gain control of the sources of their supply as well as those of their demand), we often observe their reliance upon *database marketing*. It typically involves accessing *internally generated* databases containing names and vital information of existing customers and potential customers who have expressed interest but have not yet actually made a purchase and/or acquiring *externally generated* databases from marketing support organizations, such as mailing list brokerages. And, in this day and age, mailing list contact options are no longer limited to snail mail (i.e., office or home address), and include fax and e-mail addresses, as well. Key concepts in database marketing are the *response rate* (i.e., the percentage of people who have responded to the marketing communication) and the *return rate* (i.e., the percentage of people who have been "converted" and have decided to buy). What is regarded as "acceptable" for response and return rates can vary greatly. Internally generated lists, because they are reaching existing customers, may yield as much as 15 percent or even higher, whereas "rented" lists typically yield from one-half of 1 percent to as high as 2 percent, and very rarely, a bit more. (By the way, consumer products sold in mail order campaigns must have a selling price that exceeds cost by a ratio of at least 5-to-1 if they are to be profitable.)

Although used more often in the context of information technology, the notion of *disintermediation*, commonly known as "cutting out the middleman," is getting more and more attention. For example, automobile manufacturers will supposedly reduce dealerships to merely serve as physical locations where cars are delivered and serviced—but not sold.

Retailing

Retailing involves the direct relationship between the selling intermediary and the consumer (i.e., the individual or company at the "end" of the channels of distribution). Interestingly, performance in this category is often quite dependent upon physical positioning and space: management of shelf space within the establishment as well as location of the store itself. Obviously, stores located on street corners and in high pedestrian or commuter traffic areas enjoy a considerable advantage. Similarly, the argument has been made that the more shelf space a company can capture within an establishment, the greater its sales are likely to be. This is precisely the premise that the

Coca-Cola company relied upon in its battle for market share when it introduced New Coke. Utilizing a "multibrand" strategy (Coca-Cola called it "megabrand"), the company assumed that it could increase its share of shelf space with *any combination or mix* of Coca-Cola's brands (and keep in mind that Coca-Cola doesn't mean just "Coke," but its two dozen or so other labels, including Fanta, Minute Maid, and Fresca, not to mention Diet Coke, Caffeine-free Coke, and others).

In-store marketing comprises all the merchandising activities that take place on the premises [including point-of-purchase (POP) marketing, the efforts made at the cash register or checkout counter]. This includes the usage of signs, in-window/storefront and other displays, as well as all promotional and incentive programs. It is of primary importance, especially when you consider that 70 percent of purchase decisions at retail are made "on the spot" or on impulse. In fact, you might also be surprised to know that two-thirds of soft drinks are sold at in-store locations *away from* the soft drink aisle.[14]

Do you think it is a coincidence that, in the typical supermarket, an individual must walk all the way to the rear of the store to pick out and retrieve a "staple" and frequently consumed item such as a quart of milk? The manager wants you to walk past many other items sitting on the shelves that you hadn't planned to purchase, but just might—on impulse. Perhaps a new cereal, or perhaps some chocolate syrup to try with the milk that you went there to buy in the first place. In a similar vein, do you think it is a coincidence that candy bars are typically stocked right at the checkout counter? This expectation of impulse buying helps to explain the proliferation of "scrambled merchandising," such that retailers will stock and sell items that had not been related to their product category. For example, the Old Navy clothing stores (apparel) now also sell everything from music recordings to candy bars.

In order to help differentiate the products they carry and perhaps to increase profit margins as well, some retailers incorporate a "private label" or "OEM" (original equipment manufacturer) approach, wherein they commission manufacturers of what may be well-known and respected brands to take the name of the brand off of the product and put the retailer's name on instead. This is very common with apparel in major department stores. In the durable appliance category, Sears' Kenmore line comes immediately to mind.

Multilevel (MLM) or Network Marketing

Totally circumventing the need for physical location to sell at the retail level, some organizations employ independent distributors who sell the products and recruit other "subdistributors" to sell and contribute to "downstream" income for the distributors. There are some organizations, such as Mary Kay Cosmetics and Amway, that operate well within the law and enjoy many satisfied distributors and defenders. However, MLM has come under attack because of the emergence of unscrupulous companies that make their money on recruiting new distributors and subdistributors (who may be required to make a modest or perhaps even large investment) rather than on the sales of products. This not-so-fine distinction may separate legitimate operations from fraudulent pyramid schemes.

Interestingly, MLM has become rather popular in Asia, where companies like NuSkin have been growing at a healthy pace. It has been suggested that many of the societies on that continent are more family-based than those in the West and do not have publicly funded welfare systems. Therefore, since many network marketers rely upon selling to family and friends, MLM may be more culturally compatible there.

Cyber Marketing

The Internet has revolutionized commerce, in general, and distribution of products, in particular. Online promotion and processing of orders as well as the ability to monitor performance immediately and at a glance dramatically speeds up the time it takes to sell and deliver the product. Moreover, some categories of "information" products (including entertainment, educational, and business research material) can be instantaneously delivered or "downloaded" via the Internet. This serves to virtually eliminate the costs associated with production and distribution. For example, rather than order a CD music recording and wait for it to be delivered, the encoded information might be sent or downloaded via technological formats such as MP3. This serves to eliminate shipping charges as well as CD pressing costs, making the transaction more profitable for the marketer. And, on top of these advantages, the consumer receives the product immediately and can customize what she or he wants to download. It is this element of what has been called "twitch speed" that characterizes e-commerce (electronic commerce) on the Internet. It has become the standard and requisite for success. Visit www.ecommerce.internet.com.

Promotion

Promotion involves communication of product attributes and corporate image in the most favorable light possible (without misrepresentation) to intermediary sellers (i.e., trade advertising and trade promotion) and to end users (i.e., consumer advertising and consumer promotion). Sophisticated mass-marketing organizations (Procter & Gamble immediately comes to mind) typically employ a "pulling" strategy in regard to promotion (see Figure 1.5). By heavily promoting their products directly to the consumer via advertising and sales promotion, the company hopes to create a strong demand that is then felt by the retailer who is virtually "forced" by requests from customers to order and stock the product. The retailer, in turn, pressures the wholesaler to order and stock the product, and so on. Thus, if the manufacturer has succeeded, it can be said that the product has been "pulled" through the channels of distribution by strong demand. This approach is in sharp contrast to a "pushing" strategy (see Figure 1.6), in which demand is stimulated from manufacturer to wholesaler to retailer to end user, essentially "pushing" the product through the channels of distribution. (The "pulling" strategy does not, however, preclude a strong direct selling effort. It would only tend to lessen the resistance of potential customers, since much of the influence leading to a sale will have been accomplished by advertising and promotional efforts.)

Figure 1.5 The "pulling" promotional strategy

Figure 1.6 The "pushing" promotional strategy

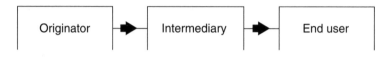

Dimensions of Advertising Effectiveness

There are the key elements we must consider in creating effective advertising:

Demographic: What type(s) of people do we want to influence?

Geographic: Where are the people we want to influence?

Impact: Is the desired message well communicated and hard-hitting enough to be memorable? To spur purchase?

Generally, advertising is designed to address the "AIR" (aware, inform, remind) concerns:

- Does it make the consumer *aware* of the product?
- Does it *inform* the consumer about the product's attributes?
- Does it *remind* the consumer about that which is already known?

Basic rules of thumb are:

1. The KISS approach—"Keep it simple, stupid!"
2. The three Ts—"Tell 'em what you're going to tell 'em."

"Tell 'em."

"Tell 'em what you've told 'em."

Reach: How many individuals or households will experience one exposure of the message?

Frequency: How many times will these people experience the message?

Reach × frequency = gross rating points

Measures total number of gross impressions of message

Target audience rating points = TARPS

Measures number of gross rating points relative to target audience/market segment targeted.

Duration: How long is the message?

Timing: When will the message be experienced?

Cost: Also known as CPM (cost per thousand). How much does it cost to reach 1,000 people or households with a single exposure?

The formula for calculating CPM, the primary measure of relative efficiencies between media options, is as follows:[15]

$$CPM = \frac{\text{Media cost}}{\text{Audience measured in thousands}}$$

For example,

	Advertising media	
	A	**B**
Cost of ad	$ 10,000	$ 30,000
Audience	100,000	600,000

so CPM is as follows:

$$A: \frac{\$10,000}{100,000} = \$100 \qquad B: \frac{\$30,000}{600.000} = \$50$$

So, as we consider placing an ad with media options A or B, we find (using the CPM formula) that B offers a more favorable CPM than does A, because in this particular case, B offers six times the audience of A at only three times the cost, in absolute dollars.

Media Options

What are the major advantages and disadvantages of the various media we may elect to use? (See www.admedia.org/internet.)

Broadcast TV

- High reach (potentially many millions of people).
- High impact (audio and video, stereo, and color. Animation is particularly important for demonstrating how a product is used.)
- High cost (in relative and absolute terms).
- Low selectivity regarding demographics (anyone with a TV can tune in, whether a millionaire or welfare recipient).

Cable TV

- Moderate to high reach.
- High impact.
- Moderate to high cost.
- High selectivity regarding demographics (cable channels can segment on the basis of special interests, such as sports, music, etc.).

Radio

- Low to high reach.
- Limited impact (audio only; but stereo is good for music programming). Listeners may experience the medium passively, while working, reading, or as "background." Nonetheless, they may become active buyers who, if driving home during rush hour, may pull off the road to purchase an impulse food item just advertised on the program they are listening to.
- Low to moderate cost.
- High selectivity regarding demographics (radio programming segments on the basis of such formats as music type, talk show, etc.).
- Lead time is generally very short. In fact, commercials can even be read live on the air, offering as much immediacy as any medium can be expected to.

Magazines

- Low to high reach.
- Moderate to high impact. (Multicolor printing on glossy paper is well-suited to upscale or aesthetically oriented items.)
- Moderate to high cost.
- Very high selectivity regarding demographics.
- Lead times of up to three months from submission of art and copy to hitting the newsstands is a major disadvantage, since timely response to market conditions might not be possible.

Newspapers

- Low to high reach.
- Moderate to high impact.
- Moderate cost.
- Moderate selectivity.
- Unlike magazines, lead times are generally very short, sometimes only a couple of days or less.

Direct Mail

- Low to high reach, depending almost entirely upon the degree to which the marketer is willing to invest in the purchase of mailing lists, postage, and other variable costs.
- Low to moderate impact.
- High cost per person reached.
- Extremely high selectivity (can cross-reference mailing lists to identify ideal prospects).

Internet

- High reach (worldwide access).
- High impact (audio and video, stereo and color, as well as animation are ideal for product demonstration).
- Extremely low cost. Although designing and maintaining a Web site may cost thousands of dollars, CPM can be extremely low.

- At first glance, rather low selectivity regarding demographics. After all, virtually anyone with a computer, modem, and connecting software can explore the Internet. However, with the adroit use of "search engines," Web publicity releases, and sophisticated "click here" options within the Web site, selectivity can actually be very high.

Out-of-Home Media

This category includes miscellaneous media, such as "Goodyear-type" blimps, billboards, and more. Can you believe that there is a company that leases the bottoms of the 18 holes of golf courses, so that golfers (who are often corporate decision makers) will bend down to pick up their golf balls out of the holes only to be greeted by a corporate "plug" like "Reach out and touch someone."

- Low to high reach.
- Low to moderate impact.
- Low cost.
- Low to moderate selectivity.

Sales Promotion Tools and Activities

Sales promotion has long been the "black sheep" in the promotion mix, and undeservedly so. It has been observed that sales promotion expenditures tend to increase as advertising expenditures decrease (during economic downturns), and vice versa (during economic upturns). The following represent key sales promotion areas of involvement:

Premiums

Gift with purchase (GWP): Involves giving an additional item for free as an incentive to buy a product (e.g., "Buy this, get that free.").

Purchase with purchase (PWP): Involves selling an additional item as an incentive to buy a product (e.g., "Buy this, get that at a highly discounted price.").

Initially, both GWP and PWP were regarded as innovations in the marketing of cosmetics. Because of their early success, however, they have become industry standards. Research indicates that consumers will often switch from one brand of cosmetics to another if the brand they have been buying fails to offer premiums as appealing as those of competitive brands.

Discounts

Simply put, a discount is a reduction in price (see "Elasticity of Demand" in Chapter 5 "Economics").

"Twofers": A "twofer" is offering two units for the price of one. In effect, this is a type of discount.

Coupons: Coupons are documents, often in the form of clippings from print media or as stand-alone promotional pieces, which entitle the bearer or presenter to discounted or free merchandise or service.

Samples: A sample strategy is giving away the product for trial at no charge. This is perhaps among the very best ways to demonstrate a product's superiority. Sampling puts it all on the line, suggesting that the consumer try the product and judge for himself or herself. This may be a particularly appropriate tactic for attracting consumers to a new brand, especially if the marketer is up against competing brands backed by heavy promotional expenditures. The potential and substantial downside, obviously, is that the brand's claim of superiority must be backed up in its product attributes. Therefore, extensive pretesting would seem to be in order.

Contests: Contests generally award prizes to winners of a competition, which may involve coming up with the slogan for a product, solving a puzzle, and so on.

Sweepstakes: Sweepstakes award prizes based upon a random drawing. Unlike contests, sweepstakes do not require skill, specialized knowledge, or creative input.

Incentives: In trade promotion (i.e., business-to-business), incentives are rewards based upon specific or targeted performance. For example, a manufacturing company may, for a specific and limited period of time, award a cash "bonus" or "spiff" to each salesperson of the retail establishments it supplies for each unit of the manufacturer's product that the individual sells. Another option is to offer a prize, be it a cash award or something of value such as a vacation, to the salesperson in each retail location who sells the most of this manufacturer's product (or a specific brand).

Product publicity: Product publicity actively brings the product to the attention of the public and/or specialized constituencies via media exposure and special events. Issuance of press releases and related marketing communications are involved. Opportunities may include:

- *Articles and/or interviews* in the broadcast and print media
- *"Staged" events* (i.e., "the world's largest …")
- *Trade/professional association lectures and demonstrations*
- *"800" toll-free telephone numbers* to provide information
- *Audiocassette or DVD programs* to provide information
- *"Freebie"* (i.e., free or complementary) *distribution* of the product accompanied by information to "opinion leaders," whose opinions are well regarded and can generate positive *word of mouth*

Sales

There are many entities that espouse a particular "method" for selling. Ultimately, all of these may be viewed relative to two models: the consultative model and the AIDA model. Neither model must be adopted in its entirety. One can "cherry-pick" the best aspects of each to come up with his or her own particular approach to best address such considerations as personal style, customer preferences, cultural and industry norms, as well as time urgency.

The consultative model: This approach is based upon keen listening skills, identification of the potential customer's real and perceived problems, and the sales professional's ability to find a solution to these problems. The major strength of this model lies in its customer-focused orientation. Its major weakness is that the sales pro tends to assume a more passive and nondirective role. In addition, time constraints (not to mention a lack of candor) may limit the opportunity for the customer to share his or her problems.

The AIDA model: AIDA stands for attention, interest, desire, and action. This approach is based primarily upon the power of persuasion and identification of the potential customer's real and perceived problems. AIDA's primary strength is that it allows the sales professional to play an active and somewhat directive role in the process. The model's primary weakness is that it may be regarded as coercive and, therefore, not sufficiently customer focused.

The sale is accomplished in stages that must follow in sequence.

1. *"A" for attention:* You must have the customer's attention. Otherwise, there is no point in proceeding.
2. *"I" for interest:* Sample gambit: "Sir, my research department and I have studied your organization and, based upon our preliminary findings, we can reduce your xxxx costs by $300,000 per month." And who wouldn't want to know how to do that?!
3. *"D" for desire:* Sample gambit: "Ms. Johnson, as you can see, using our service will save your organization a lot of money. As a further inducement—and given that we will come to agreement today—I will include an additional month of service at no extra charge."
4. *"A" for action:* After having answered any questions that the potential customer might have, the next and most important step is to close the sale or ask for the order, taking action. (And, by the way, many a sale is lost simply *because the salesperson does not know how to ask for the order* or even *completely fails to make the request*.) Sample gambit: "I'm glad that you can see the tremendous value of our service. Since we seem to be in agreement on all that's been discussed, I'd very much appreciate your approval." ("Approval" is a euphemism of sorts for "signature." Keep in mind that we live in a

litigious society and that putting one's name on paper may have a chilling effect.)

5. Once the deal is done, leave or adjourn the meeting as soon as possible. Since you have accomplished your goal, there is nothing to gain by lingering. In fact, it can only go downhill if you do.

Cross-Cultural Factors

Americans selling in Australia might be in for a big surprise in terms of the lack of receptivity they are likely to encounter. The academic sociology texts refer to the "rall poppy syndrome," which involves the seller being "cut down to size," much as the poppy is cut down. Try selling (as I have) in this culture, and it won't be long before you feel like just giving up.

In England, salespeople face the considerable challenge of convincing buyers to "trade up" to finer and more expensive products in a society that still manifests (even the vestiges) of a hierarchical class system. ("Hey lad, remember your place!")

In Singapore, the sales pro's obstacle is "Mr. Kiasu," the very popular cartoon character who has served as the stereotype of shallow hyperambition. The astute marketer is sensitive about cultural differences and adjusts his campaign and even his personal ways (e.g., manners, style) to accommodate this.

Cross-Selling

Cross-selling is a key concept for sales professionals. Since time is money and the opportunity to meet with potential or existing customers may be limited as well, it becomes all the more important to turn a single sales transaction into another or into multiples during the same sales meeting or as a direct result of it (not to mention the enhanced economies of scale that can be enjoyed; see the section "Economies of Scale" in Chapter 3).

Figuratively speaking, if customers are willing to buy peanut butter from you, they might also buy jelly from you. And if they do, they may also be interested in buying some bread from you. Now, if you are particularly skilled and the latent need is identifiable and sufficiently strong, you might even succeed in selling some fresh, cold milk—to wash it all down, of course! *Caveat:* Don't make the cross-sales unless the customer is very pleased with the primary or core product that introduced you to the cross-selling opportunity in the first place. The cross sale should not exceed 25 percent of the original/core sale. Why? Because, as sophisticated and ethical marketers, we engage in relationship-based selling, "and, psychologically, crossing the 25 percent threshold may cause the consumer to feel uncomfortable, although he or she may not be able to articulate this."

Up-Selling

Like its sibling, cross-selling, up-selling is a key concept for sales professionals. When prospective buyers are about to purchase what you have offered, you might try to persuade them (ever so gently!) to consider an "even better" (i.e., more expensive and profitable to the seller) model or option and perhaps even increase the number of units in the order. This is not to be confused with the so-called "bait and switch" practice, which is unethical, because it lures people to buy a particular item that has been advertised, only to have them find that the item is not available.

Relationship-Based Selling

We must constantly look at the big picture and our commitment to *serve the customer well over the long term.* If need be, we must be willing to walk away from the sale we know we can close if the sale would endanger our more enduring relationship with the customer; no hit-and-run approach here. This may be justified in terms of the marketing concept, idiosyncratic credit, and the true cost of losing a customer.

Factors in Marketing Analysis

After all is said and done, how do marketers ultimately determine how well they have done? They do so by measuring and analyzing the following:[17]

1. a. *Inquiries:* (By media; per marketing period; how many customer "contacts"?) Which media (e.g., TV, direct mail) are reaching prospects? Are we getting as many inquiries as (i) we usually do? and (ii) is the industry norm? The shorter the "marketing period," the more frequently we will monitor performance and analyze it. The shorter the marketing period, the more pressure we apply and the greater the likelihood of correcting errors and improving performance sooner rather than later. Some organizations monitor performance several times daily, even on an hourly basis.

   b. *Sales:* (By media; per marketing period; how many transactions and how much dollar volume?) Why is X pulling so poorly while Y is doing so well? Should we cut out the budget for X and put it into Y?

   c. *COST PER INQUIRY OR ACQUIRED LEAD:* (= total inquiries divided by total marketing costs) Are we paying too much for the lead? What can we do differently to get more responses?

   d. *COST PER SALE OR CONVERSION:* [= total (net) sales divided by total marketing costs] Are we paying too much for the sale? What can we do differently to lower costs? To increase sales volume? Okay, so we're getting a lot of good leads. But why aren't our salespeople *closing* them?

2. *Media and production costs:* (by source) Scrutinize, as above. Calculate them as one-time-only expenditures or "amortize"/spread them out over time?

3. *Representation of customer types/market segments:* Are we hearing from decision makers/purchasers? Users? Geographically, where are they? What are their personal backgrounds (age, education, race/ethnicity, gender, gender preference, values)? What kind of companies/organizations do they represent/work for (size, industry, for-profit or not-for-profit, or government agency, culture)?

4. *Representation of key titles:* Are we hearing from decision makers? Users? Or just "tire kickers" who are only curious and spinning our wheels/wasting our time?

5. *Projected dollar value of sales by customer:*
   a. Short term?
   b. Long term?
6. *Percentile analysis:* Rank our customers, from first/best to last/those having the greatest promise for more sales? When we get to Chapter 3, we will learn about the 80/20 rule. But for now, this ranking may allow us to begin to examine which of our customers (or, perhaps, which *types* or *categories* of customers) actually "butter our bread," so to speak.
7. *Bottom line:* The unavoidable and ultimate truth: Sales – costs = profits. So, what's the real deal? Did we make money or lose money? How much? What now? Hey, didn't anybody hear me? Where are my antacids? *Damn it!!!*

The Marketing and Product Management Checklist

1. How can I accumulate more idiosyncratic credit with my customers?
2. Have I adequately appraised the macroenvironment and been proactive in planning?
3. What can I do to minimize the sense of risk and maximize the sense of relative advantage that potential or existing customers may perceive regarding purchase of the products I sell?
4. Who actually makes the decision to purchase my products and who else participates in the decision?
5. Am I targeting the most appropriate market segments?
6. What can I do to differentiate my brands further from others competing against them in the same product class?
7. Are the four *P*s of my marketing mix congruent with each other, and does the mix work to the greatest advantage?
8. Do my advertising, promotional, and selling strategies best communicate the products' attributes and my commitment to customer satisfaction?

2 ACCOUNTING AND FINANCE

Finance deals with analysis of past and present data for the purpose of deploying or investing the organization's monetary and capital resources to greatest advantage. It combines day-to-day cash management responsibilities with long-term planning objectives. The function of accounting provides us with a valuable framework for management decision making toward this end, and we refer to this specialty within the discipline as *managerial accounting*. The specialty that deals with such matters as compliance with governmental regulations (such as tax and securities laws), documentation for operational purposes (i.e., record keeping or bookkeeping) as well as internal control for the safeguarding of the organization's assets is known as *financial accounting*. Our discussion of accounting focuses almost exclusively upon the managerial. And since the underlying premise here is decision making, we cover accounting and finance in the same chapter, referring back and forth to integrate the two disciplines and for ease of understanding.

Risk Management

As a preface, financial officers are charged not only with helping to identify, structure, and realize the most potentially profitable situations possible, but they are also (if not primarily) responsible for helping the firm to avoid or limit exposure to a broad range of risks. In this sense, the chief financial officer (CFO) is something of a "guardian," as well as a revenue-generating and deal-making "rainmaker." Risk management covers a dozen different areas of potential exposure, as follows:[1]

1. *Partners:* The parties with whom we do business. To what extent is the organization dependent upon them? And they dependent upon us? What kind of contractual agreements govern our relationships with them? How sensitive is the need for confidentiality? To what degree can we trust them? Is their culture similar to ours or rather different?

2. *Adversaries:* Those who compete against us in the marketplace. What is their market share? How are they pricing their offerings relative to ours? Are they spying on us and stealing trade secrets and proprietary information? Does the competition (actually, the lack of it) present legal problems (such as antitrust action)?

3. *Customers:* Those who buy our products and services. To what extent do they pose credit risks? How can we limit our exposure regarding product liability? Have we scheduled our marketing efforts to meet adequate levels of demand?

4. *Intermediaries:* Those who convey our product to our customers. Are the products and services available on a timely basis? By what means (via what path) are the offerings delivered to customers? What are the costs of distribution? To what extent are we dependent upon our distribution intermediaries?

5. *Financial considerations:* Are we vulnerable to foreign exchange rate fluctuations? To what extent is our portfolio diversified? Are we sufficiently liquid? How do interest rate fluctuations affect us?

6. *Operational considerations:* Are physical facilities safe and secure? How do abrogations of contracts interfere with "business as usual"? What measures are we prepared to take relative to acts of God/force majeure? What are the costs and corresponding benefits of our current internal methods?

7. *Human resources considerations:* What are our recruiting and hiring policies? How do we train our employees? What is the role of independent contractors? How do we forecast human resources (HR) staffing needs?

8. *Political considerations:* What is the risk of terrorism or war? What is the probability (and what is the likely consequence) of a change in regime?

9. *Legal considerations:* In what ways will we be exposed to unfavorable changes in export/import laws? Environmental laws? Intellectual property laws?

10. *Technological considerations:* How prone are we to the risk of obsolescence? Complexity? "Crash" catastrophe? What skills must our employees master in order to deal effectively with technology?

11. *Reputational considerations:* How is our corporate image vulnerable? In what ways are our brands vulnerable to attack? Are key employees "beyond reproach"?

12. *Strategic considerations:* How are resources planned and allocated? How "quick on our feet" are we? To what extent are joint ventures and mergers and acquisitions part of our plans?

Perhaps the cornerstone concept of risk management is essentially that risk be "spread" or diversified. For example, a financial specialist who manages the investments of a client might very intentionally avoid putting all of the client's "eggs in one basket." So, rather than invest only in higher-risk high technology companies (such as so-called dot-com businesses), the portfolio might spread the potential risk by investing in other sectors, including lower-risk sectors such as insurance firms and utilities.

Financial Statements

The keystone source of financial information is an organization's *annual report.* (Publicly held organizations are required by law to file these, whereas privately held entities are not required to do so.) This document includes the *balance sheet, income statement,* and *cash flow statement.* These financial statements must be prepared in accordance with *generally accepted accounting principles (GAAPs),* the body of universal standards for the accounting profession, specifically *certified public accountants (CPAs).* In addition, auditors must certify that the information contained in the statements is presented fairly, in accordance with *generally accepted auditing standards (GAASs)*, the body of universal standards specific to auditors or accountants who prepare financial statements for the annual report.

In the annual report, we find a section titled "Management's Discussion and Analysis" (MD&A). This is an important preliminary and subtle indicator of management's assessment of problems and opportunities as well as its plans for the future. While it would be unrealistic to expect management to acknowledge fault in the wake of its poor decisions and their consequences, it would be at least as troubling to investors in the enterprise if management were to rationalize the problems and/or fail to chart a credible and achievable course for the future to remedy these.

Notes to Financial Statements are "footnote" explanations to the information provided in the financial statements, but they can actually be as important as the statements themselves. These notes may disclose significant developments such as outstanding lawsuits, changes in accounting methods or officers' compensation structure, and reorganization or sales/purchases of business units.

Balance Sheet

The *balance sheet* represents a "snapshot" of a business at a particular point in time (see Figure 2.1). It reveals what the company owns (assets), what it owes (liabilities), and its net worth (shareholders' equity). The balance sheet doesn't "wipe clean" to zero at the beginning of each new period (i.e., December 31 to January 1). Assets are listed in order of liquidity, while liabilities are listed in order of claim. The synopsis of the formal "formula" for the balance sheet is:

$$\text{Assets} = \text{liabilities} + \text{shareholders' equity}$$

I believe that you will find it more meaningful, however, to move "liabilities" to the other side of the equals sign so that the informal "formula" reads:

$$\text{Shareholders' equity} = \text{assets} - \text{liabilities}$$

Figure 2.1 Balance sheet

Your Company, Inc.
(as of December 31, 2009; in millions)

Assets
Current assets
Cash	$ 15.5
Marketable securities	3.0
Accounts and notes receivable	4.0
Inventories	16.5
Total current assets	$ 39.0

Property, plant, and equipment
Buildings, machines, and equipment	190.0
Less: Accumulated depreciation	− 19.5
Land	5.5
Total property, plant, and equipment	$176.0

Other assets
Receivables due after 1 year	8.5
Other	1.5
Total assets	$225.0

Liabilities and Shareholders' Equity
Current liabilities
Accounts payable	$ 25.0
Accrued liabilities	6.5
Current maturity of long-term debt	2.0
Federal income and other taxes	12.5
Dividends payable	1.0
Total current liabilities	$ 47.0

Other liabilities	6.0
Long-term debt	27.0
Total liabilities	$ 80.0

Shareholders' equity
Preferred stock	15.0
Common stock	45.0
Additional paid-in capital	20.0
Retained earnings	65.0
Total shareholders' equity	$145.0
Total liabilities and shareholders' equity	$225.0

Income Statement

The *income statement* represents the profitability of a business over a period of time. Unlike the balance sheet, it does "wipe clean" at the beginning of each new period. The origin of the income statement has been traced back to the ancient days of Cassius, who rented slaves and used a crude form of this financial statement to record his revenues (e.g., rental fees) and expenses (e.g., fig leaves used to cover the slaves' private parts).

The "informal" synopsis of the "formula" is:

Gross income − total expenses = net profit (loss)

This formula is derived as follows:

1. Operating income (loss) = sales − total costs and expenses
   Total costs and expenses are composed of:
   Cost of goods sold
   Sales and general and administrative expenses
   Depreciation
2. Income before taxes = operating income − interest charges
3. Net income (loss) = income before taxes − provision for taxes

The legendary actor Errol Flynn had an interesting blanket interpretation of his own income statement. He said, "My problem lies in reconciling my *gross* habits with my *net* income."

Net income (or net loss) represents the net profitability of the organization. This is commonly referred to as its *bottom line*. And it is important to keep in mind that it is what you get to keep that really counts (net income) rather than what you earn (operating income).

Referring to the income statement (see Figure 2.2), let us explore and try to reach some preliminary conclusions about Your Company, Inc. In comparing figures for 2008 and 2009, we find the following.

Sales

Sales increased from $90 million to $100 million, up by about 11 percent. Not bad. However, consider the following.

Figure 2.2 Income statement

Your Company, Inc.
(year ended Dec. 31, 2009; in millions)

	2009	2008
Sales	$100.0	$90.0
Cost of goods sold	59.0	50.0
Sales, general, and admin. expenses	15.0	20.0
Depreciation	12.0	10.0
Total costs and expenses	$ 86.0	$80.0
Operating income	$ 14.0	$10.0
Interest charges	0.5	1.0
Income before taxes	$ 13.5	$ 9.0
Provision for income taxes	5.0	4.0
Net income (loss)	$ 8.5	$ 5.0

Cost of Goods Sold

Cost of goods sold increased from $50 million to $59 million, up by about 18 percent. This hike outstrips the rate of inflation and, perhaps more important, is in excess of the percentage increase of sales. Perhaps we should ponder the following:

- Can we reduce the cost of goods sold by renegotiating our deals with suppliers or by finding new and less expensive suppliers?
- Can we reduce the cost of goods sold by purchasing in larger quantities, and, if so, would this be efficient?
- Can we substitute different substances, materials, or products for the ones we are currently buying?
- Can we raise the price of our product?

Sales, General, and Administrative Expenses

This category decreased from $20 million to $15 million, down by about 25 percent. As a general rule, when expenditures decline dramatically (as is this case), it can be assumed that this is the result of deliberate management action. (Conversely, substantial growth in expenditures may be the result of "creeping decimalism," wherein management is not sufficiently sensitive to the notion that increments in spending, however small, ultimately can add up to a large sum.) We might ask:

- Does the decrease reflect a diminution in labor? In other words, were people fired, or was the company downsized? If so, what were the direct and indirect costs associated with severance, outplacement, and replacement?
- Does the decrease reflect a reduction in salaries or commissions payable to the organization's salespeople or independent sales agents?
- Does the decrease reflect a tightening of the purse strings regarding employee expense accounts or employee benefits?
- Does the decrease reflect reductions in such areas as office rental, utilities (e.g., telephone, electric), and insurance? If so, what are the trade-offs?
- Does the decrease reflect a cutback in research and development? If so, how is this likely to affect future earnings?

Total Costs and Expenses

This category increased from $80 million to $86 million, up by about 7.5 percent. We might question:

- How does this rate compare with that of inflation?
- How does it compare with standards for the industry?
- Can this category of expenditures be pared down further without adverse effects?

The adoption of an activity-based costing (ABC) method could only serve to improve performance. ABC is used to apportion costs to specific tasks, materials, products, services, and customers. Analysis can reveal a disproportion between input and output. Management can then make decisions to boost profitability.

Depreciation

Depreciation increased from $10 million to $12 million, up by about 20 percent. Given that depreciation is indicative of the potential for tax reduction arising from wear and tear or obsolescence of equipment or property (more on this later in the chapter), we might ponder whether the increase reflects additional purchases of equipment or property, or does it reflect a change in the method of depreciation that is used?

Operating Income vis-à-vis Net Income

Operating income (i.e., income before interest charges and taxes) increased from $10 million to $14 million, up by about 40 percent, a substantial rise. Yet net income (i.e., income after interest charges and taxes) increased at an even greater rate, 70 percent. Does this suggest that management was able to reduce its indebtedness and/or take greater advantage of tax-reduction opportunities in the second year? Or was it a stroke of luck that interest rates (and, therefore, interest expense) went down? It is noteworthy that, in absolute dollars, interest charges are relatively low and were reduced by about 50 percent. And, although provision for income taxes is substantial relative to income before taxes (which increased by about 50 percent), it increased at a rate of about 20 percent, rather less than the rates of increase for operating income, income before taxes, and net income.

Cash Flow Statement

The *cash flow statement* depicts sources and uses of cash over a given period of time. Focus is on generating income and honoring obligations (e.g., loans and other debts). It is of the utmost importance to differentiate the concepts of profitability and cash flow. An organization's balance sheet may reveal assets that substantially outweigh liabilities (i.e., profitability). However, if these assets are not collectible (e.g., bad debts or accounts receivable in arrears) or liquid (e.g., inventory) within a given time frame, then it is more than just theoretically possible that the organization might be unable to meet its obligations and be forced to file for bankruptcy even though financial statements indicate "profitability." As the saying goes, "Positive cash flow, not profit (on the books), pays for lunch."

Cash flows fall into any of three categories: *operating activities, investing activities,* and *financing activities.* Referring to the cash flow statement (see Figure 2.3), let us continue to explore and try to reach additional preliminary conclusions about Your Company, Inc. Given that figures in parentheses indicate money that is spent whereas figures without parentheses indicate money that is received, we observe that operating activities yielded $12 million, positive cash flow thus far. However, investing activities indicate that $15.5 million was spent in excess of that which was received. What might have precipitated this? The expenditure of $16 million for property, plant, and equipment suggests that the organization is implementing a plan for expansion.

Figure 2.3 Cash flow statement

Your Company, Inc.
(Year ended Dec. 31; in millions)

	2008
Cash flows	
Sources: operating activities	
Net earnings	$ 8.5
Accounts and notes receivable	(2.5)
Inventories	(5.0)
Depreciation	12.0
Accounts and notes payable	0.0
Federal income and other taxes	(1.0)
	$ 12.0
Sources: investing activities	
Marketable securities	0.5
Property, plant, and equipment	(16.0)
	$ (15.5)
Sources: financing activities	
Preferred stock (sale)	3.0
Common stock (sale)	2.5
	$ 5.5
Cash, net change	$ 2.0
Cash, on January 1	$ 13.5
Cash, on December 31	$ 15.5

This possibility is supported by the sale of $5.5 million in preferred and common stock under financing activities. Why sell stock to raise capital rather than take a bank loan? Perhaps the organization wanted to avoid paying interest on the principal, or (as we will see in the later section on key financial ratios) maybe it couldn't qualify for a loan. Ultimately, the organization posted a net positive cash flow of $2 million. In other words, although some activities may have contributed to positive cash flow while others may not have, the result is that more money was received than was spent.

Tax-Reduction Considerations

Referring to the income statement (see Figure 2.2), it is clear that an organization's net income or bottom line can be enhanced by a reduction in tax obligations much as it is by increased revenues and operating income. Essentially, the organization typically accomplishes this on a number of different fronts.

Structure of the Organization

Assuming that the entity is a corporation (rather than a partnership or sole proprietorship), different categories of the organization (e.g., "C" or "S") are taxed at different rates. The types include: limited liability company, limited partnership, C corporation, and S corporation. Other considerations must also be weighed, including: the extent to which liability is limited, who is eligible to run the organization, the number of participants allowed, to what extent ownership is transferable, and how many different types of stock can be issued. It may even make sense to switch from one type to another as tax status changes. In addition, the state (or province) in which the corporation is chartered can similarly influence tax liability.

Timing of Purchases

Most accounting is done on what is known as the *accrual basis*. Using this method, revenues are recognized on transactions during the tax period in which they actually occur. Conversely, if revenues are recognized during the period in which payment is made, we can assume that accounting is done on what is known as the *cash basis* (see Figure 2.4). Deferring the transaction even a single day (from December 31 to January 1, based on a January 1 fiscal year) essentially causes revenues to be recognized in the more recent year.

If income is high in a given year, the organization may benefit from being able to write off deductible expenditures against such income in the same year, effectively reducing its taxable income. If, however, income was very low or the organization has already written off a great deal for this year, it may elect to defer additional purchases until the following year when it can "use" the deductions.

Figure 2.4 Revenue recognition

Method	When revenue is recognized	Purchase (or) payment December 31	January 1
Accrual	At time of purchase	X	
Cash	At time of payment		X

Timing of Bad-Debt Write-offs

Accounts receivable that are substantially in arrears may, in fact, be uncollectible. Conceptually similar to the previous example of timing of purchases, the organization may elect to recognize such write-offs at a point in time when these deductions can be taken to full advantage. (It is interesting to note that Citicorp's write-off of $3 billion in Latin American debt in 1987 may have held strategic implications beyond those relating to the reduction of potential tax liability. Citicorp was at the time the largest U.S. bank, with assets far in excess of the vast majority of its competitors. Since market conditions dictated that these competitors would have to "follow the leader" and write off their own Latin American debt, Citicorp enjoyed a relative advantage. Its size allowed it to "take the hit" or bear the loss better than its competitors.)

Depreciation

The government allows the organization to reduce its tax liability by acknowledging the decrease in value of equipment and property relating to wear and tear or obsolescence. Depreciation policies can change to reflect the attempts of government to stimulate growth of particular industries or of the economy, in general.

There are two depreciation methods. Using a purchase of $80,000 in equipment and a life span of four years, for example, the methods are:

1. *Straight line:* Simply divide the purchase price of the item by the number of years over which it is to be depreciated. So, when we divide $80,000 by 4, we find that $20,000 is the amount that we can depreciate for each of the four years.

   Year 1: $80,000 × $^1/_4$ = $20,000
   Year 2: $80,000 × $^1/_4$ = $20,000
   Year 3: $80,000 × $^1/_4$ = $20,000
   Year 4: $80,000 × $^1/_4$ = $20,000

2. *Double declining balance:* Take the straight line and double it. In the previous example, one-fourth of the depreciation takes place in each of the four years; in this instance, we depreciate at the rate of one-half of the (remaining) value for each year.

   Year 1: $80,000 × $^1/_2$ = $40,000 (balance carried to year 2)
   Year 2: $40,000 × $^1/_2$ = $20,000 (balance carried to year 3)
   Year 3: $20,000 × $^1/_2$ = $10,000 (balance carried to year 4)
   Year 4: $10,000 × $^1/_2$ = $ 5,000 (balance is not exhausted)

You will notice that the value has not been fully depreciated by the end of the fourth year, since the balance is repeatedly multiplied by a fraction and is, therefore, almost infinite. So, when you reach the year when the straight-line method offers greater depreciation than the double-declining balance method, you may elect to switch over to the straight-line method to exhaust the value in its entirety.

As you can see, these methods differ in the rate at which depreciation is paced. Generally speaking, we would prefer to accelerate depreciation as much as possible to reduce income taxes.

Depletion

Similar to depreciation, the government may allow deductions relating to the depletion or exhaustion of natural resources, as in mining and logging.

Amortization

This is the policy of writing off the cost of an asset over time, usually fixed amounts at regular intervals. A simple example of amortization in banking or real estate would be assumption of a mortgage, making payments on a monthly basis until the mortgage is paid off.

Inventory Valuation: LIFO/FIFO

The means by which we assign value to our inventory also can have tax-reduction implications. Since inventory falls into the category of assets and is reflected in the income statement under cost of goods sold, diminishing or enhancing inventory will affect the bottom line. Let's assume that we operate a furniture store and have a total of three identical chairs. One chair was purchased in February for $12, another in March for $14, and still another in April for $17. If we sell a single chair, we might ask whether this item was the one we bought in February for $12 or the one bought in April for $17. If we decide that the "February" chair (the item purchased earliest or first) is the one that we will sell first, then we are using the *FIFO method (first in, first out)*. If, on the other hand, we decide that the "April" chair (the item purchased most recently or last) is the one that we will sell first, then we are using the *LIFO method (last in, first out)*. In this situation, the FIFO method enhances the value of the inventory, as shown in Figure 2.5, whereas the LIFO method diminishes it.

Since LIFO relatively understates the value of inventory, it may serve to reduce taxable income. However, management might prefer FIFO if, for example, a key priority is raising capital. In this case, the relatively overstated value of inventory may serve to enhance net worth in the balance sheet, due to the increase in the value of inventory, an asset. It may also serve to enhance net income, reflected in the income statement as a reduction in the cost of goods sold. And this might appeal to potential lenders and investors. (FIFO and LIFO assume that prices increase with time as a result of inflation. In the absence of inflation, both methods would be set aside, in favor of the weighted moving average (WMA) method. More about this soon, when we get to Chapter 4, "Statistics.")

Figure 2.5 Impact of LIFO/FIFO on value of inventory

		Value of Inventory	
		FIFO	LIFO
1 chair bought in February	for $12	(Sold)	$12
1 chair bought in March	for $14	$14	$14
1 chair bought in April	for $17	$17	(Sold)
		$31	$26

"Creative" Accounting

Obviously, presenting fraudulent information in financial statements subjects the offenders to civil and perhaps even criminal penalties. However, the current state of the art in financial reporting tolerates a considerable degree of discretion as to what is allowed. Skilled accountants may be able to present information that distracts attention from poor performance or incompletely states the information so as to create an inaccurate impression while nonetheless stopping short of actual fraud. Let's outline some red flags to keep in mind when you review financial statements (as in an annual report):

- *Growth in accounts receivable exceeds growth in sales.* Sales are "made" too aggressively. ("Chainsaw Al" Dunlap was cited for this while he was CEO of Sunbeam Corporation. His approach was to sell many seasonal items on credit way in advance, boosting revenue *on the books*, but minimizing *actual incoming cash flow*. The shenanigans eventually caught up with Dunlap, and he was soon ousted from his job.) See income statement and balance sheet.

- *Growth of inventories exceeds growth of sales.* Sales levels are falling. This might suggest products that are not competitive, poor marketing effort, or economic downturn. See income statement and balance sheet.
- *Ordinary expenses are included in restructuring charges.* As a result, earnings in the future are overstated. See income statement, management discussion and analysis, and footnotes.
- *Restructuring charges are taken frequently.* As a result, earnings growth will be overstated. (A prime example is Eastman Kodak with "serial" write-offs of $4.5 billion over six out of seven years, which, by the way, is more than the company earned over the previous nine years.) See income statement, management discussion and analysis, and footnotes.
- *In-process research and development (R&D) charges are written off by the purchaser at the time of acquisition.* (If the R&D is in process.)
- *Revenue recognition* (see Figure 2.4).

Internal Control

The organization must establish and implement policies and procedures to safeguard assets. The following measures are time-honored and widely accepted:

- *Make responsibilities as clear and discrete as possible.* For example, only one salesclerk should be assigned to a given cash register per shift, and that individual should be held accountable for any shortage.
- *Create a division of labor in areas where there is a potential for abuse.* For example, don't allow an employee to control cash if he or she also functions as the bookkeeper or to control inventory if he or she is the shipping department manager.
- *Set up a system of checks and balances.* For example, require two signatures on checks, for access to lockboxes, and for authorization of electronic funds transfers (EFT).

- *Hire reliable and ethical personnel.* Toward that end, job interviewers should view the reference check as more than just a minor and routine procedure. Off the record, I suggest that interviewers pose the following "acid test" question near the end of the reference check protocol: "Would you rehire him if he were available?" Any hesitation or response short of unequivocal endorsement is a red flag.
- *Document control procedures wherever and whenever possible.* These measures are ideally immediate, complete, and tamper-proof. For example, cash register receipts must be given to each customer to document and ensure that each transaction is actually rung up by the clerk rather than pocketed by that individual. It is also a good idea to post a notice conspicuously at the cash register to let customers know that they are entitled to a store credit (of, say, $10) if the clerk fails to hand them a register receipt. This provides an incentive to the customer to report an unrecorded transaction.
- *Rotate duties periodically.* This enables management to observe whether or not a problem stops when an individual is temporarily removed. If it does stop, this suggests that the individual may be culpable. Vacations provide such an opportunity. (For this reason, bank officers are required to take a vacation of at least two consecutive weeks in duration.)
- *Utilize independent checks.* Hire outside specialists such as certified public accountants (CPAs) in the capacity of auditors to inspect for irregularities or flaws in the system.
- *Supervise closely* (as needed) *and monitor performance* (periodically, albeit regularly).

Other People's Money (OPM)

Savvy businesspeople understand the importance of the concept of other people's money. In simplest form, OPM suggests that you arrange to receive money due to you (i.e., receivables) at the earliest possible moment, and you arrange to send money that you are obligated to pay (i.e., payables) at the last possible moment. In this way, you are able to enjoy the *float* or interest earned on this money. OPM policies are associated with improved cash flow as well as profitability.

Want some examples of OPM that are "everyday" points of reference, yet don't immediately come to mind as ways to use other people's money? In other words, funding that costs the astute user of OPM little or next to nothing?

- *Gift certificates:* You buy a gift certificate at a department store for, let's say, $100, but choose not to use it right away. If you wait one year, the department store has enjoyed one year of interest in their bank accounts— on your money. (And what if you lose the certificate?)

- *Traveler's checks (TCs):* You go on vacation, but don't use up all of your TCs. You put them in your drawer and anticipate using them on your next vacation in one year, rather than redeem or cash them in now. As a result, the TC company collects interest on *your* money over the duration of that year.

- *Commemorative stamps:* Postal services around the world periodically issue special editions of stamps, often celebrating or memorializing popular individuals or themes, involving such areas as sports, the arts, and politics. Why do they issue this type of stamp instead of just the "regular" type? Because many of the people who buy commemoratives *never use the stamps as postage*! They collect them. Of course, postal services are thrilled about this. After all, what could be better than having a business that involves selling "coupons" (i.e., stamps) that entitle the buyer to mail delivery service, but the buyer rarely redeems the coupon?

- *Celebrity personal checks:* When the great artist Picasso dined at restaurants or went to the local store to buy bottles of wine, loaves of bread, and such, he would typically ask the proprietor of the establishment to accept payment in the form of a personal check. Put yourself for a moment in that proprietor's shoes: First of all, do you want to offend Picasso and lose him as a customer by refusing his check? Of course not. But, you know something?

Picasso's check in the amount of, let's say, $10, is worth considerably more than that to collectors of such memorabilia.

By the way, wouldn't you be likely to frame and proudly display Picasso's check, for all to see? Sure you would. If so, you will never cash that check. Can you just imagine how many meals and provisions Picasso got for *free* over the course of his life?

Improving Cash Flow

The following methods are time-honored and widely used. While MBAs may learn these in classrooms, successful "shirtsleeves" managers often know these intuitively or learn them on the job.

Incoming Money

Incoming money includes accounts receivable, that is, money that is owed to you. There are several ways to encourage prompt payment:

- *Have payments electronically wired directly into your bank account via electronic funds transfers (EFT).* This can be done almost instantaneously. If this is not possible or feasible, have payments mailed directly to the bank (i.e., lockbox) rather than to you. The day or two saved in this process allows your money to be earning interest that much longer.
- *If your organization has many locations or branches, use the concentration method.* Funds from all areas are instantaneously transferred to a main or central bank account. As a result, your organization will pay less in fees for bank services while collecting more interest.
- *Allow cash discounts for early payment.* You might, for example, grant a 2-percent discount for payment within 10 days (i.e., "2 percent, net 10 days"). *Caveat:* The author is reluctant to suggest this because even 2 percent, net 10 days is the equivalent of more than 24 percent annualized. Moreover, creditors may pay you late and take the discount anyway.

- *Bill customers on a timely basis.* "Monitor" your accounts, tracking them to see if they are past due and, if so, 30, 60, or 90 days past due or more. As the saying goes: Aging is fine for wine, but not for receivables. Rules of thumb: The odds of never collecting an account that is 90 days delinquent are better than 1 out of 4. The odds of never collecting an account that is 180 days delinquent are better than 4 out of 10. If sufficiently delinquent, immediate payment may be demanded and further credit denied. Billing should be on a cyclical basis (e.g., weekly). In this way, pressure on the accounts receivable function is eased and operations tend to run more smoothly.
- *Make an active collection effort.* This may involve progressive steps ranging from initial telephone calls and letters to sterner demands and warnings of legal action.
- *Deposit receipts on a daily basis.* In addition to the OPM factor, this makes good sense from the standpoint of internal control as well. (Cash, checks, and credit card forms can be lost or stolen.)
- *Factor accounts, if necessary.* Essentially, this involves selling your accounts receivable to a financial services company at somewhat less than face value. Of course, the factor then assumes full responsibility for collection.

Outgoing Money

Outgoing money includes accounts payable, that is, money that you owe. Some tips for accounts payable include:

- *Centralize accounts payable.* Pay at the last possible moment. (See the section, "OPM" earlier in this chapter.)
- *Draw checks on out-of-town banks to take advantage of the "float,"* since it will take longer for the checks to clear.

Budgets

The budget represents the official position of management relative to anticipated financial activity within a given time frame (generally, quarterly and annually). It may be used to authorize action (i.e., spending as the budget allows), to assess performance (i.e., using the budget as a standard of measure), and to motivate (i.e., granting financial awards such as a bonus to those who surpass the budget standard).

There are, of course, different types of budgets to suit different purposes. *Operating budgets* govern everyday expenses, while *capital budgets* govern major investments and are more closely linked to strategic rather than operational planning (see Chapter 8, "Strategic Planning"). Zero-based budgets require decision makers to start from scratch (i.e., zero dollars), assuming that previously accepted expenses are not automatically included in the upcoming budget. Each expense must be justified in its own right, regardless of how it was represented in previous budgets. (This method, associated with a cost-cutting or "bean counter" mindset, is commonly employed within certain rigid organizational cultures and seems to become even more widely used during periods of economic downturn. While this approach can uncover areas of unnecessary spending, it more often than not generates excessive paperwork and is, ironically, more costly in the end.)

Time Value of Money (Discounted Cash Flow)

Albert Einstein, when asked to identify the most powerful force in the universe, replied that it is *superannuation*. That is a fancy word for *compound interest*. No less than John D. Rockefeller referred to it as the eighth wonder of the world. If a kindly uncle had put away for you $5,000 on the day you were born and just let it lay to earn compound interest at the rate of, let's say, 12 percent per year after tax—earnings upon earnings—you would be a millionaire at the relatively young age of 47![2]

Simply put, $1 today is worth less than $1 a year from now because of inflation. Clearly, the value of money diminishes with the passage of time. With this in mind, we factor (or "discount") these future cash flows to reflect this diminution in value.

Investment Appraisal

Organizations must acknowledge the reality of *limited funding resources* (as reflected in budgets, for example) in the face of what may seem to be an abundance of investment opportunities. This area of endeavor is known as *capital rationing*. It implies that financial decision makers sometimes reach a fork in the road, so to speak, and must choose one investment or another, but not both. The potential benefit associated with the foregone option is known as an *opportunity cost*. Conversely, a chosen investment may, in time, come to be regarded as an undesirable and irrevocable action (as in the decision to buy equipment that has unforeseeably become obsolete and whose value will not be recouped). This potential burden is known as a *sunk cost*. There are basically three methods of assessing potential investment opportunities. Two of these, *net present value (NPV)* and *internal rate of return (IRR)*, address the issue of discounted cash flow. The *payback* method does not.

Net Present Value (NPV)

NPV weighs the investment in absolute dollars against its return in discounted cash. The formula for NPV is:

NPV = Discounted incoming cash flows (revenues)
− outgoing cash flow (investment) at the outset

Let us assume that we are presented with an investment opportunity that would cost us $3,800 in today's money. Let us further assume that we can reasonably expect to generate $1,000 in income per year for each of five years and that the prevailing cost of money or interest rate is 8 percent.

Do we accept or decline the opportunity?

The answer lies in comparison of the discounted (incoming) cash flows to the initial (outgoing) cash investment. We multiply each year's projected incoming cash flow by its discount factor (see area under "8%" in the present value table, Figure 2.6). If the sum of the

Figure 2.6 Present value of $1

Period	1%	2%	3%	4%	5%	6%	7%	8%	9%	10%	12%	14%	15%
1	.990	.980	.971	.962	.952	.943	.935	.926	.917	.909	.893	.877	.870
2	.980	.961	.943	.925	.907	.890	.873	.857	.842	.826	.797	.769	.756
3	.971	.942	.915	.889	.864	.840	.816	.794	.772	.751	.712	.675	.658
4	.961	.924	.889	.855	.823	.792	.763	.735	.708	.683	.636	.592	.572
5	.951	.906	.863	.822	.784	.747	.713	.681	.650	.621	.567	.519	.497
6	.942	.888	.838	.790	.746	.705	.666	.630	.596	.364	.507	.456	.432
7	.933	.871	.813	.760	.711	.665	.623	.683	.547	.500	.452	.400	.376
8	.923	.853	.789	.731	.677	.627	.582	.540	.502	.467	.404	.351	.327
9	.914	.837	.766	.703	.645	.592	.544	.500	.460	.424	.361	.308	.284
10	.905	.820	.744	.676	.614	.558	.508	.463	.422	.386	.322	.270	.247
11	.896	.804	.722	.650	.585	.527	.475	.429	.388	.350	.287	.237	.215
12	.887	.788	.701	.625	.557	.497	.444	.397	.356	.319	.257	.208	.187
13	.879	.773	.681	.601	.530	.469	.415	.368	.326	.290	.229	.182	.163
14	.870	.758	.661	.577	.505	.442	.388	.340	.299	.263	.205	.160	.141
15	.861	.743	.642	.555	.481	.417	.362	.315	.275	.239	.183	.140	.123
16	.853	.728	.623	.534	.458	.394	.339	.292	.252	.218	.163	.123	.107
17	.844	.714	.605	.513	.436	.371	.317	.270	.231	.198	.146	.108	.093
18	.836	.700	.587	.494	.416	.350	.296	.250	.212	.180	.130	.095	.081
19	.828	.686	.570	.475	.396	.331	.276	.232	.194	.164	.116	.083	.070
20	.820	.673	.554	.456	.377	.312	.258	.215	.178	.149	.104	.073	.061
25	.780	.610	.478	.375	.295	.233	.184	.146	.116	.092	.059	.038	.030
30	.742	.552	.412	.308	.231	.174	.131	.099	.075	.057	.033	.020	.015

Period	16%	18%	20%	24%	28%	30%	32%	40%	50%	60%	70%	80%	90%
1	.862	.847	.833	.806	.781	.758	.735	.714	.667	.625	.588	.556	.526
2	.743	.718	.694	.650	.610	.574	.541	.510	.444	.391	.346	.309	.277
3	.641	.609	.579	.524	.477	.435	.398	.364	.296	.244	.204	.171	.146
4	.552	.516	.482	.423	.373	.329	.292	.260	.198	.153	.120	.095	.077
5	.476	.437	.402	.341	.291	.250	.215	.186	.132	.095	.070	.053	.040
6	.410	.370	.335	.275	.227	.189	.158	.133	.088	.060	.041	.029	.021
7	.354	.314	.279	.222	.178	.143	.116	.095	.059	.037	.024	.016	.011
8	.305	.266	.233	.179	.139	.108	.085	.068	.039	.023	.014	.009	.006
9	.263	.226	.194	.144	.108	.082	.063	.048	.026	.015	.008	.005	.003
10	.227	.191	.162	.116	.085	.062	.046	.035	.017	.009	.005	.003	.002
11	.195	.162	.135	.094	.066	.047	.034	.025	.012	.006	.003	.002	.001
12	.168	.137	.112	.076	.052	.036	.025	.018	.008	.004	.002	.001	.001
13	.145	.116	.093	.061	.040	.027	.018	.013	.005	.002	.001	.001	.000
14	.125	.099	.078	.049	.032	.021	.014	.009	.003	.001	.001	.000	.000
15	.108	.084	.065	.040	.025	.016	.010	.006	.002	.001	.000	.000	.000
16	.093	.071	.054	.032	.019	.012	.007	.005	.002	.001	.000	.000	
17	.080	.080	.045	.026	.015	.009	.005	.003	.001	.000	.000		
18	.089	.051	.038	.021	.012	.007	.004	.002	.001	.000	.000		
19	.080	.043	.031	.017	.009	.005	.003	.002	.000	.000			
20	.051	.037	.026	.014	.007	.004	.002	.001	.000	.000			
25	.024	.016	.010	.005	.002	.001	.000	.000					
30	.012	.007	.004	.002	.001	.000	.000						

discounted cash flows is a higher figure than the amount invested, it would seem (other factors aside) that we should accept the deal. If the sum is lower, it would seem (other factors aside) that we should decline the deal. In the example at hand, we would accept, since the difference between the two, the NPV, is a positive figure, 193. In choosing between several investment options, we would generally select the one with the highest NPV (other factors aside).

Investment (outgoing cash flow) $3,800
Revenues (incoming cash flows):
$$
\begin{array}{llll}
\text{Year 1:} & \$1,000 \times 0.926 & = & \$\ 926 \\
\text{Year 2:} & \$1,000 \times 0.857 & = & \$\ 857 \\
\text{Year 3:} & \$1,000 \times 0.794 & = & \$\ 794 \\
\text{Year 4:} & \$1,000 \times 0.735 & = & \$\ 735 \\
\text{Year 5:} & \underline{\$1,000} \times 0.681 & = & \underline{\$\ 681} \\
& \$5,000 & & \$3,993 \\
& \text{(Not discounted)} & & \text{(Discounted)}
\end{array}
$$

$3,993 (discounted income) − $3,800 (initial investment) =
$193 (NPV)

Note: If additional outgoing cash flows were to be incurred in subsequent years, they too should be discounted. In such an instance, the previous NPV formula would be modified as follows:

NPV = Discounted incoming cash flows (revenues)
− outgoing cash flow (investment at the outset)
− discounted outgoing cash flows (investment in
subsequent years)

Economic Value Added (EVA)

EVA, devised by consulting firm Stern Stewart & Associates, is employed by decision makers to help measure internal performance and to optimally allocate resources. It involves the discounting of cash flows and, as such, NPV will serve much the same purpose. EVA reveals how net operating profits after tax (NOPAT) compare to the cost of capital during a given time period. This metric is widely used to link productivity to performance (e.g., bonus), formulate budgets, and analyze acquisitions and divestitures. It is not the absolute EVA level that counts, but the *change* in level that really is of interest to us. The formula for EVA is:

$$\text{EVA 5 net operating profits after tax (NOPAT)}$$
$$- \text{book value} \times \text{cost of capital}$$

Market Value Added (MVA)

A "sister" of EVA, MVA serves as a measure of wealth creation. All the capital contributed by lending entities and shareholders over time is measured against the firm's market value. In other words, what is the net amount or return that contributors can walk away with if they were to "cash in their chips"? The formula is:

$$\text{MVA 5 cash in (investor and lender contributions)}$$
$$- \text{cash out (what they could sell their interests}$$
$$\text{for today/now)}$$

More Alphabet Soup?

Critics of EVA are quick to suggest several flaws. According to a communication by Eric Olsen of the Boston Consulting Group, EVA:

1. Is biased against new assets. When an investment is incurred, EVA is artificially low.
2. Encourages managers to "milk the business." It punishes behavior that is associated with growth, while it rewards behavior that is not associated with it.
3. Is biased in favor of large, low-return organizations. Size counts.

So, in response, *alternative measures of value* have emerged:[3]

TSR (total shareholder return): Represents the change in capital value during an annual period, plus dividends, expressing a percentage gain or loss relative to the level at the outset.

TBR (total business return): Looks at CFROI (cash flow return on investment) and the growth in invested cash. (By the way, TBR was devised by the Boston Consulting Group.)

EBITDA: Represents earnings before interest, taxes, depreciation, and amortization.

EBITDAMN: Represents earnings before interest, taxes, and I don't give a damn!

Excuse the "cuss" word, but keep in mind that the world of financial analysis is also governed by the rules of marketing. In other words, financial consulting firms have to *differentiate* themselves from their competitors, just as players in any product class must do. So they come up with new methods or metrics, each of which has strengths and weaknesses.

Personally, as primitive as it may reveal me to be, I still like to use the almost ancient metric of ROI (return on investment), that is, operating income divided by assets.

Variants of this include:

ROCE (return on cash employed): That is, earnings divided by book capital.

RONA (return on net assets): That is, net income divided by net assets.

Internal Rate of Return (IRR)

Unlike net present value, internal rate of return weighs the investment relative to the cost of money or interest rate, which herein is an unknown. IRR assumes that NPV is zero. In other words, IRR asks us to determine the rate of interest that would cause the discounted (incoming) cash flows to be equal to the investment (i.e., zero difference).

Using the example for NPV, we would calculate to find the rate that would, in effect, reduce $3,993 to $3,800. That figure is your IRR and is calculated by trial and error. In this particular instance, that rate is slightly higher than 9 percent (see area under 9% on the present value table, Figure 2.6). The investment would be judged desirable to the extent that the IRR exceeds those of alternative investment options.

Investment (outgoing cash flow) $3,800
Revenues (incoming cash flows):

Year 1: $1,000 × 0.917	=	$ 917
Year 2: $1,000 × 0.842	=	$ 842
Year 3: $1,000 × 0.772	=	$ 772
Year 4: $1,000 × 0.708	=	$ 708
Year 5: $1,000 × 0.650	=	$ 650
$5,000		$3,889
(Not discounted)		(Discounted)

The amount—$3,889 (discounted income at 9 percent)—is still a little higher than the $3,800 (initial investment). To reduce the discounted income by $89 and set it equal to the initial investment ($3,800 = $3,800, zero difference), we would require an IRR of slightly higher than 9 percent.

Payback

The payback method helps us to calculate the point in time at which we can expect to recoup our investment. Unlike net present value and internal rate of return, however, payback does not discount cash flows. (If the deal takes place within a short time frame, say, one year, then the time value of money would probably not be as significant a factor and, for this reason, payback is a commonly used "quickie" method or as a preliminary "screen," or hurdle of sorts, to ascertain whether or not to consider the opportunity further and go to the next level.) Also, payback does not evaluate the upside or profitability of one investment option as compared with another. Let us compare Deal A, which yields income of $50,000 per year for 7 years, with Deal B, which yields $50,000 per year for 10 years (see Figure 2.7). Each deal requires an investment of $250,000. Using the payback method, we would rank these options equally, since each recoups its investment or reaches payback in 5 years (i.e., $50,000 per year for each of 5 years). However, Deal B generates $500,000 (i.e., $50,000 per year for each of 10 years), whereas Deal A generates only $350,000 (i.e., $50,000 per year for each of 7 years), a difference of $150,000 without discounting of cash flows.

The formula for payback is:

$$\text{Payback} = \frac{\text{Investment}}{\text{Yield}} = \frac{250,000}{50,000} = 5 \text{ years}$$

Figure 2.7 Comparison of investments using the payback method

	Investment	Annual yield	Years of return	Years for payback	Total income
Deal A	$250,000	$50,000	7	5	$350,000
Deal B	250,000	50,000	10	5	500,000

Office Politics and the Funding of Budgets

Pretend for a moment: You ask your boss for a certain amount of money for a project that you are very optimistic about. She tells you that she agrees with you that it is a good idea and worthy of being funded, but unfortunately she cannot spare the money because there's not enough cash on hand. This is known as a *plowback* position. Of course, it is entirely possible that the company really is experiencing financial difficulties or some other emergency situation. (We would refer to that as a *putback* situation.) But if this is not the case, you might actually prevail and get your funding by *tactfully* (underline: *tactfully*) reminding your boss that the cost of capital when you borrow funds actually costs less than equity capital when you consider that the interest on such loans is usually tax deductible. And, of course, what about the *opportunity cost* involved in passing up your proposed project? After all, wouldn't it be awful if one of your competitors seized the opportunity and succeeded in the marketplace simply because our company chose not to?

Special Considerations Regarding Foreign Investment

In addition to using the appraisal methods we have just discussed, it is necessary to weigh certain factors specific to foreign investment and operations. For example, *fluctuations in currency exchange rates* can render an otherwise profitable situation unprofitable. (For exchange rate information, visit www.xe.net/currency.) *Unfavorable tax structure* can have a similar effect. In addition, some countries place *restrictions on outbound transfer of funds*, making it difficult or impossible to withdraw capital for reinvestment or redeployment. And, of course, *political instability* may portend nationalization of industries or other seizures of assets.

Predicting devaluations in foreign currency requires more than street smarts.[4] Keep your eye out for these red flags:

1. *Current account deficits.* This occurs when outgoing cash flow exceeds incoming cash flow/exports.
2. *Level of foreign exchange (FX) reserves.* Countries with substantial reserves or money in the bank are better able to avoid devaluations.
3. *Condition of the home currency versus currencies of trading partners.* Exchange rates that do not fluctuate much tend to encourage capital inflows, hence domestic growth.
4. *The nature of foreign capital inflows and outflows.* Direct foreign investment of the "bricks and mortar" variety is preferable to short-term investments in bonds and equities.
5. *Money supply growth.* Rapid growth puts a lot of cash into circulation, and lending institutions that are so liquid may have lax credit requirements.

6. *Local condition of real estate markets.* Particularly in developing nations, real estate is widely regarded as the most reliable means of wealth accumulation. However, "asset inflation" is associated with further *unnecessary* building and, ultimately, the gluts that result. Write-offs of failed real estate loans weaken currency.

7. *Solvency of banking and financial institutions.* Central banks find it difficult to raise interest rates for the purpose of defending currency when the institutions are in poor condition.

8. *Dissent on financial policy.* Central banks not seeing eye to eye with the ministry of finance or its equivalent is a red flag. Deciding to devalue currency is an easy way out, given political realities and decision maker self-interest.

9. *Forward FX market.* Keen observers keep a close watch on the spread between bids and offers. Widening of spreads might suggest a coming devaluation.

10. *Sophistication of technocrats and central bankers.* Reputations of central bank policy makers and their track records should be factored in.

Key Financial Ratios

We can learn a great deal about an organization by compiling ratios culled from its financial statements. These ratios are strong indicators of the organization's solvency (i.e., ability to meet its financial obligations), efficiency, or profitability. While the standards (i.e., what is regarded as "good" or "bad") for some ratios may apply across industry lines, they do tend to differ by industry. To find guidelines or parameters on an industry-specific basis, the following sources can refer to *Almanac of Business and Industrial Financial Ratios* by Leo Troy or *Annual Statement Studies* by The Risk Management Association.

Personally, I have found the following formulas to be particularly important (and apply them to the financial statements for Your Company, Inc.),[5]

Working Capital or Current Ratio

The working capital or current ratio (see Figure 2.1, the balance sheet, on page 57) is a measure of short-term solvency, in relative terms. The formula that expresses this is:

$$\text{Working capital} = \frac{\text{Current assets}}{\text{Current liabilities}}$$

Placing the values from the balance sheet (see Figure 2.1) into the formula yields:

$$\text{Working capital} = \frac{\$39 \text{ million}}{\$47 \text{ million}} = 0.83$$

Generally, the ratio should be greater than 1:1. Your Company's current ratio is only 0.83. So the firm might attempt to restructure its debt, deferring some of it further into the future (see debt-to-equity ratio, which follows).

Net Working Capital

Net working capital (see Figure 2.1, the balance sheet) is a measure of short-term solvency, in absolute terms (i.e., dollars). Although it is not in strict terms a ratio, it is a practical indicator of likely credit-worthiness, since banks and other lending institutions typically require certain minimum levels of net working capital. The formula that expresses this is:

Net working capital = current assets − current liabilities

Placing the values from the balance sheet (see Figure 2.1) into the formula yields:

Net working capital = $39 million − $47 million = −$8 million

Your Company's net working capital is $-\$8$ million, a negative figure. So the firm may have to generate capital by other means, such as selling its assets or stock. Incidentally, one of the most common causes of new business failure is undercapitalization. Fledgling enterprises with solid product lines and good marketing efforts may nonetheless require a great deal of funding, especially in capital-intensive industries, such as manufacturing.

Liquidity Ratio or Quick Ratio

The liquidity ratio or quick ratio (see Figure 2.1, the balance sheet) is another measure of short-term solvency, in relative terms. It is a conservative indicator, given that the assets represented in the numerator of the ratio do not include inventory, which is difficult to liquidate quickly. The formula that expresses this is:

$$\text{Liquidity ratio} = \frac{\text{Cash} + \text{accounts receivable} + \text{marketable securities}}{\text{Current liabilities}}$$

Placing the values from the balance sheet (see Figure 2.1) into the formula yields:

$$\text{Liquidity ratio} = \frac{\$22.5 \text{ million}}{\$47.0 \text{ million}} = 0.48$$

Your Company's quick ratio is only approximately 0.48. This ratio should always be greater than 1:1. It can even be as high as 4:1 (sometimes even higher, depending upon the industry).

Debt-to-Equity Ratio

The debt-to-equity ratio (see Figure 2.1, the balance sheet) is a measure of long-term solvency, in relative terms. The formula that expresses this is:

$$\text{Debt-to-equity ratio} = \frac{\text{Total liabilities}}{\text{Total shareholders' equity}}$$

Placing the values from the balance sheet (see Figure 2.1) into the formula yields:

$$\text{Debt-to-equity ratio} = \frac{\$\ 80\ \text{million}}{\$145\ \text{million}} = 0.55 = 55\%$$

Generally speaking, the debt-to-equity ratio should be less than 0.80. Your Company's debt-to-equity ratio is approximately 0.55. Not bad. So this figure suggests that the firm might possibly be able to "trade off" its long-term obligations against its short-term obligations (by renegotiating the terms of loan repayment, for example).

Incidentally, indebtedness or leverage is not a bad thing per se. In fact, it can be said that a firm with absolutely no debt is not optimally managed. To use a point of reference in our personal financial lives, buying a home for cash is not generally as advantageous as taking a loan to finance the purchase, since the mortgage payments are tax deductible and can be paid from future earnings. This, in effect, reduces the initial cash outflow.

Operating Profit Margin

Operating profit margin (see Figure 2.2, income statement, on page 59) is a measure of profitability before interest charges and taxes, in relative terms. The formula that expresses this is:

$$\text{Operating profit margin} = \frac{\text{Operating income}}{\text{Sales}}$$

Placing the values from the income statement (see Figure 2.2) into the formula yields:

$$\text{Operating profit margin} = \frac{\$\ 14\ \text{million}}{\$100\ \text{million}} = 0.14 = 14\%$$

The standard may vary by industry. For example, 5 percent might be the norm for supermarket chains, whereas 40 percent might be more appropriate for cable TV multisystem operators.

Inventory Turnover

Inventory turnover (see Figure 2.1, the balance sheet) is a measure of efficiency. The higher, the better. The formula that expresses this is:

$$\text{Inventory turnover} = \frac{\text{Total inventory}}{\text{Average level of inventory}}$$

Using the values from the balance sheet (see Figure 2.1) and assuming that the average level of inventory is 1.65 (since that figure is not presented in the financial statements), the formula yields:

$$\text{Inventory turnover} = \frac{\$16.5 \text{ million}}{\$1.65 \text{ million}} = 10$$

The standard differs by industry. Low turnover may suggest a noncompetitive or obsolescent product. However, low turnover is not always bad. For example, art galleries that deal in high-priced, high-profit margin items may sell their entire inventory of extremely expensive paintings at auction only once or twice a year.

Sales-to-Employees Ratio

The sales-to-employees ratio (see Figure 2.2, the income statement) is a measure of efficiency. It may implicitly indicate the extent to which an organization is automated. Or it may suggest the skill level of the organization's sales (and marketing) personnel. The formula that expresses this is:

$$\text{Sales-to-employees ratio} = \frac{\text{Sales}}{\text{Number of employees}}$$

Using the values from the income statement (see Figure 2.2) and assuming that the number of employees is 500 (since that figure is not presented in these particular financial statements), the formula yields:

$$\text{Sales-to-employees ratio} = \frac{\$100 \text{ million}}{500 \text{ employees}} = \$200,000 \text{ / employee}$$

The higher the ratio, the better, as long as the customer-focus orientation is not diminished.

Return on Assets (ROA)

Return on assets, or ROA (see Figure 2.1, the balance sheet and Figure 2.2, the income statement), is a key measure of management productivity, an indicator of how well the firm's assets are being utilized. The formula that expresses this is:

$$\text{Return on assets} = \frac{\text{Net income}}{\text{Assets}}$$

Placing the values from the balance sheet (see Figure 2.1) and the income statement (see Figure 2.2) into the formula yields:

$$\text{Return on assets} = \frac{\$\ 8.5 \text{ million}}{\$225.0 \text{ million}} = 0.037 = 3.7\%$$

Your Company's ROA is 3.7 percent. The standard for ROA varies by industry. Some years ago, an accountant hired by Universal Pictures was escorted to the lot where many of the company's feature films were shot. As the story has it, he found the movie set very exciting. He asked his host/new boss what was done with the studio set when films were not actually in production only to be informed that the gates were locked and security guards posted to prevent theft and vandalism. The new hire then suggested that it would make a fascinating tour for vacationers and other visitors (creative management thinking). And that suggestion gave birth to what we know today as the famous Universal tour.

Another entertainment industry story: As a young man working for his family's funeral parlor business, Steven J. Ross noticed that the limousines used for funeral services laid idle in the evenings. So he arranged for a livery service to hire the vehicles during what would otherwise have been considered "downtime." It was this type of resourcefulness and astute deployment of assets that enabled Ross to grow a small car rental business, merge it with a garage firm (and the family's funeral parlor business), and acquire a motion picture and record company, transforming this entity into Warner Communications and, ultimately, Time Warner, Inc.[6]

Return on Equity (ROE)

Return on equity or ROE (see Figure 2.1, the balance sheet and Figure 2.2, the income statement) is a key measure of profitability. The formula that expresses this is:

$$\text{Return on equity} = \frac{\text{Net income}}{\text{Shareholders' equity}}$$

Placing the values from the balance sheet (see Figure 2.1) and income statement (see Figure 2.2) into the formula yields:

$$\text{Return on equity} = \frac{\$\ 8.5\ \text{million}}{\$145.0\ \text{million}} = 0.059 = 5.9\%$$

Your Company's ROE is 5.9 percent. The standard for ROE varies by industry. The higher, the better. However, the investor may weigh an organization's ROE against the yields of "passive" investment options (e.g., money markets or commercial paper) or those of other "active" investment options.

Return on Investment (ROI)

Return on investment or ROI (see Figure 2.1, the balance sheet and Figure 2.2, the income statement) is a key measure of profitability, relative to the firm's basic operations, an indicator of what management guru Peter Drucker would characterize as management's effectiveness ("doing the right things") and efficiency ("doing things right"). The formula that expresses this is:

$$\text{Return on investment} = \frac{\text{Operating income}}{\text{Assets}}$$

Placing the values from the balance sheet (see Figure 2.1) and income statement (see Figure 2.2) into the formula yields:

$$\text{Return on investment} = \frac{\$\ 14\ \text{million}}{\$225\ \text{million}} = 0.062 = 6.2\%$$

Your Company's ROI is 6.2 percent. Although the standards vary by industry, ROI yields of 0 to 10 percent are generally viewed as low, 10 to 20 percent as medium, and anything in excess of 20 percent as high. *Note:* Analysts differ as to the "proper" formula for ROI. Some prefer to use "net income" as the numerator (i.e., a more conservative indicator), while others prefer to use "operating income." Similarly, analysts interested in long-range funding might tend to favor "assets minus current liabilities" as the denominator, rather than "assets."[7] In this sense, the definition of the formula is subjective and open to interpretation.

Price-to-Earnings (P/E) Ratio

P/E is a key measure of profitability, particularly from an investor's perspective. The formula that expresses this is:

$$P\ /\ E = \frac{\text{Price per share of common stock}}{\text{Earnings per share (EPS) of common stock}^*}$$

So if we have net income of $8.5 million and we have 4.25 million shares of common stock outstanding, we have EPS of $2. If the price of a share is $30, then the P/E is 15. High-growth industries tend to have higher P/E, because higher earnings are anticipated in the future.

So, what then, of the company that has a *market capitalization* or *book value* (i.e., number of outstanding shares multiplied by price per share) well into billions of dollars and is considered a "category killer" and huge success, while it has actually been *losing money* every year since its inception? Those who support such a firm explain that the profits will come in the future. If you factor in industry "shake out" (i.e., failure of competitors) as well as dramatic growth, this is plausible. However, others are skeptical and have referred to such companies' P/E ratio as a "price-to-fantasy" ratio.

* EPS = net income divided by the number of common stock shares

So what's a company worth? Modigliani and Miller won the Nobel Prize for addressing this query about corporate financing. The duo theorized that value is better decided by investment choices than by investment decisions. Hmm.

Baseball legend Yogi Berra was asked whether he wanted his pizza pie cut into six or eight slices. Yogi confidently answered, "Eight. You get more that way." Mr. Berra, meet Professors Modigliani and Miller!

Dividend Payout

The dividend payout ratio reveals common stock earnings that are paid as dividends, and reflects the company's dividend *policy*. Is the firm plowing earnings back into the business (an anticipation of growth), or are dividend payments quite liberal?

$$\frac{\text{Dividend per share}}{\text{Earnings per share (EPS) of common stock}}$$

Some Equity Terms (Reference)

Common stock: Ownership shares in a firm. These shareholders have the right to vote for directors and on important issues.

Preferred stock: Also, ownership shares in a firm. These shareholders are entitled to receive dividends before those who own shares of common stock, but they are not entitled to vote.

Beta: The measure of a stock's sensitivity to market change. For example, if the market goes up 30 percent and your stock has a *beta* of 1.5, its price should increase by 45 percent (1.5 × 30).

Book value: Total assets minus total liabilities.

Call option: The right to buy a predetermined amount of stock on or before a predetermined date, upon which this right terminates.

Put option: The right to sell, rather than buy, a predetermined amount of stock on or before a predetermined date; the opposite of a "call option."

Hedging: Taking measures to minimize potential losses. Toward that end, we have heard a lot about ...

Derivatives: These investments take the form of a contract whose value is based on other, underlying assets. They present, for the issuing company (as James Leung so nicely put it), "The prospect of turning a risk you don't like into a risk you like ... or can accept." Nonetheless, derivatives can be extremely complex and pose serious risks that are not easy to identify beforehand. Moreover, they are not typically traded over securities exchanges and, therefore, not subject to the rules of such governing bodies.

Capitalization: The total value of a firm's securities, including all stock, bonds, and other securities.

Mezzanine financing: Transitional or "bridge" funding [e.g., to facilitate an initial public offer(ing) (IPO)].

Lease versus Buy versus Rent

Lease/buy/rent decisions are made on the basis of five criteria (see Figure 2.8): cash flow, commitment, cost, tax impact, and obsolescence risk.

Figure 2.8 Lease/buy/rent decisions

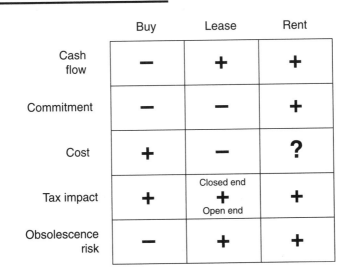

	Buy	Lease	Rent
Cash flow	–	+	+
Commitment	–	–	+
Cost	+	–	?
Tax impact	+	Closed end + Open end	+
Obsolescence risk	–	+	+

Cash Flow

When we buy (i.e., cash price), our cash flow is immediately and adversely affected, equivalent to the purchase price. To lease or rent, in contrast, involves outgoing cash flow in smaller payments over time.

Commitment

When we buy, we are locked in to the purchase (unless, of course, we have bought on a trial basis and can return the item within a limited time period). Lease arrangements may allow us to terminate the deal. However, the penalties usually incurred do not make it worthwhile to do so. Rental suggests no commitment. (One can rent day to day or month to month, etc.)

Cost

With the time value of money as a factor, buying is actually less expensive than leasing, since the latter involves interest built in to installment payments. Rental may or may not be cost-effective, depending on the nature of usage. For example, rental of tables and chairs for a once-a-year "season's greetings" party might justify rental, whereas regular daily usage of an automobile by a sales representative would probably not.

Tax Impact

With purchases and leases, the transaction would allow for depreciation and the potential for reduced tax liability. Rentals are not depreciated but can be deducted as expenses nonetheless.

Obsolescence Risk

As this relates to commitment, purchases do not allow us to exchange the item for a newer, better version. However, leases often do. And rentals provide a great deal of flexibility to upgrade or switch.

Funding

Simply put, capital (along with talent, of course) is the fuel that runs the business enterprise. To the extent that growth is sought, fuel must be expended. It is interesting to note that a large percentage of business start-ups fail not because of poor general management skills or the lack of product integrity, but rather as a result of inadequate funding. In fact, many would-be entities never materialize at all due to such inability. The irony is that there are many excellent sources that go virtually untapped, often because a surprising number of those who seek funding are not even aware that they exist, much less how to approach them. These sources include the following:

Self

Entrepreneurs can tap their bank accounts, securities, insurance policies, and retirement plans and draw upon their home equity in the form of loans as well. While this may be an easily accessible source for many individuals, the magnitude of the potential risk is great for the individuals and their families. (What will happen if I lose my home?)

Some years ago, the talented (but at the time, struggling) actor Robert Townsend was trying to get the money to finish shooting a motion picture that he was producing on a shoestring, with no other investors. Having no other financing alternatives, as he viewed it, Townsend "maxed out" his credit cards to the tune of just under $100,000, in order to help pay for production costs, such as film processing and editing. The resulting film, *Hollywood Shuffle*, was a better-than-moderate critical and financial success.

Off the record, in observing entrepreneurs, it is interesting to note just how many of them (particularly the successful ones) are willing to stake everything and "go for broke." I'm especially impressed by the number of MBAs who are betting their entire personal savings, even though they are taught in business school to rely more so on "other people's money" or "OPM."

Family and Friends

Gifts, loans, or equity involving loved ones as a source are also easily accessible for many individuals. Once again, however, doing business with loved ones may hold the potential for risks of the emotional variety. (If the deal goes sour, will my relative or friend and I still be on good terms, or will it damage the relationship?)

Informal Private Investors (IPI)

Using informal private investors is a popular way to fund various enterprises. In fact, some industries or fields of endeavor rely heavily on IPIs, such as Broadway and the theatrical world with its ad hoc syndicates of funding "angels," who acquire equity interests in plays. While angels may be capable of underwriting the venture, they do not generally offer expertise in addition to their capital.

Suppliers (of Goods or Services)

Suppliers commonly extend trade credit to fledgling business enterprises. Also, they may be candidates for *barter arrangements,* wherein you would receive their goods or services in return for your goods or services. "Taking a percentage in trade" is a common practice in the service sector. Certain industries, such as media, advertising, restaurant/hotel/hospitality, and equipment rental are heavily dependent upon barter. Barter exchanges or service organizations link traders in return for annual "membership" fees plus a small percentage of the cash value of each transaction that is arranged. (It should be noted that, under the regulations of the Internal Revenue Service, barter transactions are taxable just as cash transactions are.)

Employees

Some of the folks on your payroll might actually be eager to invest in the firm. The employee with an equity stake has an incentive to be more productive. Also, this funding approach allows the employer to tap a source of low-cost capital. The key consideration may be the extent to which owners are willing to relinquish equity and control.

Sellers (of Business Enterprises)

Sellers of businesses represent a largely untapped source of funding and, for that matter, of finding a business to purchase and operate. There are a great many small and small-to-midsized companies (i.e., $500,000 to $5 million) that are forced to liquidate because their owners are ill, wish to retire, or simply have no heirs or successors to take over. These enterprises typically are liquidated for 15 to 20 percent of their true value. Such situations present a perfect opportunity for those who wish to buy a business for little or no money down.

Licensees

An organization may be able to raise capital by licensing rights to its product or service. This may be on a limited basis, such as the exclusive right to offer the product or service in a foreign country. There is virtually no direct or immediate cost involved in granting licenses. However, it may be difficult to "police" the licensee. As a result, the integrity of the product or service and, ultimately, the reputation of the licensor may be jeopardized. In fact, licensing rights has proven to be extremely profitable for some companies, a business in its own right. For example, Coca-Cola's sales of licensed merchandise is in excess of $1.1 billion while Harley-Davidson is not far behind at the $1 billion level. (When I lectured in Malaysia several years ago, I had the pleasure of meeting the manager of Harley-Davidson's licensee in that country. She attended my seminar and invited me to visit the Harley-Davidson office and showroom. I was stunned to find that her organization had in stock something in the vicinity of 1,000 SKU's (stock-keeping units) or different items, ranging from apparel to eyeglasses, attaché cases, and even women's lingerie!) And speaking of the automotive industry, Ferrari, manufacturer of expensive precision cars, is said to obtain more than 10 percent of its total profits from licensing and merchandising.

Customers

Clients or patrons may help to capitalize enterprises in a variety of ways, perhaps without even realizing that they are doing so. In the early days of the home video rental industry, entrepreneurs typically charged customers a "membership" fee of $25 to $100. That fee actually financed the purchase of video programs/movies that these "members" later rented. Similarly, many direct mail entrepreneurs order their merchandise only after receiving payment in advance from customers. Discounts can be offered as further inducements toward this end.

Banks

Commercial bank loans may be a viable alternative. However, the cost of capital may be high, and the bank may place certain restrictions on the borrower. Then, again, money may be tight and application by a new enterprise (without a substantial credit history) may be declined.

Although standards may vary from one bank to another, creditworthiness is typically judged on the basis of several criteria including how long the company has been in business, its average monthly bank account balances, past payment history, and past history of lawsuits and judgments.

Government

States and municipalities operate business development units with the express purpose of luring business. They can arrange for substantial tax breaks, free or very inexpensive facilities, labor, and other direct or indirect funding. The federal government provides loans through its Small Business Administration (SBA) and awards outright grants through its other agencies. Of course, foreign governments offer similar inducements to attract commercial activity.

Venture Capital

Unlike most other investors, venture capitalists are generally "dedicated" professionals whose sole activity is funding business enterprises in return for equity positions. They may command a large minority or even a majority interest in the organization. In addition to providing capital, they often bring to the table many years of specialized experience in a particular industry along with numerous valuable contacts.

Corporate Underwriting/Alliance

A *corporate underwriting/alliance* is essentially a joint venture or partnership with a large corporation. Funding may be only one of several important advantages offered by the partner. Others may include access to markets, sales representation, and sophisticated support for research and development.

Private Placement

Private placement involves the private sale of equity or may involve a combination package of equity with cash. This may be adequate to fund the enterprise, but it may also serve as a prelude to an initial public offering (IPO).

Initial Public Offering (IPO)

The organization may be able to raise a great deal of money by selling shares in the enterprise publicly on the stock market ("going public"). In fact, the original owners/entrepreneurs of cyber firms such as Yahoo! and Netscape made many millions of dollars virtually overnight this way, epitomizing the term "paper millionaire." Taking a company public via an initial public offering is often a difficult and expensive task in light of hefty lawyers' fees, underwriters' shares, and such, and it typically requires outlays of $500,000 or sometimes considerably more.

A "backdoor" method to the IPO can involve what is commonly known as a *reverse merger*. In this type of deal, an operating private firm buys a public company that is typically inactive. As a result, the private company *becomes* public.

Direct Public Offering (DPO)

As a less expensive and less complicated alternative to the IPO, one might consider the *direct public offering*.[8] This is a "do-it-yourself" method well-suited to small businesses in need of cash. The U.S. Securities and Exchange Commission now permits businesses with annual revenues of less than $25 million to raise money without having to incur underwriters' and most lawyers' fees. The filing fee is only in the $500 range. Its total cost is usually a little more than 5 percent of funds raised, whereas an IPO's total cost is about 13 percent, more than double. One can set up a DPO using an easy method known as SCOR (small corporate offering registration). This method is legal in almost all states in the United States. Considering setting up a DPO? Visit www.datamerge.com.

Partial Public Subsidiary (PPS)

Taking an organization's subsidiary public is not an option for small organizations. However, the opportunity provides inexpensive equity capital. It also tends to increase motivation of the subsidiary's employees. The poorer the performance of the subsidiary prior to going PPS, the more likely it is to succeed as one. (The PPS has most recently been referred to as an "equity carve-out," particularly when the minority stake that is available via IPO does not exceed one-fifth of the voting stock.)

Bonds

Unlike IPO and DPO, which involve the issuance of stock or ownership shares in the company, bonds represent the company's obligation to repay money that is loaned to it. "Securitization of debt" has been popularized by issuance of the so-called "Bowie bonds," bonds that were sold for $55 million to Prudential Insurance Company and backed by revenues from the future sales of rock star David Bowie's recordings.[9] Securitization is attractive because (1) it can facilitate the sale of assets that are not liquid, (2) almost any kind of payment stream can be securitized, (3) securities can be structured to accommodate any degree of risk, and (4) even the most unattractive assets can obtain the highest bond rating (AAA).

On the other hand, (1) issuing companies may, nonetheless, fail, perhaps due to overreliance on credit creation, (2) anticipated cash flows may be much lower than expected due to inaccurate forecasts of consumer spending, and (3) liquidity may not be easily facilitated during extreme economic downturns.[10]

Leveraged Buyout (LBO)

Leveraged buyouts are purchase arrangements that involve more debt and less equity than are commonly accepted to finance a business purchase.

This investment increases the assumption of risk, because the heavy interest expense serves to reduce future net income. If future earnings can't cover repayment of the debt, the organization may be forced into bankruptcy. Common approaches to an LBO include the issuance of "junk bonds" that offer the potential of high yields to offset the risk.

Documentation

The submission of *pro forma statements* to potential investors is standard practice. These documents include assumed or projected figures or facts. In addition to employing pro forma materials to gauge an investment opportunity objectively, savvy investors may also use these as indirect indicators of just how realistic or candid and trustworthy the management team really is. Figure 2.9 provides a suggested outline for presentation of pro forma statements.

Figure 2.9 Sample cover sheet and table of contents for a pro forma statement

(Cover Sheet)

A BUSINESS PLAN
FOR
YOUR COMPANY, INC.
ANYTOWN, ANYSTATE

Jane Doe
President
(999) 555-5555

or

A FINANCING PROPOSAL
Submitted to

Last National Bank
of Anytown

by

YOUR COMPANY, INC.
ANYTOWN, ANYSTATE

Jane Doe
President
(999) 555-5555

Figure 2.9 (Continued)

Table of Contents

STATEMENT OF PURPOSE

I   THE BUSINESS
    Description of the Business
    Market and Competition Analysis
    Products
    Services
    Manufacturing and Service Delivery Facilities/Operations
    Location
    Marketing Plan
    Future Change Strategies
    Management Team
    Operating Personnel
    Venture Development Schedule
    Proposed Uses of Funds Requested
    Critical Risks and Problems
    Summary

II FINANCIAL DATA
    Sources and Applications of Funds
    Capital Equipment List
    Pro Forma Balance Sheet as of Commencement of Business
    Breakeven Analysis

    PRO FORMA INCOME FORECASTS
    3-Year Summary
    Detail by Month, Year 1
    Detail by Quarter, Years 2 and 3
    Notes of Explanation

    PRO FORMA CASH FLOW ANALYSIS
    3-Year Summary
    Detail by Month, Year 1
    Detail by Quarter, Years 2 and 3
    Notes of Explanation

    PRO FORMA BALANCE SHEETS
    By Quarter, Year 1
    Annual, Years 2 and 3

III PRODUCTS AND SERVICES
    Appendix I Product and Service Program Outlines
    Appendix II Marketing Plan
    Appendix III Background of Principal(s)
    Appendix IV Material Resources and Operations

Some Tips

It should be noted that I am momentarily going "off the record." The following information or advice may be very helpful if you are trying to get an enterprise or project funded. However, it is not generally covered within the MBA curriculum.

Adler's Laws

Fred Adler, a venture capitalist, lived by some of the philosophies listed below.[11] I hope you find them helpful.

1. The likelihood of an organization's success is inversely proportional to the amount of publicity it receives prior to initial product/service introduction.
2. An investor's ability to talk about his or her winners is an order of magnitude greater than the ability to talk about his or her losers.
3. If you don't think you have a problem, you have a *big* problem.
4. Happiness is positive cash flow. Everything else will come later.
5. The likelihood of success of a small company is inversely proportional to the size of the president's office.
6. Would-be entrepreneurs who pick up the check are usually losers.
7. The longer the investment proposal, the shorter its chances of acceptance.
8. There is no such thing as an overfinanced company.
9. Managers who worry about voting control usually have nothing worth controlling.
10. There's no limit on what a (person) can achieve if that individual does not mind who gets the credit.

Sobel's Suggestions

Though I am not a venture capitalist or a highly sophisticated investor, I have given my students and consulting clients the following advice and I have been told that it was helpful:

- When a prospective investor agrees to meet with you and asks what time is good for you, request before 7:00 A.M. or after 8:00 P.M. You are likely to be met with either of two responses: the individual will express shock that you want to meet so early or so late. This provides you with the perfect opportunity to explain that you put in very long hours. This indicates your seriousness of purpose and commitment to the business.

- When you take a meal at a restaurant with a potential investor, don't be quick to pick up the check. That does not mean that you shouldn't pick up the check, only that you shouldn't be eager to do so (unless, of course, you specifically invited the investor to be your guest). Eagerness to pay the tab may be construed as spendthrift behavior (not good). Moreover, your willingness to gain favor may also welcome more requests or demands for concessions than you would otherwise need to grant.

- When you take a meal at a restaurant with a potential investor, be sure to taste your food before you season it. This may strike you as odd advice but, I assure you, investment pros look for cues that indicate to them whether or not you are a good candidate. And seasoning your food before tasting it suggests that you may have preconceived notions about things and may not be open-minded or flexible enough to succeed. As a matter of fact, the late Admiral Hyman Rickover, father of the U.S. nuclear navy, was known to invite promising young naval officers to lunch for the purpose of interviewing them for positions in his then-new and elite organization. Those who "seasoned before they reasoned" found that their luncheon meeting would come to an abrupt end.

The Accounting and Finance Checklist

1. Can I take greater advantage of tax-reduction strategies?
2. Can I do more to improve my internal control procedures to better safeguard my assets?

3. Is my current cash flow strategy optimal, or can it be improved?
4. Have I calculated key ratios to compare my company's performance to others in the same industry?
5. Have I chosen the best investment options?
6. Should other or additional funding sources be identified and considered?

3 HUMAN RESOURCE AND OPERATIONS MANAGEMENT

Human Resources Management

Human resources management (HRM) is concerned with maximizing employee competency and motivation, the desired end being enhanced productivity. Let us review the history or evolution of the discipline.

Prescientific Era (up to 1910)

HRM has been traced as far back as the eighteenth century BC, to the Code of Hammurabi and the establishment of what we regard today as a minimum wage. More complex compensation structures began to emerge following the Arsenal of Venice in 1436, which distinguished between per diem and piecework rates, depending upon the nature of work performed.

Scientific Management Era (1910–1940)

Early in the twentieth century, Frederick Taylor (1911) introduced the so-called *scientific approach to management* and, along with it, the intention of establishing management as a discrete field of endeavor, thus "professionalizing" the discipline. In fact, it was during this period that the term "efficiency expert" came into being. Emphasis was on improving the task. Toward this end, time-and-motion studies were introduced to eliminate any extraneous steps involved.

In 1916, Henri Fayol introduced the *process approach*. This is characterized by a shift in emphasis from improving the worker's performance of tasks to developing management's skills.

This was followed in 1927 by the work of Elton Mayo. His Hawthorne studies, which were conducted at a Western Electric plant in Hawthorne, California, indicated that workers' productivity did not decline despite adverse physical working conditions. They realized the importance of their participation in the experiment, underscoring the role of motivation toward productivity.[1]

Human Relations Era (1940–1960)

Perhaps the hallmark of this period is the *hierarchy of needs model* advanced by Abraham Maslow in 1954 (see Figure 3.1). This concept emphasizes that employees (actually, any individuals, vocationally or avocationally) may be at differing levels of attainment or need at different points in their lives.[2] So it is implicit that the enlightened

Figure 3.1 Maslow's hierarchy of needs model

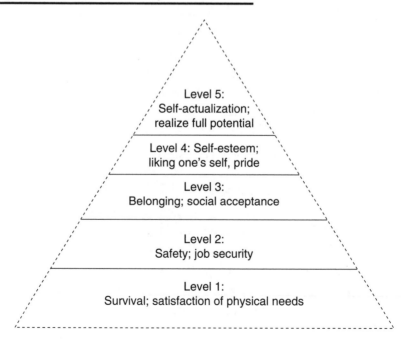

manager identify each subordinate's level of attainment within the context of a hierarchy of needs and motivate him or her toward greater productivity on an individualized basis.

There are two basic limitations of the model. First, it assumes that as a "lower" need is met, a "higher" need is amplified. While this may technically be true, it suggests that the satisfaction of needs is sequential when, in fact, it is concurrent. An individual may have satisfied the self-esteem need although the safety need has not yet been satisfied. Second, it assumes that the pecking order of this sequence is accurate and universally applicable. Clearly, culture makes a difference. While a typical American of European descent is likely to more readily satisfy the survival need before the self-actualization need, the reverse might be true of the typical Indian, who might realize full potential although he or she is starving.

Managers may employ the following "motivators" to help satisfy needs:

Level 1: Survival	Raise in salary
	Bonus
	Better working conditions
	Periodic medical examinations
	Recreation
Level 2: Safety	Stock options
	Insurance
	Tenure
	Verbal and written acknowledgment
	Promotions
Level 3: Belonging	Invitation to special events
	Task force opportunities
	Committee opportunities
	Membership in organizational "clubs"
	Transfers

Level 4: Self-esteem   Awards
                              Letters of commendation
                              Titles
                              Publicity exposure
                              Serve on management council

Level 5: Self-actualization   Sabbatical leaves
                              Leading task forces
                              Educational opportunities
                              Teaching assignments
                              Coaching assignments[3]

In 1960, Douglas McGregor introduced the concepts of *Theory X* and *Theory Y*, the former is indicative of an autocratic management style, and the latter is indicative of an egalitarian management style.[4] Based upon our assumptions of human behavior, all of us have some kind of management style, whether or not we know it or wish to acknowledge it. The autocratic and custodial management styles reflect the Theory X mindset, whereas the participative and collegial management styles reflect the Theory Y mindset (see Figure 3.2). An interesting aspect of management style is that each of us not only has a particular management style (or has management styles, plural), but we have a *style* to the way we manifest our style(s). For example, a manager whose *intention* is clearly Theory X may obscure this by, for example, "inviting" his staff's opinions (especially in a leading way) and ending up with the result he wanted from the outset anyway (Theory X?). Conversely, a Theory Y manager whose *intention* is clearly Theory X may obscure this by, for example, "ordering" his staff to make decisions on their own (Theory Y?).

Moreover, it may be appropriate to manifest different styles with different people. For example, if one of your staff is a "star" and always gets the job done early and well, it might be best to give that person a lot of space and input (more consistent with Theory Y), whereas if another staff member forgets to do the job (if not reminded by you) and tends to complete it late and poorly, it might

Figure 3.2 Management styles

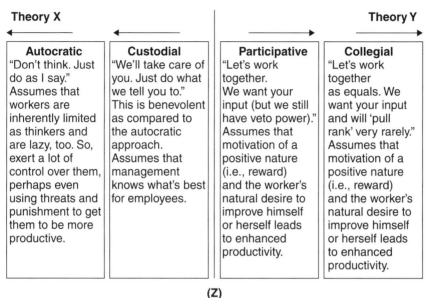

Theory X			Theory Y
Autocratic	**Custodial**	**Participative**	**Collegial**
"Don't think. Just do as I say." Assumes that workers are inherently limited as thinkers and are lazy, too. So, exert a lot of control over them, perhaps even using threats and punishment to get them to be more productive.	"We'll take care of you. Just do what we tell you to." This is benevolent as compared to the autocratic approach. Assumes that management knows what's best for employees.	"Let's work together. We want your input (but we still have veto power)." Assumes that motivation of a positive nature (i.e., reward) and the worker's natural desire to improve himself or herself leads to enhanced productivity.	"Let's work together as equals. We want your input and will 'pull rank' very rarely." Assumes that motivation of a positive nature (i.e., reward) and the worker's natural desire to improve himself or herself leads to enhanced productivity.

(Z)
Neutral

be appropriate to (relatively) breathe down his neck, supervising closely and exerting your authority, as necessary (more consistent with Theory X).

In any event, the most astute managers understand that it may be necessary to wear different masks for different occasions. In fact, the "best of the best" are able to skillfully wear masks—underneath their obvious masks. Charles Schwab, chairman of U.S. Steel in 1918, was a shrewd man. As the story goes: "Schwab asked a man from the day shift how many heats they had made that day. 'Six, sir,' was the reply. Getting a piece of chalk, Schwab chalked a big '6' on the floor. When the night shift arrived, they were curious what the '6' meant, and they were duly informed. The next morning, Schwab saw a bigger '7' in place of the '6.'

"On his next visit, the '7' was gone, replaced by a big '10.' The mill, which had been the poorest producer in the plant, became the chief producer."[5] Would you describe this as Theory X or Theory Y?

In terms of political correctness, what I am about to state "off the record" is not popular. Business schools don't teach it, but the truth is that while "teamwork" is appropriate much of the time and in many circumstances, sometimes what works best is a single leader with authority who can direct (i.e., as courteously as possible, order) people to do what must be done. It is not democratic and not necessarily pretty, but it can be the way to go. This is especially so when (1) the business unit or organization is under great time constraints (as in the face of a crisis) or (2) the leader's experience base and/or skill base is markedly superior to those of other members.

Humanistic Psychology Era (1960–1970)

During this decade, V. H. Vroom, Porter and Lawler, and others wrote extensively about *expectancy theory*, maintaining that management can effectively motivate workers toward desired goals by providing appropriate incentives. In a similar vein, Lawrence and Lorsch and others wrote about *contingency theory*, asserting that there is no "one best way" or single style of management that would be suitable on a universal or generalized basis; it all depends upon the particular situation. This would not even preclude the so-called KITA approach, an acronym for "kick in the ass." Herzberg, who introduced the term, suggests that even "nice guys [and gals]" sometimes have to adopt a harsher management style in order to deal with a particular type of worker or work condition.[6]

How can we gauge management or work style relative to personality type? Perhaps the most widely used measurement tool for this purpose is the *Myers-Briggs Type Inventory (MBTI)*. It is based upon Carl Jung's *theory of psychological profiles* and relies upon self-reported preferences in terms of 4 personality dimensions (see Figure 3.3), which allow for 16 permutations or possible personality types:

1. Interaction with the environment (extroverted) in contrast to quiet reflection (introverted).
2. Conceptual approach coupled with gut feelings (intuitive) in contrast to experiential approach with "here and now" orientation (sensing).
3. Emphasis on personal values (feeling) in contrast to practical and objective considerations or "what will work" (thinking).

Figure 3.3 Myers-Briggs type inventory®

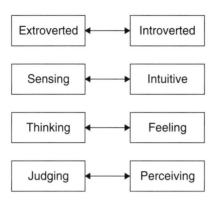

Source: Jean M. Kummerow, *Verifying Your Type Preferences,* Centers for Applications of Psychological Type, Gainesville, FL, 1987.

4. Open-end exploration (perceiving) in contrast to decisions and closure (judging).[7]

This enables the test taker to gain insights regarding inclinations and associated strengths and weaknesses. It might seem that individuals who share the same or similar type are likely to get along better than those who do not. However, getting along and working together productively is another matter entirely. In fact, the complement of opposite types is probably very healthy, and MBTI allows dissimilar individuals to understand each other better and work together more effectively. *Off the record:* Using my own marriage as a metaphor for teamwork in organizations, let me share with you an example of how differences in personality type present themselves and how situations can be improved.

One day, at the end of the workday, my lovely wife warmly greeted me and asked: "Hi, Sweetheart! How was your day?"

I told her that I had a particularly interesting day and (in my enthusiasm) began to elaborate on this. Soon, in the middle of a sentence, my wife cut me off, saying: "Milo, don't take me on a trip to Mozambique! I just want to know: Was it a good day—or not?"

Well, it was a good day, I said, but my mood was a bit deflated by her brusquely cutting me off. Some time later, my wife and I discussed this episode and agreed that it probably occurred because my wife is a "judging" ("J") type who primarily values the "product" or coming to closure—crossing the finish line, in runner's parlance—whereas I am a "perceiving" ("P") type who primarily values the process, enjoying the activity of running with less regard for whether I win the race.

We decided to improve our communication—and our relationship—by agreeing to a compromise, of sorts. When asked, "How was your day?" I would answer with a brief "pretty good" or "not so great," followed by one or two sentences to *briefly* explain. At that point, I ask my wife: "Would you like to hear more about it?" And she usually says: "Sure, a little more."

Some critics of MBTI view the test as a means of typecasting individuals so that they are precluded from consideration for opportunities based solely upon their profile. (For this reason, it can reasonably be argued that it should not be used as an appraisal tool by management, only confidentially by the individual for his or her own insights.) Others contend that since MBTI is based upon self-reported assessments, the lack of objectivity or bias may render the test invalid. Moreover, participants may rationalize the findings if they don't like the implications. And most interesting and controversial is the assertion that individual personality plays a very small role as a determinant of group performance.

Would you like to take the Myers-Briggs test online? All you have to do is answer 70 multiple-choice questions. Then add up your score to find out your personality type. Just go to http://www.humanmetrics.com/cgi-win/JTypes1.htm (right now or after you're done studying today).

Management by objective (MBO), developed by George S. Odiorne, came into widespread usage during the same general period that MBTI was introduced. MBO is intended to provide a framework for planning the tasks an employee is expected to perform and the goals that individual is expected to achieve within a particular time frame. Theoretically, the manager will meet with the subordinate, and together they will discuss and jointly decide what the subordinate will be expected to accomplish within the upcoming business period. So it can be said that the MBO ostensibly provides the opportunity for agreement and for documentation of such agreement as this relates to accountability.[8]

In practice, however, the MBO is all too often abused. For example, a manager might try to flatter or coerce the subordinate into "signing off" on tasks or objectives that are unreasonable or unattainable or that the subordinate is otherwise unwilling to perform or actualize. Moreover, circumstances beyond the subordinate's control that prevent successful completion are not necessarily factored into evaluation of performance.

Even more troubling, though, is the potential for portions of the MBO to be purposefully interpreted out of context to undermine the subordinate's subsequent appraisal. For example, the MBO may include a seemingly innocuous question, such as, "What skills would you like to improve?" At the time of appraisal, the manager may try to justify a poor (and unfair) evaluation by claiming that the subordinate lacked certain skills—that the individual even implicitly conceded this in the MBO. For these reasons, abuse of the MBO has been referred to as *management by terror (MBT)*.

Companies are increasingly adopting the usage of what is commonly known as *360-degree feedback*, which allows participants to receive input and a cumulative appraisal from their peers and subordinates, as well as from their immediate supervisors. This approach is popular because it facilitates evaluation of the individual's performance from several different perspectives. Therefore, it is rather less likely that a (single) boss's biased evaluation would carry as much weight in the face of several other differing and unbiased reviews given by coworkers.

But wouldn't it make more sense to help individuals improve their performance along the way, on a day-to-day basis, rather than allow things to deteriorate and have poor job appraisals come as a surprise to these folks? Toward that end, I suggest the following:[9]

Tulgan's Fast Feedback Approach

a. Incorporate feedback into routine meetings.

b. Address performance in routine memoranda.

c. Include feedback in each work-in-progress (WIP) or final result that you oversee.

d. Make the feedback medium convenient to use (e.g., voice mail, e-mail, brief notes).

e. Devote time at regular intervals (e.g., daily or weekly) to give feedback.

f. Reward your employees for precision and truly address requests voiced in their feedback.

Tulgan's Feedback Reality Check: A Suggested Format (Variant)

a. Name of employee

b. Subject for feedback

c. Duration of time elapsed following performance

d. Verification of information prior to giving feedback (Y/N)

e. Most recent prior feedback (date)

f. Feedback medium (e.g., in person, e-mail)

g. Summary of feedback

h. Subsequent action (to be) taken

Systems Era (1980–Present)

The systems era is almost synonymous with the theme of *total quality management (TQM)*. The cornerstones of TQM include a striving toward constant and ongoing improvement, setting long-term objectives, empowering employees, and utilizing the team approach.

Although the preeminent TQM "gurus" may differ over how it can be accomplished, all seem to agree that it is critical to "do it right the first time" and to satisfy and perhaps even surpass the expectations of clients. Aside from the fact that doing it right the first time is congruent with a customer-focused orientation, it often costs a great deal more to correct or undo an error than to avoid making one in the first place. TQM guru Philip Crosby places this cost at approximately one quarter of total revenues.

Benchmarking is a popular concept in the TQM world. Simply put, managers are encouraged to observe the ways that their counterparts in other organizations can shed light on how they themselves can improve performance in their own organizations. As you might imagine, competitors are not likely to be sharing with one another. However, it may very well be appropriate for managers in allied or unrelated industries. Etiquette dictates that you should be willing to reveal the same type of information that you request from your counterparts.

A frequent phenomenon associated with TQM is reduced cycle time. By minimizing mistakes and turnaround time in production situations, for example, a manufacturing run can be completed more quickly, and the product can be brought to market sooner. In a similar vein, adding value or utility to tasks is also stressed. Toward this end, one of Motorola's quality experts is said to have the following outgoing message on his voicemail (to paraphrase): "If speaking with me will add value for you or for me, leave a message. If not, hang up now."

It is no surprise that much of the tremendous success of Japan's manufacturing is attributable to TQM efforts. It is ironic, however, in light of relatively lackluster performance in the United States, that TQM as we know it was introduced to the Japanese many years ago by an American, W. Edwards Deming. In fact, Deming was so revered in Japan that the country's most prestigious award for quality control, the Deming prize, was established in his honor more than 40 years ago by the Japanese Union of Scientists and Engineers. In addition, eligibility for the Japan Quality Control Award, which was established almost 30 years later, is limited to winners of the Deming prize. Deming, who died in 1993, had long enjoyed the reputation of a curmudgeon, purportedly refusing to continue working with executives who failed to learn as quickly as he would have liked. The key points of Deming's platform are:[10]

- Drive out fear.
- Get rid of numerical goals (e.g., quotas).
- Train on the job (OJT).
- Deemphasize short-term profits.

Over the past decade or so, Philip Crosby has popularized the term "zero defects" as a quality control orientation. This approach calls for 100 percent error-free performance as a goal. Crosby contends that to establish any level of defects as "acceptable" tends to have the effect of making that level (or higher) a self-fulfilling prophecy; if employees know that it is "okay" to operate at a certain error level, they will come to view the level as a standard. Of course, this standard is suboptimal.[11]

The story is told of Crosby attending his daughter's lavish wedding and abstaining from indulging in even a single celebratory alcoholic toast. His explanation: zero defects (ZD). He was on a diet at the time and to depart from his regimen, even for a special occasion, would constitute a ZD lapse. But if you had to quantify some defect rate above zero as "acceptable," what would that be? The crafty folks at Motorola, as pioneers in quality improvement, introduced to the world their (trademarked) concept and program known as *Six Sigma*, which regards no more than 3.4 defects per million parts as "acceptable." This is equivalent to a 99.9999998-percent success rate. In practice, as you might imagine, Six Sigma can be problematic. A client of mine shared with me that his Six Sigma–trained company fell considerably short of quality standards, not just because virtually zero defects (VZD) is a lofty goal, but because it takes time to learn the necessary skills and for the organization to truly embrace the new culture. Moreover, the press of time (in the form of unreasonable rush orders and accelerated "impossible" deadlines) can contribute to unacceptably high (but understandable) defect rates.

A caveat involves cross-cultural perceptions of ZD, insofar as it may be used as a selling point to prospective customers. In certain cultures, error-free performance is an alien concept and inconsistent with a belief system that generously factors in human fallibility. So, while zero defects policies enable organizations to satisfy their customers better, it is ironic that communication of this approach to customers does not necessarily go over as well as expected.

A contemporary of Deming, Joseph Juran, liberally expanded the definition of "customer" to include internal entities, such as coworkers. When coworker A passes the unfinished product to coworker B on the production line, coworker B becomes coworker A's "customer." Actually, any coworker or individual within the organization who can be helped or served by other employees may be regarded as their customer. Juran emphasized the value of problem-solving and brainstorming teams. Unlike Deming, however, he contended that fear can be a positive motivating influence.[12]

In light of the universal acknowledgment of the importance of quality, it was only a matter of time until internationally accepted standards would be established and companies that would be willing to meet these requirements would be *certified* or *registered*. The best known of these standards is known as *ISO*, a designation granted by the International Organization for Standards based in Geneva, Switzerland. The designation does not vouch for the quality of the designee's product or service. It only claims that the firm has properly articulated and detailed its quality-control methods and "practices what it preaches." The assumption is that if the company has a good approach, properly implements it, and continues to do so, the resulting products or services will be of high quality.

As a consultant, I particularly take note of what I will refer to as "markers" of quality. These are seemingly unimportant details that *implicitly* (not explicitly) suggest that quality standards are high and are being met. You might not notice or care about any single one of them, but the cumulative effect of all these details can be impressive. For example, when I lecture in Asia, I often stay at the Shangri-La

Hotel in Singapore. When I stepped into the elevator, I noticed that the carpeted floor had spelled out on it, in bold letters, the day of the week, "Tuesday." The following day, I looked down and read "Wednesday." That's right: They change the elevator carpet every single day! Similarly, the ashtrays in the hallways were typically emptied every hour. How do I know that? Hotel staff used a simple handheld device to make an impression on the sand in the ashtrays, in the shape of the Shangri-La logo. If I saw cigarettes put out and other refuse lying in the ashtray (having messed up the logo design in the sand), I would return an hour later to find an empty ashtray with a brand new logo!

It was reported that the rock group Van Halen had a clause in their contracts requiring that M&M candies be provided in their dressing room backstage prior to their performance. As rock star demands go, this doesn't seem unreasonable, but a lot of eyebrows were raised by their requirement that *all of the brown-colored pieces had to be discarded!*

A member of the group reasoned that, since the brown M&Ms hadn't been removed (that being what I'd call a quality "marker"?), there were likely to be errors affecting the musical and audio equipment used in the performance, too. As it turned out, these concerns were quite justified: The stage actually did collapse, causing a lot of damage. Fortunately, nobody was injured.

As I tell my clients, it's often the aggregation of many little details rather than the broad strokes of the brush that truly make a big difference.

Postsystems Era (1990–Present)

The influence of Deming was profound. In fact, TQM has been embraced universally. However, its aspect of *kaizen* or "continuous improvement" has, in many circles, been supplanted by a harsher approach. I am referring to the so-called "slash-and-burn" methods associated with the *reengineering concept* introduced to us by Messrs. Hammer and Champy. This approach is not incremental, as is TQM. Organizational hierarchies are flattened and, in the course of doing so, organizations are "downsized" (i.e., people lose their jobs) in the name of efficiency.

Proponents of reengineering argue that those who lose their jobs can be retrained and are then able to work at other jobs that might not have existed were it not for the increased efficiency and productivity that results from reengineering.

What about the contention that most of those who lost jobs may get rehired—doing *some* kind of work, but that many will not earn nearly as much as they did before? A controversy surrounds this point and we will not resolve it here.

But, allow me to share a personal opinion, off the record, if you will: Let's look at the big picture. Clearly, reengineering gurus have often been able to make companies more profitable by transforming fat and sluggish operations into lean-and-mean competitive machines. In microcosm, this is impressive even if you might have to fire 25 percent of your employees.

However, in macrocosm (i.e., as an entire society or as a civilization), if *every company* "succeeds" at reengineering and 25 percent of each company's work force is to be put out of work, who then will be able to buy the company's products and services produced? I am suggesting that, as paradoxical as it may seem, the widespread success and overreliance upon reengineering may, if unchecked, irreparably tear the very fabric of society.

As a consultant, I have witnessed more than my share of executives who regard "reducing head count" as a sort of blood sport. Too many of them take an insensitive pride (not a sadistic pride, just an insensitive pride) in their success at this, with little regard for the human toll involved. What many people lose sight of is that, ultimately, profitability (and I mean dramatic increases in it) would more appropriately arise from *innovation* rather than reengineering. Just food for thought.

Dimensions of Managerial Effectiveness

It is difficult to generalize about the components of managerial effectiveness because many of the necessary skills are "soft" and subjective and difficult to assess. These include leadership, motivation, people skills, and administrative and strategic skills.

Leadership

At the very least, managers must be able to exert their authority. Ideally, subordinates will follow a manager's directives solely on the basis of their respect for that individual's personal integrity and/or professional attainment rather than the formal authority that accompanies a title. In this sense, it can be said that the best of managers lead by example, providing role models for their staffs. As I reflect on leaders whom I have worked for or worked with, one in particular comes to mind as extraordinary. His subordinates respected and admired him to such an extent that, in the face of a less than excellent performance on their part, they would immediately express concern about how this might affect their boss. (The vast majority of employees would, of course, focus instead on their own self-interest.)

Motivation

The best managers make it a point to know what makes their subordinates tick and then to create incentives to get them to be as productive as possible (see Figure 3.1, Maslow's hierarchy of needs, on page 106). This requires managers to wear different hats with different employees at different points in time. An increasingly important aspect of the manager's role involves the training and development of staff. Cultivation of talent is necessary for succession planning and may even be viewed as an entitlement or condition of employment by those who are hired. It is ironic that managers withhold guidance out of fear that their subordinates might threaten their jobs if they learn too much. Ultimately they threaten their own jobs. These disenchanted employees will probably be less productive or leave for more promising jobs, reflecting poorly on their managers' performance.

3M Corporation has been able to motivate its employees, decade after decade, by carrying out the following policies:[13]

The 3M Way

- *Keep divisions small enough* so that division managers know each of their employees by their first names. When a division reaches approximately $300 million in sales, it is divided into smaller divisions.
- *Tolerate failure* so that experimentation and taking risks are encouraged. As a result, the firm has an unwritten rule that at least 25 percent of its sales should come from products that were launched during the previous five years.
- *Support the idea/product "champions"* by giving employees who come up with ideas to recruit a group to help him or her develop it. Compensation and promotions may be linked to success of the project. If an idea isn't adopted by any of 3M's divisions, these employees can spend 15 percent of their time to justify the project and may apply for $50,000 grants to help fund the effort.
- *Share the wealth.* Regardless of where in the organization technology is developed, it "belongs" to everybody in the firm.

People Skills

Diplomacy and charm count for a lot. In the corporate world, style may be just as important as substance. One of my senior colleagues, an extremely successful management consultant and keen observer of top executives who are considered for CEO positions, shared with me his empirical finding that the individuals who ascend to the top are not necessarily the best or the brightest. They tend to be nominally competent, but are skillful at getting along with everyone and alienating no one.

Administrative and Strategic Skills

If you manufactured violins and were interviewing for a salesperson, would you hire a violinist and teach her to sell or would you hire a salesperson and teach him to play violin? This question may seem rhetorical, but I assure you, it is commonly posed in corporate boardrooms. Here's a classic example. John Scully, the former chairman of Apple Computers, was recruited from Pepsi-Cola. He had very little knowledge of the computer industry, but he was a "professional manager," the kind that business schools turn out, one who supposedly can manage any type of organization, given that management is a universally applicable skill. Contrast Scully, if you will, with television's "Lou Grant" character, a veteran newsman who knows the particulars of his chosen field "in his sleep." Why didn't Apple bring in a Lou Grant, a computer pro, rather than an industry "outsider" like Scully? Perhaps the Apple board of directors felt that, since the computer industry was maturing, it was no longer necessary to have a "visionary" and computer pro like former Chairman Steven Jobs at the helm. In contrast, Chrysler's board faced considerable criticism when it hired a top executive from General Motors to succeed Chairman Lee Iacocca. The newcomer was a respected automobile pro, yet hiring someone from outside the company was regarded by many as sacrilege. Clearly, the controversy of professional manager versus industry professional will not be resolved here, but it merits further discussion.

Work versus Play

To put it simply, work is not fun and play is (see Figure 3.4). It is only natural that we gravitate toward that which we regard as pleasant or fun. So, to the extent that we must engage in work, the enlightened manager tries to create a work environment that is playlike if not actually playful. Care less about how a job is accomplished, as long as it is completed on time and done well. Give employees the opportunity to make choices whenever possible. After all, it is only fair that if people are to be held responsible for their actions, they also have authority commensurate to the degree of their responsibility. (By the way, considerable responsibility without much authority would explain the feelings of frustration and futility common among many midlevel managers. To paraphrase management guru Tom Peters, "Middle managers are cooked geese. Raise hell and at least go down in flames. You'd be better off getting fired for doing something interesting rather than laid off for doing something boring."[14])

How is the morale in your place? Smiles? Laughter? Genuine cooperation? Well, perhaps it's time for a Morale Audit.[15] You might want to have your staff participate, too. Respond to each of the following 15 questions with a numerical rating of 3 frequently, 2 occasionally, or 1 rarely or never.

(Scoring information is printed at the bottom of the questionnaire.)

_____ 1. People who work here stop and casually talk with each other.

_____ 2. We speak about the goals and vision of the organization.

_____ 3. Managers and their staffs work together to plan important workplace changes.

_____ 4. Employees feel free to make suggestions—and actually do so.

_____ 5. We complement each other on jobs well done.

_____ 6. The entire staff tries to build consensus on important issues and projects.

_____ 7a. Concerns are discussed openly, courteously, and respectfully.

_____ 7b. Disagreements are discussed openly, courteously, and respectfully.

_____ 8. Employees participate in activities away from the job altogether.

_____ 9. Employees are given the opportunity to lead special projects or activities, regardless of their rank.

_____ 10. Employees enjoy coming to work.

_____ 11. There is laughter and a *visible* sense of camaraderie in the workplace.

_____ 12. Employees are willing to—and do—adjust to each other's changing needs.

_____ 13. When problems occur, managers and employees deal with them quickly and honestly.

_____ 14. Employees display personal photographs and mementos in our work areas.

Scoring:

30–35: Outstanding

25–29: Good

20–24: Fair

11–19: Poor

  0–10: Very poor

Figure 3.4 Work versus play

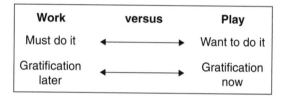

Psychological Contracts in the Workplace

That was then; this is now.

Once upon a time, it was a reasonable assumption that if you did your job well, you could keep that position until you were promoted to a better job, took retirement, or died while on the payroll. The world was a more predictable place, and continual growth was expected. Now, nobody's job is secure. Not even the CEOs' of the largest organizations, especially in light of the shareholders' rights movement (which is dedicated to maximizing the value of owners' stock shares) and related restructurings, cost-reduction programs, as well as mergers and acquisitions.

Given this state of relative uncertainty (if not, in the worst-case scenarios, chaos), companies now tend to "purchase" workers for specific skills and talents that are perceived as needed in the short term, rather than hire and develop people for the long term. In fact, an interesting phenomenon is the growing popularity of *ad hoc* or *interim* managers and specialists, who are hired to work—perhaps at premium compensation—under the terms of a contract that has a duration of perhaps three or four months. When the time period is up, the interim employee is generally gone, unless, of course, the company wants to extend the duration of the agreement or perhaps even hire the individual on a permanent basis. This is more likely to occur when there is a market shortage for specialized types of labor or interim personnel are of outstanding caliber. Clearly, organizations now try to remain as flexible as possible in their staffing options. Also, in the past, benefits such as life insurance, health insurance, and retirement pensions were provided by and at the expense of the company. Now, employees are often required to fund such plans, in whole or part.

Psychological contracts, not unlike any other kinds of contracts, involve a *quid pro quo* or mutual agreement to the effect that, "I'll give you this in return for you giving me that." So it should come as no surprise that employees are not automatically loyal to their organizations in light of the perceived downgrading of contemporary working conditions by many. Nonetheless, many employees are surprised (and very unprepared) to find that their skills are no longer adequate to meet market demands when they look elsewhere for work. This underscores the notion that, in the course of a lifetime, people may have several different careers and that job training is a periodic if not continual process, and not necessarily a linear one.

Line versus Staff

Line jobs are those with direct authority and profit center orientation, such as sales and production positions. *Staff positions* support line functions, such as market research and personnel positions. The designation of a particular job in terms of line or staff depends upon the industry. For example, a security officer or specialist employed by Pinkerton would probably be regarded as line, whereas a security officer deployed internally by a bank would probably be regarded as staff. Similarly, a market researcher employed by Nielsen (the folks who conduct television ratings surveys) would probably be regarded as line, whereas a market researcher employed by a manufacturing company would probably be regarded as staff. However, the distinctions are becoming blurred in the midst of a trend toward integration of line and staff.

Increasingly, staff people will be assuming responsibility for the profitability of specific accounts, while their line counterparts will be playing more supportive roles that may involve less direct authority.

Communication

Since the Tower of Babel, humankind has posted an unimpressive track record in the person-to-person conveyance of information and ideas. I do not believe, even in today's sophisticated business arena, that MBAs necessarily communicate very effectively, or, for that matter, appreciably better (if at all) than their colleagues. Therefore, I now offer some very basic, practical advice in this area, even though the subject is not generally covered in the MBA curriculum.

Writing Memos and E-Mails

1. Do not write unless it is necessary. Inundating colleagues with junk memos and e-mails is a surefire way to get them angry.
2. Respond promptly. Within 24 to 48 hours, if not much sooner.
3. Get to the point immediately. Their time is valuable.
4. Be brief.
5. Use simple language.
6. Keep sentences and paragraphs short.
7. Be clear and specific.
8. If you want something, ask for it. It's okay to request action and a reply.
9. Personalize and gear your approach to appeal to the reader's self-interest, not yours. Keep "I" and "my" to a minimum.[16]
10. It should be embarrassing for you to listen to someone like me lecturing to you about something that you certainly would have

learned in Sunday school at whatever your house of worship or should have learned at home as a child. Also, sometimes we forget some of the things that are too important to forget. Here goes: Be nice to people *all the time*, not just when you need them to do something for you. Send a note or card to: congratulate a colleague on a promotion or even on a job well done, express condolence upon a loved one's death, share information that will be of interest or value, simply stay in touch if you can't otherwise think of a good enough reason. And if you are such a tightwad that you can't bring yourself to spring for a greeting card and postage, go to www.egreetings.com or other such sites on the Internet and send an e-card at no cost.

11. Be sensitive to "netiquette" (Internet etiquette). For example, do not use all uppercase characters unless you wish to be perceived as shouting.

12. If in doubt, leave it out. In other words, any material that might be perceived as sensitive (particularly in regard to legal issues) may not be appropriate to transmit via written hard copy or electronic conveyance.

Preparing for and Conducting Meetings

John Cleese of Monty Python fame wrote and was featured in a very funny—albeit quite honest—training film entitled "Meetings, Bloody Meetings." At the outset, Cleese's wife is disturbed that he is doing paperwork in bed, preventing her from falling asleep. When she asks him, annoyed, why he can't do the work at work, he explains, "I can't do that. Don't you understand that I'm in meetings all day?!"

Time is money. If you are devoting time to unnecessary or unproductive meetings, you are poorly deploying the assets (human capital) of the organization and you are wasting money. The 3M Corporation commissioned a study to identify the "typical" meeting in corporate America.[17] According to 3M's findings, it can best be characterized by the following:

Type/Purpose/Features	Percentage of Meetings in This Category
• A staff meeting	45
• A task force meeting	23
• An information-sharing meeting	20
• In the organization's conference room	74
• Starting at 11:00 A.M.	N/A
• Having a duration of an hour and thirty minutes	N/A
• Attended by nine employees (two managers, four coworkers, two subordinates, and one person from outside of the company)	N/A
• Providing no advance notice	33
• Providing up to 60 minutes advance notice	44
• Providing up to one day advance notice	19
• Providing up to seven days advance notice	4
• Providing more than seven days advance notice	1
• Having no written agenda distributed in advance	63
• Being somewhat or very informal	76
• With most or all attendees participating actively	72
• Distributing materials (i.e., handouts)	47
• Covering the entire agenda	53
• Time spent on irrelevant matters	11

It is interesting to note that despite the obvious shortcomings of the "typical" meeting, as much as 20 percent of participants were "very satisfied" and 52 percent were "satisfied," while as little as 16 percent were "neutral," 11 percent were "dissatisfied," and 2 percent were "very dissatisfied." Which only goes to show how many people (in addition to Nero) can fiddle while Rome burns. So here are some tips for scheduling and conducting meetings:

1. Clearly establish and state in advance the meeting's objectives and agenda. Distribute pertinent material. This enables participants to prepare properly.

2. Set a time limit.
3. Limit the number of participants to those who can add value and to those who have a stake in the meeting's outcome. Keep in mind that the inclusion of each additional "unnecessary" participant may serve to increase dramatically the likelihood of disagreement (not necessarily a bad thing).
4. Prioritize or rank topics to be addressed. If time constraints are the primary concern, proceed from "most important" to "less important." If agreement is the primary concern, proceed from "most likely to be agreed upon" to "least likely to be agreed upon."
5. To help generate support for your "political" position or cause, it may be appropriate to enter into a dialogue with selected participants privately and in advance.[18]
6. Start on time. It is unfair to penalize those who arrive punctually in consideration of others who do not. Moreover, it sets a precedent. Show that you mean business. You might even want to close, or in some special cases, even *lock* the conference room doors at the outset so that those who come late will have unwelcome attention brought upon themselves or, in the latter case, be prevented from entering at all. Certainly, this would send a clear and powerful signal as to expectations and obligations for how future meetings will be conducted.

Have you ever considered holding real-time *electronic* meetings that allow participants at remote locations to exchange their documents? This can be easily arranged by using tools that also facilitate the scheduling, documentation, and management (control?) of the meetings. See www.webex.com for more information.

Negotiating

1. Confirm that the party you are dealing with does, in fact, have the authority to grant you what you want.
2. Begin with those points most likely to be agreed upon and then proceed in descending order of what is likely to be agreed upon.

3. Never give up "something for nothing." Always link something that you are asked to give up with something that you want.
4. Try to see the other person's side.
5. Accept the individual's stated feelings as though they were facts.
6. "Save face" for them if you want them to give in. Avoid backing people into corners and offending them with phrases like, "Take it or leave it."
7. Periodically repeat and summarize what they are saying so they will realize that you are taking them seriously and actually listening to them.
8. Let the other party know that you are seeking a win-win resolution so that both parties gain rather than one party winning at the expense of the other.[19]

Giving Praise and Criticism

1. Praise publicly. Making employees look good in front of coworkers goes a long way toward building positive PR for you as well as the obvious recipient of the kind words.
2. Criticize privately. Humiliating an individual in front of others serves no useful purpose, and the damage often cannot be undone.
3. In the immortal words of Lyndon Johnson, "Don't tell 'em to go to hell unless you can send them there."[20]

Managing Staff Conflicts

1. First of all, be objective. Don't take sides.
2. Meet privately with each of the involved parties and get each person's version of the truth.
3. Focus on the present. Do not allow previous events or old gripes or grievances to enter into the picture.
4. Allow the parties to express their feelings—to a degree. However, you must keep the conversation on track and require statement of the facts.
5. Relate what has been said to the standards set forth in company policies and/or job requirements.
6. Judge the issue, not the person.

7. Let them know what outcome you want and ask each party how that can be accomplished.
8. (After deliberating) Bring the parties together and either inform them of your decision and the actions that must be taken or moderate their negotiation of a solution (if, in your judgment, the parties are not very far apart and are rational, fair-minded people who will act in good faith).

An interesting alternative method to the above that can be used when one party complains to you *privately* about (i.e., behind the back of) a rival, is to summon that rival to your office and have the complainant repeat what he or she has told you to the individual's face. You'd be surprised how this type of practice can minimize office politics. David Ogilvy, a true legend of the advertising field, is credited with promoting this approach. Yet Ogilvy suggests that the *environment* that fosters such an unhealthy, strife-ridden situation can be avoided by your commitment not to play favorites and by establishing a luncheon club within the organization.[21]

Compensation

While salary usually comprises the lion's share of a total compensation package, other components have grown in importance so that salary in major corporations comprises only 65 to 75 percent of the compensation pie. The proportions differ by employment stratum, reflecting what is necessary to attract, motivate, and/or keep employees at each level. Check out www.employease.com for more information.

There is major criticism involving the contention that distribution of compensation within a corporation is often highly inequitable. In larger corporations, the most senior executive or CEO can earn 70 times more than the employees at the lowest rung of the ladder. And to buttress further the claim that large corporations serve the interests of senior management elites, critics need only point out that when senior executives lose their jobs, they often receive "golden parachutes" or generous severance packages while rank-and-file employees can expect to receive far more modest packages.

At the other end of the spectrum, Ben & Jerry's ice cream company represents commitment to industrial democracy, the participation of rank and file in decision making and profit participation, including ESOPs, or employee stock ownership plans. More than 25 years ago, the company had a policy that precluded the most senior executive from earning more than 5 times the lowest-paid employee. However, as entrepreneurs Ben and Jerry (of Ben & Jerry's Ice Cream) *now* concede, it became necessary to raise the ratio considerably higher in order to attract top managerial talent at the "going market rate."

It is particularly interesting to note that much of the compensation of Japanese senior executives is typically deferred until the twilight of their careers, ostensibly to promote long-range decisions (and lower turnover) that are ultimately in the best interests of the organization as well as the executives. American senior executives operate all too often under compensation systems that allow for "quick hits" and relatively immediate gratification. These compensation structures promote short-range decisions wherein the interests of the organization and of its senior management can be mutually exclusive. In terms of motivation of the "rank and file," the Lincoln Electric Company serves as a noteworthy case study. Although the company offers employees little in the way of "automatic" benefits, the compensation structure apparently is successful at linking productivity to earnings, such that an assembly-line worker who is willing to work overtime can earn as much as $100,000 per year or more. I mention this because it is an important yet surprisingly difficult challenge to successfully index productivity to compensation.

Also, the rags-to-riches potential of Internet-driven businesses in comparison to that of relatively modest "brick-and-mortar" (or traditional) businesses has altered the perception of compensation, particularly as it pertains to recruiting younger, high-potential prospects. In the old days, the best students from the best MBA programs sought positions with the top consulting firms or major investment banks, at six-figure salaries with many perks or benefits and the shot of becoming a partner. Today, this phenomenon may exist to a lesser degree due to the boom and bust of the economy. Students often have no choice but to start entrepreneurial ventures. Ideally, they would prefer to get industry experience under their belt by working with one of the top firms in their field. And then, after having learned as much as they can on the job—they break out on their own to become better seasoned entrepreneurs. Of course, there has been, and always will be "the company man." The top consulting firms, such as McKinsey, are said to be addressing this issue by including these select new employees in Internet "start-up" investments in which the company is involved. Keep in mind that partners of the consulting firms themselves have been bitten by the dot-com bug, too, such that the firms are now openly willing to accept part of their total compensation from clients in the form of stock or stock options. After all, wouldn't you have been willing to get in on the ground floor of such Internet start-ups (and now, institutions) such as Amazon, Google, Priceline, and Yahoo!?

Learning

Learning is a continuous and ongoing process. The best organizations know this and make substantive commitments to this effort in three areas: training, education, and development.

Training is learning that is applicable to the individual's current job.

Education is learning that is designed to groom the individual for future jobs he or she may assume.

Development is learning that is geared toward "general growth" of the individual and/or that of the organization and is not directly linked to the person's current position or an identified future job.[22]

The perceived appropriateness of any type of learning program is weighed in terms of its perceived risk and reward. The time lag that occurs between the learning and its observable benefits appears to be a key factor. Management typically is most favorably disposed toward training, since its benefits are observed on the job and short term, if not immediately. Receptivity toward education is often less enthusiastic, since its benefits are generally regarded as midterm.

And attitudes toward development tend to be even less positive, since the benefits are viewed as long term and questionable or difficult to measure.

In your role as a successful manager and content expert, you may at some point be called upon to share your considerable knowledge with others in a classroom setting. In anticipation of this, enrolling in a "train-the-trainer" course might be a wise career investment. (You realize, of course, that mastery of the material doesn't necessarily mean that you can teach it well. Just think of the awful instructor or two who you had in college or graduate school.) So, if you have the opportunity to be a learning facilitator (i.e., "instructor") and are unable to attend a "train-the-trainer" program to develop your skills, the following guidelines should be helpful.

Thirty-three Dos of Adult Learning

1. Begin with introductions of you and the adult learners.
2. Share some of yourself (i.e., humor, experiences, feelings, self). Be honest, authentic, and self-disclosing.
3. Make sure that the learners' first experiences with the subject or class are as positive as possible.
4. Relate learning to adult interests, concerns, and values.
5. Selectively emphasize and deal with the human perspective of what is being learned, with applications to the personal daily lives of the adult learners whenever possible.
6. Give learners a needs assessment to determine the felt needs and actual needs of the learners using assessments administered by the instructor and self-assessments by the adult learner.
7. Provide opportunities for self-directed learning where adults can participate in setting objectives, selecting instructional methods, self-evaluating, and analyzing their performance.
8. Make the learning goals as clear as possible and as appropriate to the learners as possible.
9. Give the rationale for assignments, procedures, and instructional methods.

10. When possible, clearly state or demonstrate the learning that will result from learning activities.

11. Ensure successful learning by planning instructional activities that match the needs and objectives of adult learners.

12. Encourage and challenge the learners.

13. Make learner reaction and active participation an essential part of the learning process.

14. Provide frequent response opportunities for all adult learners on an equitable basis.

15. Promote learners' personal control over the context of learning by involving them in the planning and setting of goals, self-evaluation and determination of their strengths and weaknesses, and recording and analyzing progress.

16. Make the criteria for evaluation as clear as possible.

17. Use consistent feedback to learners regarding their mastery, progress, and responsibility in learning.

18. When it is necessary, use constructive criticism.

19. Effectively use praise and reward learning.

20. Plan with the motivation of the learners in mind. Don't assume that the content or the teacher will maintain motivation.

21. Create a learning environment that is organized and orderly.

22. Be aware of the needs of adults: their physiological, safety, love and belongingness, and self-esteem needs and curiosity, sense of wonder, and need to explore.

23. Remove or reduce components of learning situations that lead to failure and fear.

24. Introduce the unfamiliar through the familiar.

25. Use unpredictability and uncertainty to the degree that learners enjoy them with a sense of security.

26. Use disequilibrium to stimulate learning by using such methods as contradiction and "leaving them wanting more" and playing the role of the devil's advocate.

27. Use collaboration as an instructional technique to develop and maximize cohesiveness in the group.

28. Create components in the learning environment that tell learners they are accepted, respected members of the group.
29. When appropriate, plan activities that allow adults to share and to display publicly their projects and skills.
30. Provide variety in presentational style, methods of instruction, and learning materials.
31. Selectively use breaks, physical exercise, and energizers.
32. Use humor liberally and frequently.
33. Use examples, stories, analogies, and metaphors.[23]

Diversity and Discrimination

HR management professionals acknowledge the widespread overrepresentation of white, middle-aged males in the ranks of management. Exclusion of minorities may be subtle or not so subtle. For example, a minority employee can be "promoted" to a position that is either not very visible (and unlikely to showcase the individual's talents) or assigned to one that is doomed to failure. Other variants of the "glass ceiling" may entirely preclude mobility of any substantive kind. While racism and sexism often receive the most attention, other "isms" are no less worthy of our attention. These include discrimination on the basis of age, sexual orientation, and physical or mental disability.

In any event, discrimination in employment is not just against the law. It subjects the employer to possible monetary penalties and damages, as well as adverse publicity. Figuratively speaking, skilled employees (as human capital) are categorized as assets. By failing to deploy these valuable assets properly (or perhaps even driving them from the firm), the manager who discriminates, in effect, devalues the organization's asset base and, therefore, its net worth.

Senior management must, in no uncertain terms, make clear to all employees that discrimination is not acceptable and will not be tolerated. Training programs can be an important component in a more comprehensive plan designed to sensitize employees, to respect one another, and perhaps even to celebrate their differences.

Crisis Management

Given the ever-increasing complexity of the business landscape and the extremely high stakes involved, organizations not only plan to realize their objectives, but they also actively plan to confront their most dreaded possible scenarios.

Crisis management is a specialized area and is to the practice of management what emergency medicine is to the practice of medicine. Both involve the compression of time, and the stakes can be extremely high. The best crisis managers are proactive, anticipating possible catastrophes with various contingency plans to accommodate many scenarios. They have also assembled special task forces that can be sent into action almost without delay. The manager, as spokesperson for the organization, must immediately be prepared to be the source of bad news rather than the defensive receiver of it, and must reassure customers, constituents, and the general public that their well-being is more important to the company than any profits that may be lost as a result of the catastrophe. Johnson & Johnson did a superb job when its Tylenol product was tampered with, and innocent people died as a result of ingesting the poisoned medication. The company's CEO, James Burke, was very visible from the outset and reassured everyone that extreme measures were already being taken to safeguard lives, and he revealed the specific plans to everyone. His concern for public safety was sincere and convincing.

This is in sharp contrast to Audi's handling of the crisis caused by sudden acceleration of its automobile. The company added insult to injury by blaming the drivers, accusing them of stepping down on the wrong pedal. Similarly, after publicly announcing that some of the chips it had recently manufactured and distributed were defective, Intel Corporation made a terrible error by initially refusing to grant exchanges to all purchasers of the chip. After the public outcry that followed, Intel was forced to grant exchanges to all customers who requested one.

To summarize, the basic tenets of crisis management are:

- Anticipation/proactivity
- Timely response
- Genuine concern
- Honesty
- Reassurance

Operations Management

Thus far in this chapter, we have discussed the "soft" skills associated with human behavior in the workplace. In contrast, operations management (OM) is composed largely of "hard" skills and addresses the optimal utilization of material, as well as human resources. OM techniques are crucial in areas such as the production of goods (e.g., assembly-line efficiencies) and the delivery of services (e.g., reducing waiting time for customers). We examine key concepts and formulas, including economies of scale, crossover analysis, breakeven analysis, linear programming, network analysis, queuing theory, and the Just-in-Time production approach. In this chapter, computation of formulas is generally quite simple, requiring only basic arithmetic skills. The sole exception is for linear programming (LP), which involves an algebraic equation. However, even this formula is reduced to basic arithmetic and presented step by step. And, in practice, LP is virtually always computed by machine.

In the real world, almost all of the quantitative problems related to operational aspects of manufacturing and providing service can be addressed via ERP (that is, enterprise resource planning) software.

Logistics and the Supply Chain

Much of this chapter emphasizes the ways by which *value is added* to the product (and for the customer), from the point at which the materials for a product are sourced to the point at which it is delivered; in other words, throughout the *supply chain*. The ultimate goal is to deliver the product in the best condition possible, in a timely manner, and at the lowest possible cost. The area of *logistics* addresses these concerns.

Inbound Logistics

- *Ordering*
  Frequency of orders
  Quantity of orders
- *Sourcing materials*
  Specifications or technical requirements
  Time frame for delivery (urgency)
  Cost
- *Negotiation*
  Policies and options (open or closed bid vs. direct negotiation)
  Special terms (discounts, payment conditions, termination/nullification, and other clauses)
- *Transportation*
  Mode (air, land, sea)
  Time frame for delivery (urgency)
  Cost
- *Receiving (accepting delivery)*
  Facilities
  Inspection of goods
  Documentation
- *Inventory control*
  Security (theft, vandalism)
  Maintenance (physical conditions affecting shelf life/spoilage; acts of God/force majeure)

Outbound Logistics

- *Inventory control (of finished goods)*
  (of works-in-progress)
  Analysis of activity (what is moving and what is not)
  Avoiding "stock-outs" (very important!)

- *Valuation (LIFO, FIFO, weighted average, other)*
- *The same considerations as for* Inbound Logistics, *but with a different perspective*
  Ordering
  Materials
  Negotiation
  Transportation
  Receiving (making delivery)

Economies of Scale

It is important to know the degree to which a larger quantity of units to be produced or purchased will result in a lower average cost per unit (see Figures 3.5 and 3.6). *Economies of scale*, the cost savings that result from dealing in larger quantities, can be increased to the extent that fixed costs (those not sensitive to variations in volume) are absorbed by each additional unit that is produced or purchased.

Note: Scale curves, as depictions of economies of scale, are not the same as experience curves (also known as learning curves). *Experience curves* reflect situations in which costs decrease as experience

Figure 3.5 Economies of scale: the effect of quantity on cost

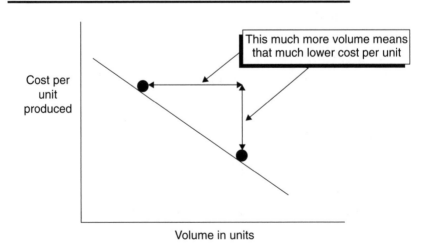

Figure 3.6 Economies of scale: the effect of fixed and variable costs on unit costs

	Project A		Project B
Fixed cost	= $1,000	Fixed cost	= $250
Variable cost	= 5	Variable cost	= 8

	Unit Cost	
Quantity	Project A	Project B
250	9.00	9.00
500	7.00	8.50
750	6.33	8.33
1,000	6.00	8.25
2,000	5.50	8.13
5,000	5.20	8.05
10,000	5.10	8.02

increases. Thus the longer we perform a task (given proper training), the better we become at it. We require less time, there are fewer defects or errors made, and, ultimately, costs come down. *Concentration curves* reflect situations in which output (productivity) is disproportionate to input (deployment of resources).[24] This is roughly analogous to the 80/20 rule (see "The Pareto Principle: 80/20 Rule" later in this chapter).

Assuming that you operate a "fast-food" restaurant, rent, insurance, equipment, furnishings, and utilities are examples of fixed costs, since they do not vary with volume. In other words, they remain pretty much the same regardless of how many orders are filled or how many meals are served. On the other hand, paper cups and napkins are examples of variable costs and are volume-sensitive, since the number of these items used directly corresponds to the number of drinks that are served. So each additional drink that you serve during a meal period costs less than the one before it, until the economies of scale are exhausted. Moreover, if your restaurant has been open for dinner only, you might entertain the notion of offering lunch as well. After all, your fixed costs (with the exception of an additional shift for your cook, waiters/waitresses, and cashier) would already have been borne. Your variable costs would, in effect, be limited to those associated with food portions actually served.

The most commonly used methods for enhancing economies of scale are mergers and acquisitions, joint ventures, compressed scheduling, and cluster management. We discuss each method in the context of hospital management.

Mergers and Acquisitions

By consolidating two previously discrete entities into a single one, administrative expenses can often be dramatically reduced. For example, the merger of two hospitals into one would allow the elimination of duplicated efforts (i.e., two human resources departments would not be necessary).

Taking the hospital example a step further, a large health-care company (or perhaps one that merely *intends to become* large) might institute a *roll-up strategy*, wherein it would buy up many hospitals (i.e., units of the same kind). This is differentiated from a *build-up strategy*, wherein the acquisition-oriented company would buy different but related units, for example, companies that manufacture hospital supplies and companies that provide medical malpractice insurance, in addition to hospitals.

Joint Ventures

If two separate entities are performing the same function and both are operating at a level substantially below full capacity, they can join forces to perform jointly the same function at a level close to full utilization. For example, two neighboring hospitals may decide to share a single CAT scan unit.

Compressed Scheduling

Let's assume that a hospital offers a particular outpatient and elective service 8 hours per day for 7 days per week, but actually delivers this service an average of only 5 hours per day. Since demand or utilization is only at about the 62 percent level, it might be more cost effective to close the facility 2 days per week (thereby reducing such costs as labor and utilities), so that service would be provided 7 hours per day for only 5 days per week, near to full utilization.

Cluster Management

If two departments within that hospital are sufficiently related in function (e.g., obstetrics and gynecology), administration might be handled under a single umbrella (clustering). Redundancy of labor would be eliminated, and purchasing costs would go down as the result of quantity discounts.

Crossover Analysis

Crossover analysis is a quantitative tool that allows us to determine at what point we should switch from one product or service to a competing option. This relates to economies of scale in that we are dealing with fixed and variable costs.

Example: We can buy a Xerox copying machine for $1,000 that costs 3 cents per copy to operate. We can buy an IBM copying machine for only $800, but it costs 4 cents per copy to operate. At what level of activity (number of copies made) does one option offer a cost advantage over the other? Which machine should we start with and which machine should we switch to? The formula for this calculation is:

$$N = \frac{FC2 - FC1}{VC1 - VC2}$$

where

N = crossover point
$FC2$ = fixed cost of machine 2 (IBM; $ 800)
$FC1$ = fixed cost of machine 1 (Xerox; $1,000)
$VC2$ = variable cost of machine 2 (IBM; $0.04)
$VC1$ = variable cost of machine 1 (Xerox; $0.03)

Putting the variables from our hypothetical situation into the formula, we get:

$$N = \frac{800 - 1000}{.03 - .04} = \frac{-200}{-.01} = 20,000 \text{ units}$$

N, the *point of indifference*, also known as the *crossover point*, is equal to the fixed cost (or purchase price) of machine 2 ($FC2$) minus the fixed cost (or purchase price) of machine 1 ($FC1$).

Divided by the variable cost (cost per copy) of machine 1 ($VC1$) minus the variable cost (cost per copy) of machine 2 ($VC2$).

We can see that, if we were to make exactly 20,000 copies, it would make no difference which machine we would choose. In practice, the machine with the lower fixed cost would generally be preferred for quantities below the crossover point.

Double check: To find the machine that would be better for fewer than 20,000 units, we would compare the total cost of each machine at 19,999 units (1 unit less than the point of indifference) and at 20,001 (1 unit more than the point of indifference). We then find that the IBM machine is preferable for quantities up to the point of indifference, whereas the Xerox machine is preferable for quantities at or above the crossover point. The formulas for these calculations are:

$FC + VC \times$ (one unit *below* the point of indifference)

Xerox: 1,000 + .03(19,999) = $1,599.97
IBM: 800 + .04(19,999) = $1,599.96
IBM is less expensive for *less than* 20,000 units.

$FC + VC \times$ (one unit *above* the point of indifference)

Xerox: $1,000 + .03(20,001) = \$1,600.03$
IBM: $800 + .04(20,001) = \$1,600.04$
Xerox is less expensive for *more than* 20,000 units.

Crossover analysis has several major limitations. It does not factor the time value of money into calculations. Also, in practice, we may not be able to forecast the number of copies that we will need to make within a particular time frame. Moreover, it assumes that both options are equivalent in specifications. (This refers to such variables as copy quality, serviceability, duration of warranty, and so on.)

Breakeven Analysis

Breakeven analysis allows us to determine the point at which we can expect to recoup an investment. The calculation for breakeven can be based on (1) the quantity of units which must be produced/served, (2) total sales volume generated, or (3) selling price per unit (see Figure 3.7). Typically, costs exceed revenues (i.e., operating in the red) at the outset of an undertaking, and this gap is narrowed until revenues meet costs (at the breakeven point) and eventually exceed costs (i.e., operating in the black).

Quantity

To find the breakeven point based on the number of units that must be produced/served, we divide the fixed cost by the price minus the variable cost. The formula for this calculation is:

$$Bq = \frac{FC}{P - VC}$$

Figure 3.7 Charting the breakeven point

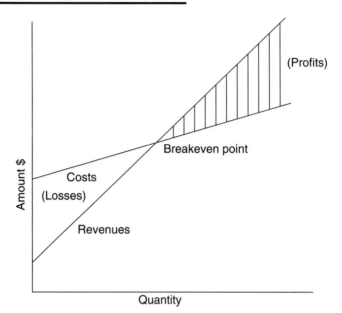

where

Bq = breakeven quantity (the B/E point expressed in units)
FC = fixed cost, at $800
P = price, at $6 per unit
VC = variable cost, at $2 per unit

Putting the variables from our hypothetical situation into the formula, we get:

$$Bq = \frac{\$800}{\$6 - \$2} = 200 \text{ units}$$

Two hundred units would have to be sold to break even.

Sales Volume

To find the breakeven point based on sales volume, we add the fixed cost to the variable cost multiplied by the number of units. The formula for this calculation is:

$$Bs = FC + VC(Q)$$

where

Bsv = breakeven sales volume (expressed in sales revenues)
FC = fixed cost, at $800
VC = variable cost, at $10
Q = quantity, at 200 units

Putting the variables from our hypothetical situation into the formula, we get:

$$Bsv = \$800 + \$10(200) = \$2,800$$

The $2,800 in sales revenues would have to be generated in order to break even.

Unit Price

To find the breakeven point based on selling price, we add the fixed cost to the variable cost multiplied by the number of units and then divide this sum by the number of units. The formula for this calculation is:

$$BP = \frac{FC + VC(Q)}{Q}$$

where

B = breakeven price (the B/E point expressed as the selling price)
FC = fixed cost, at $800
VC = variable cost, at $10
Q = quantity, at 200 units

$$Bp = \frac{\$800 + \$10(200)}{200} = \$14$$

A price of $14 per unit would have to be charged to break even. The major limitation to breakeven analysis is that it doesn't factor in the time value of money. (As with the payback method, this may not be a significant issue if time horizons for recouping investments are relatively short.)

Linear Programming

Linear programming (LP) allows us to determine the optimal mix of competing options in an investment or production environment, to increase profits in the face of financial and/or physical constraints (see "Capital Rationing" in Chapter 2, Accounting and Finance). If, for example, we are in the construction/real estate business building tennis courts and golf courses, we would like to know how many of each to invest in. Or, as in Figure 3.8, we are musical instrument manufacturers who produce only guitars and pianos.

Note that in real life, it would be difficult to calculate the solution for a situation involving more than two unknowns without the use of a computer. Therefore, the following hypothetical case has been simplified for illustrative purposes so that the production of musical instruments involves only two tasks or steps in the production process. In actuality, production involves many more tasks. With a computer, arriving at a solution would be very simple. LP computation is virtually always done by machine.

It takes 2 hours to assemble each guitar (A) and 1 hour to paint it (B), while it takes 1 hour to assemble each piano and 3 hours to paint it. We have only 1,000 hours to assemble guitars and/or pianos, and only 1,200 hours to paint guitars and/or pianos. We anticipate that we will make a profit (C) of $200 on each guitar and $300 on each piano. So our linear programming questions are:

How many guitars should we make?
How many pianos should we make?
How much profit will we make?

To find the answers to these questions, we translate the aforementioned "givens" [(A), (B), and (C)] into the simple algebraic language that you learned in high school [(a), (b), and (c)]. We find for one unknown P (for piano) by taking equation $2G + 1P \leq 1,000$ (A) and

Figure 3.8 Linear programming

Given:

[Tasks]	Guitar	Piano	Capacity
(A) Assembling	2 hours per unit	1 hour per unit	1,000 hours
(B) Painting	1 hour per unit	3 hours per unit	1,200 hours
(C) Unit profit:	$200 + $300		
(c) Objective function:	$200G + $300P = profit		

Questions:

How many guitars and pianos should we manufacture?

How much profit should we make?

(A) Constraints: $2G + 1P \leq 1,000$

(B) $1G + 3P \leq 1,200$

Algebraic computations:

$1P \leq 1,000 - 2G$

$1G + 3(1,000 - 2G) \leq 1,200$

$1G + 3,000 - 6G \leq 1,200$

$-5G = -1,800$

$G = 360$

$2(360) + 1P \leq 1,000$

$720 + P \leq 1,000$

$P = 280$

Answers:

Manufacture 360 guitars and 280 pianos.

Anticipate $72,000 profit on guitars and $84,000 profit on pianos.

moving $2G$ to the other side of the equal sign so that $1P < 1,000 - 2G$ (a). P is equal to or less than $(1,000 - 2G)$, and we substitute $(1,000 - 2G)$ (b) for P on the second line of "algebraic computations," which corresponds to (B). We find that since G and P represent the optimal number of guitars and pianos to make within the limits of production capacity, we should make 360 guitars and 280 pianos. When we multiply these figures by the projected profit for guitars ($200 times C) and for pianos ($300 times C), we find that we can anticipate receiving $72,000 and $84,000, respectively.

Although LP is a very valuable tool, it does carry with it a major limitation: Not all situations can be viewed as linear. (Sophisticated computer programs can adjust for this, if they include a so-called "step" component.) Nonlinearity can reflect, for example, a bottleneck in production due to physical breakdown or work stoppage. Moreover, the projected unit profit would have to change as a result of changes in wages (e.g., overtime) or other costs (e.g., quantity discounts).

Network Analysis

Network analysis helps us to forecast the points of completion for projects we may choose to undertake. It provides analytical frameworks or formulas that can be used to transform subjective or "soft" information (or opinions) into somewhat more tangible projections or "solutions" to planning problems. Critical path and PERT are the most popular of the network analysis methods. Critical path allows us to identify junctures at which delays are likely to occur. PERT (project evaluation and review technique) enables us to factor in optimistic and pessimistic (i.e., early and late) projections of project completion time.

Critical Path

Critical path depicts a series of linked or critical paths that lead to project completion. The critical path is the longest path of them all and represents the amount of time necessary to complete the project. The technique was originally introduced at E. I. du Pont de Nemours.

Figure 3.9 represents the critical path involved in building a scientific research center. Tasks A through F must be successfully accomplished to complete the project. In addition, certain steps must be completed before others can be started. We refer to these as "predecessor" steps. In situations in which tasks overlap (as with tasks B and C), we count only the longer/longest of these tasks, since counting more than one could have the effect of overstating the time necessary to complete the project. We may be able to accelerate completion by enhancing overlapping of tasks.

Figure 3.9 Identifying the critical path for building a research center

Given:

Tasks		Time	Predecessor
A	Forecast demand	2 months	—
B	Design facilities	5 months	A
C	Select equipment	4 months	A
D	Construction	7 months	B
E	Installation	3 months	C, D
F	Fine-tuning	1 month	E

Question:

How long will it take to complete this project?

Answer:

It will take 18 months.
But if tasks A, B, and C can be performed simultaneously,

Answer:

It will take only 16 months.

Project Evaluation and Review Technique (PERT)

PERT was first used by the military in development of the Polaris submarine. The method exists in two forms. As a deterministic technique (i.e., one in which all activity times are assumed to be known with certainty), it is virtually indistinguishable from the critical path method "and the differences, if any, are only historical."[25] However, as a stochastic technique (i.e., one in which all activity times are assumed to be random variables), project managers are called upon to assign three subjective time estimates for each component or task. The optimistic estimate (i.e., early) is multiplied by 1, realistic by 4, and pessimistic by 1. These three weighted estimates are added together and then divided by 6. The formula for this calculation is:

$$Tc = \frac{a + 4b + c}{6}$$

where

Tc = time of completion for each task

a = optimistic estimate

b = realistic estimate

c = pessimistic estimate

Referring to the example provided for critical path and using totally arbitrary numbers to illustrate an application (see Figure 3.10), we can use this formula to calculate the time of completion for each task. By adding the values of each of the tasks comprising the critical path (note that path C is not a part of the critical path), we can obtain an estimate of how long the project will take.

The Pareto Principle: 80/20 Rule

The noted economist Vilfredo Pareto was an avid amateur gardener. In active pursuit of his avocation, he observed that roughly 20 percent of the peapods in his garden yielded 80 percent of the peas that

Figure 3.10 Pert calculations for estimation of project competition time

Given

Task	Optimistic	Realistic	Pessimistic
A Forecast demand	1 month	2 months	4 months
B Design facilities	3 months	5 months	6 months
C Select equipment	2 months	4 months	5 months
D Construction	5 months	7 months	9 months
E Installation	1 month	3 months	4 months
F Fine-tuning	½ month	1 month	2½ months

$$A \quad \frac{1+4(2)+4}{6} \quad = \quad \frac{13}{6} = 2\frac{1}{6}$$

$$B \quad \frac{3+4(5)+6}{6} \quad = \quad \frac{29}{6} = 4\frac{5}{6}$$

$$C \quad \frac{2+4(4)+5}{6} \quad = \quad \left(\frac{23}{6} = 3\frac{5}{6}\right): \text{not counted}$$

$$D \quad \frac{5+4(7)+9}{6} \quad = \quad \frac{42}{6} = 7$$

$$E \quad \frac{1+4(3)+4}{6} \quad = \quad \frac{17}{6} = 2\frac{5}{6}$$

$$F \quad \frac{\frac{1}{2}+4(1)+1\frac{1}{2}}{6} \quad = \quad \frac{6}{6} = \frac{1}{17\frac{5}{6} \text{ months}}$$

If we sum the subtotals for tasks A, B, D, E and F, we find that the project is likely to take $17\frac{5}{6}$ months to complete.

could be harvested. As abstracted and applied to human resources management and operations management in the context of quality (TQM), the 80/20 rule suggests, for example, that relatively few errors (i.e., input) can typically cause the lion's share of defects (i.e., output). The 80/20 rule is also widely used by marketers to illustrate, for example, that relatively few of a company's salespeople may account for the majority of its sales volume or that relatively few of the brands in a company's product line may account for the majority of the firm's profits.

Queuing Theory

The *queuing theory* allows us to minimize the amount of time that customers (i.e., anyone we serve) must spend waiting (on line or in a queue) before they are served. Bank managers use queuing models to deploy human resources (i.e., tellers) efficiently, to minimize the time that customers must wait to be served. Facilities managers also program the computers that control multiple-elevator systems in large buildings so that the average time spent waiting for an elevator can be anticipated and minimized.

There is no single queuing formula. However, each is based upon prior experience. In other words, they consider the number of customers who can be expected to wait on line or be served at a given point in time, along with the likelihood that the size of the queue will substantially exceed the ability to accommodate customers in a timely manner. While the reduction of waiting time may incur increased costs, this must be weighed against the potential loss of customers resulting from poor service.

The Walt Disney amusement parks (such as Disneyland) are considered to be among the best-run facilities in terms of queuing considerations. While Disney's operations engineers are secretive about the methods they employ, some basic rules of queue management are commonly accepted:

- *Establish a standard for maximum waiting time.* Disney's is 15 minutes.

- *"Distract"* those who are waiting. Disney management knows that waiting time doesn't seem as long to customers if they are being entertained while waiting. (I recently visited an extremely popular restaurant for brunch. About ten parties were waiting to be seated before my guests and me, suggesting a wait of more than 15 minutes. Management astutely dispatched hostesses into the queue to serve complementary coffee.)

- *Conceal the queue.* If potential customers can observe the line, they may be put off by it and decide not to wait on line at all. The better facilities are physically designed to "camouflage" or deflect attention from the queue.[26]

Monte Carlo Simulation

The discussion of statistics in Chapter 4 underscores the importance of randomness in polling or testing. Toward that end, *Monte Carlo simulation* is a technique that has been widely employed to generate random numbers. (As you might imagine, the name is inspired by the gaming tables of Monaco.) It involves the use of mathematical formulas and is generally performed via computer. Given that randomness in sampling is linked to reliability of test results, applications of Monte Carlo abound in science, military strategy, and many other areas of endeavor, including business planning (e.g., forecasting prices and such). Employed to help forecast the probability of an event's occurrence, Monte Carlo has been particularly popular with production quality specialists as a means of identifying the point in time that a machine is likely to break down. For example, I am told that the U.S. Postal Service (USPS) uses similar statistical methods to forecast when parts in its optical character readers and other types of equipment are likely to fail. Having established a predictive maintenance program, the USPS is able to replace the parts shortly before they fail, thus averting processing stoppages. (*Note:* Critics of Monte Carlo simulation assert that the approach often generates nonrandom sets of numbers. Although such nonrandomness may be very subtle or "slight," it could be enough to cause an erroneous result.[27]) So a refinement, commonly known as a quasi-Monte Carlo has been gaining much attention.

Just-in-Time (JIT) Production System

Developed by Taiichi Ohno of Toyota, inventory used in production is delivered to assembly lines just in time to avoid a stoppage in production. The benefits associated with this approach include enhancement of cash flow (as a result of reductions in inventory levels) and quality control (as a result of identification and correction of defects prior to or early in the production process).[28] Application to the food processing industry would seem particularly appropriate, in light of perishable inventory.

However, other fields have employed Just-in-Time with considerable success. For example, the Benetton clothing chain purportedly employs a variant of JIT. The firm manufactures sweaters without immediately dyeing them until orders indicate color preferences, at which point it dyes the items to meet demand.

Some critics of JIT, while appreciating the theoretical benefits of the approach, contend that in practice the process requires that inventory be ordered more frequently and in smaller quantities. (This suggests that economies of scale are not likely to be enjoyed.) So, they argue, the approach not only incurs additional ordering and carrying charges (i.e., costs) but is ultimately a rather cumbersome system, since it requires more labor, as well.

Moreover, the consequences of underestimating customer demand (and the corresponding required inventory) may call for managers to employ a Just-in-Case (JIC) approach, one that provides for a "cushion" or overage to accommodate additional demand.

Economic Order Quantity (EOQ) and Reorder Point (ROP)

The formulas for economic order quantity and reorder point were designed to help us determine the most cost-effective size of an order (EOQ) for merchandise and the point in time at which we should reorder (ROP), respectively. In practice, however, both formulas are greatly limited in their application since they are based upon the premise that we can forecast demand and lead time with precision, which we unfortunately cannot do.[29] (As you might imagine, EOQ and ROP are not congruent with JIT).

Clearly, our examination of JIT, EOQ, and ROP underscores the keystone importance of economies of scale as a business issue. These approaches share in common their association with costs of one type or another. JIT may incur purchasing inefficiencies in the interest of product or service quality, whereas EOQ and ROP may incur quality deficiencies in the interest of purchasing efficiencies.

Ultimately, a business should be geared toward optimizing its capacity or resources. In Tokyo, where real estate is extraordinarily expensive, some restaurants have begun to charge customers based upon how much time they take to eat their meals, rather than which foods they select or how much of these foods they actually consume. (Yes, that's correct. They start timing the customers using a punch clock, of sorts, from the time the customers are given access to an all-you-can-eat buffet table!) In London, movie theaters charge different prices for seats, depending upon location within the theater. In contrast, the vast majority of movie theaters in New York seat customers on a first-come/first-served basis. Yet, in the world of mass transportation, it is common practice for airlines to help induce the sale of otherwise-unsold seats (e.g., on less attractive routes or less convenient times) by offering "frequent flyer" points and similar incentives. Coca-Cola once announced plans to vary the price of a can of soft drink from vending machines, such that the price of each can of soft drink would increase as the temperature rises. Before the launch, they wisely rescinded this decision. (*My personal opinion:* Though a typical consumer may be willing to pay an exorbitant price for the first can of soft drink to quench thirst on a very hot day, I doubt that this individual will purchase a second unit at this high price once the severe thirst is at least somewhat satisfied. Also, Coca Cola seems to assume that competitors' brands will not be available at the same or nearby locations, at a reasonable price. Ultimately, this is certainly not a customer-focused strategy and it is bound to reap a lot of negative backlash. The only thing worse than charging customers based upon the temperature would be, as one of the critics cleverly put it, using an X-ray machine to determine how much money the customer has in his pocket and to charge him that amount!)

The Human Resources Management Checklist

1. Do I motivate my subordinates based upon their needs as individuals as well as my needs as their manager?
2. What motivates me?
3. Can I be more sensitive to the personality characteristics of my subordinates? Can I deploy my staff more effectively as a result?
4. Does my personality relate to my strengths and weaknesses as a manager?
5. Should I use an MBO program or something like it to plan and evaluate performance?
6. How can I improve my communication skills?
7. What can I do to embrace total quality management (TQM)?

The Operations Management Checklist

1. Have I done all that I can to enhance economies of scale? Why might I deliberately not want to do so?
2. Can I readily calculate the breakeven points of my projects?
3. Do I know when to switch from one machine to another in the interest of cost-effectiveness?
4. Am I making optimal use of my production and processing facilities?
5. Can I forecast completion dates of projects more accurately?
6. Can I minimize waiting time for internal as well as external customers?
7. Can I reduce inventory while improving quality standards?

4 STATISTICS

Statistics involve the gathering, organization, and mathematical analysis of information. Statistical methods enable business decision makers to characterize a given entity/population quantitatively, compare it to another or others, and arrive at meaningful insights. Arriving at insights is commonly known as *statistical inference,* since we are often able to deduce or infer certain conclusions on the basis of statistical evidence.

In today's sophisticated business environment, virtually all types of statistically relevant data can be readily and easily retrieved and analyzed through the use of computers and a wide variety of programs generally available at computer software dealers. The user does not have to crunch numbers and plot out elaborate formulas. Instead, he or she need only plug in raw numbers and program the process. In other words, don't sweat the calculations. Nevertheless, the decision maker should have a sufficient conceptual understanding of statistics to know which process (i.e., formula) to program, given its strengths and limitations.

When I studied statistics as a requisite part of my MBA curriculum, I really hated it, and now I realize why. Statistics, as typically taught in business schools, does not necessarily address "real-world" business concerns. Students learn formulas and punch these out on handheld calculators in the hope of arriving at "correct" answers on exams and assignments. They don't, however, learn to "play detective" and use statistics to address practical, everyday situations. Nor, for that matter, do they learn to anticipate the "political" nuances relating to the presentation of statistical information. After all, one may elect to present a glass as half empty or half full. In this regard, we will be sensitized to the notion that information can be organized and presented by us to further our cause, or organized and presented by others to our detriment. You will learn the distinction in this chapter.

Conducting a Research Project

How do managers obtain the information necessary to make optimal decisions? Welcome to the wonderful world of research! Areas of application include:

- Forecasting revenues.
- Gauging competitive threats.
- Examining consumer attitudes.
- Evaluating advertising effectiveness.
- Establishing pricing policy.
- Gauging quality control.

The information that management decision makers seek comes from a variety of sources and may be categorized as either primary research or secondary research. *Secondary research* is generally more readily available and less expensive. It is preexisting and can often be obtained from the following sources:

- Market research firms
- Advertising agencies
- Sales promotion firms
- Public relations firms
- Trade associations
- Professional associations
- Governmental agencies
- Quasigovernmental agencies
- Professional journals and publications

- Trade journals and publications
- Newspaper research departments
- Magazine research departments
- Mailing list firms
- Academic institutions

Primary research is not as yet created and must be made to order, so to speak. It can often be commissioned and obtained from a number of the aforementioned sources, or you can conduct your own market research project.

Steps in a Research Project

1. Define the problem.
   a. State the questions that are begging for answers.
   b. Be as specific as possible.
   c. Try not to accomplish too much at one time.
2. Formulate a plan and choose from among the following research methods.
   a. *Questionnaire Survey:* The question-and-answer approach—open or closed ended or a combination—may be used as follows:
   Q: Do you own a DVD player?
   A Yes (or no).
   Q: If "yes," what brand?
   A: Brand X.
   Q: Why did you choose that brand?
   A: Because ...
   b. *Observation:* This method—watching subjects using the product—is used with great success in the toy industry. (Researchers know that kids can find the most unusual ways of playing with toys and develop ingenious new applications— or unsafe ones.) Generally, however, ethical and legal issues may arise involving observation without informed consent.
   c. *Experimentation:* Changing one variable (such as price) while keeping the others constant may be used in a test market

situation prior to formal launch of the product and its broader distribution.

d. *Focus group:* Group discussion involving current or potential users or customers requires a skilled moderator to "probe" effectively yet not in an obvious manner. For example, a major household appliance manufacturer conducted focus groups to determine how it might modify its product line to best satisfy consumers. Findings suggested that consumers wished they had more surface area on the countertops. So the manufacturer decided to mount the entire new line of appliances under the kitchen cabinets.

3. Collect data.

a. *Telephone:* Immediate online entry of responses into databases can be facilitated. Interviewer may probe beyond initial answers for richer information, but this method can be expensive.

b. *Mail:* Callers can reach a highly targeted survey sample, but response rates may be low. (In this single instance, "response" means participation.) Moreover, this method lacks interactivity and does not permit probing for additional information.

c. *In person:* The human element enhances the opportunity to obtain rich information. However, interviewer cheating may occur. (Low-paid students who are often hired to conduct interviews in the field may falsify or distort interviews to complete more interviews on a piecework compensation basis.)

4. Analyze data. The raw information is organized and examined. Quantitative methods may be employed, especially in terms of probability and the relatedness of variables, or findings may be expressed more simply. For example, "Nine out of ten respondents said they preferred our experimental new brand to Brand X."

5. State conclusions and make recommendations. Based upon the findings arising from analysis, marketing implications will emerge. For example, since nine out of ten respondents preferred the brand we are testing, we may decide to launch it on a national basis.

Basic Terminology

Statistics can be a complex subject, but here are some basic key terms you'll need to know.

Populations, Samples, Randomness, Bias, and Representativeness

Political polls are a kind of study that we are all familiar with. It is impractical, if not actually impossible, to ask all voting members of a *population* or an entire group in which we are interested (i.e., the total universe) what candidate they intend to vote for. Therefore, the poll taker must choose a *sample* or small percentage of the population on a *random basis*, so that *bias* is unlikely to distort the result of the study. In other words, the sample should, in microcosm, be *representative* of the entire voting population. A classic example of a study that failed to achieve this was the poll for the 1948 presidential election. Apparently, pollsters chose and relied upon a sample that was *unrepresentative* and biased in favor of Dewey, who ultimately lost to Truman.

Validity and Reliability

Obviously, a test must be able to measure accurately whatever it is designed to measure (*validity*) and to do so repeatedly (*reliability*).

Sometimes, tests are both invalid and unreliable. More dangerous, though, are tests that are invalid and reliable. It has been argued, for example, that exam questions dealing with sports points of reference can reflect a bias against females (who tend to find these points of reference unfamiliar because of cultural norms).

The various statistical tests outlined in this chapter help us to analyze data and to infer certain conclusions about the subject of our research. These tests yield numerical values (e.g., t values for t-test; F for analysis of variance) and are listed in statistical tables, similar to the way mortgage payment schedules are listed in financial tables. When these values fall within certain parameters, we may be able to draw conclusions from the data. For example, we might find that the relationships being tested are very strong or significant and that they (in a sense) validate our *hypothesis*, the assumption or hunch that we are testing.

But to what extent is the test result reliable? In other words, we want to know what the *margin of error* or *confidence interval* is. This is often expressed as a p or *probability value*. P values usually appear in any of three forms:

$P \leq .01$ indicates that the findings are likely to occur at least 99 percent of the time and that the margin of error is not likely to be greater than 1 percent.

$P \leq .05$ indicates that the findings are likely to occur at least 95 percent of the time and that the margin of error is not likely to be greater than 5 percent.

$P \leq .10$ indicates that the findings are likely to occur at least 90 percent of the time and that the margin of error is not likely to be greater than 10 percent.

The selection of a confidence interval should be appropriate to the circumstances at hand. For example, the standard for conducting an exploratory study might be less stringent than the standard for a more critical or definitive follow-up project. So it might be more practical to use .05 than .01. (If we want to increase the confidence level, that is, decrease the margin of error, we would use a larger sample. However, this might prove to be more expensive or require more time.) If, on the other hand, you are reviewing a vendor's specifications regarding the integrity or performance of his product, you might require a probability value of .01 rather than .05 in your capacity as a discriminating customer.

Frequency Distributions

In analyzing the information we gather, we would certainly be interested in the degree to which the *observations* (i.e., the people polled in the survey) are clustered or dispersed, similar or different. The degree of variation in the data is commonly referred to as *dispersion*. This characteristic may be depicted graphically and is known as a *distribution*.

Distributions generally take on any of three forms: symmetrical, skewed, and bimodal.

Symmetrical

A *symmetrical distribution* takes on the shape of a normal or bell curve, with most observations appearing at the midrange and other observations falling equally on both sides. (See Figure 4.1.) Clothing manufacturers, for example, go with a production run that yields a relatively small proportion of very small as well as very large sizes, a larger proportion of somewhat small as well as somewhat large sizes, and the greatest proportion of sizes in the range of what is "average" (and we will define and calculate "average" very shortly).

Skewed

A *skewed distribution* takes on the shape of a curve that "favors" a certain range of values over others. (See Figure 4.2.) For example, the distribution in Figure 4.2(a) can be said to be skewed downward, and conversely, the distribution in Figure 4.2(b) can be said to be skewed upward. For example, if the range of values represent income levels for each of two communities, ranked lowest to highest (left to right) and the range is the same for both communities, we would conclude that the community represented by Figure 4.2(a) seems to be relatively impoverished, whereas the community represented by Figure 4.2(b) seems to be relatively wealthy.

Bimodal

Bimodal distribution takes on the shape of two mirror curves that have been joined together. (See Figure 4.3.) It represents a situation in which there are two "clusters" or many observations at each of two values. Figure 4.3 could represent test grades for a particular class marked by a preponderance of grades that are "low" and "high," with considerably fewer grades that fall somewhere in between.

Figure 4.1 Symmetrical distribution

Figure 4.2 Skewed distribution

(a)

(b)

Figure 4.3 Bimodal distribution

Key Statistical Measures

While distributions are useful in that they characterize how observations appear in the aggregate and can be depicted graphically, other measures allow us to quantify information and to organize it so that we can make better decisions. Such measures include the following.

Measures of Central Tendency

The *measure of central tendency* refers to the value that is expected, a value that can measure a collection of data in three different ways—through the mean, median, and mode.

Mean

Mean is a fancy word for average. The way we figure out an average is to divide the total or sum of all observations by the total number of observations. Let's assume that there are 7 salespeople (or observations) in a sales department. The number of product units sold by these individuals in June is $1 + 9 + 10 + 12 + 13 + 17 + 17 + \ldots$, or 79, if you add them. If we divide 79 by 7, we find that the average number of sales per salesperson in June is 11.28 units.

If we were sales managers, we might compare the mean number of sales for June with the means for previous months to see if there is some kind of trend. An advantage to using the mean for this purpose rather than absolute sales volume measured in dollars is that it would allow us to examine the level of productivity of the sales force. Specifically, sales volume might increase merely because more people were hired to sell, not because they did a better job. So if there were 14 salespeople employed next June (twice the number working this year, a 100 percent increase) and total sales dollars increased by 50 percent, productivity and profitability would have declined despite an increase in sales revenues.

In Chapter 2, "Accounting and Finance," we briefly mention the *weighted moving average (WMA)* as an alternative to LIFO/FIFO. How does it work" Let's use the same scenario as the one we used for LIFO/FIFO, but to better illustrate the point, let's add inventory purchased in May (1, at \$15) and June (1, at \$16). If today is July 1 and we sell one chair today, what is the value of our chair inventory using WMA

$$\frac{\text{Total \$ value of remaining chairs}}{\text{total number of remaining chairs}} =$$

$$\frac{\text{February (\$12) + March (\$14) + April (\$17) + May (\$15) } [not \text{ including June (\$16)}]}{4 \text{ remaining chairs}} =$$

Value of inventory = \$58, or an average (weighted moving average) of \$14.50 per chair.

Median

The *median* is the middle number in a series of numbers when ranked in value from low to high. We calculate the median by taking the number of observations +1 and then dividing that sum by 2. In the previous example, we have 7 salespeople. 7 + 1 (or 8) divided by 2 equals 4. The fourth number in the sequence is the median. In this instance, the median is 12.

$$1, 9, 10, [12], 13, 17, 17$$

The median tends to screen out extreme values. As we review the performance of our 7 salespeople, we notice that one of them turned in a performance considerably lower than all the others, selling only one single unit in June. A median would serve to "camouflage" this poor performance, as evidenced in this instance by a median of 12.0 compared to a mean of only 11.28. The sales manager who wishes to put his or her best foot forward, so to speak, would obviously prefer to use the median. If, however, the salesperson who sold only one unit had sold 35 units instead, the sales manager would prefer to include or even highlight this outstanding performance in his or her report rather than deemphasize it. Therefore, the mean would be preferred.

Mode

The *mode* is simply the number that appears most often. In this case, the number 17 happens to appear more often than any other number, so it is the mode.

$$1, 9, 10, 12, 13, [17], [17]$$

Identifying the mode can help you decide how to prioritize and where to concentrate your efforts. This can readily be applied to marketing, regarding the concentrated marketing strategy. To take best advantage of limited financial resources, for example, a manufacturer may decide to produce an initial production run in a single color. Given that this variable may be "coded" numerically (i.e., 1 = red, 9 = blue, 17 = green), the mode for the color variable would suggest the color of choice.

Measures of Dispersion

Measures of dispersion refers to the variance in a collection of data, which can be determined through the range or the standard deviation.

Range
Range simply describes how much of a "spread" there is between the highest and lowest numbers, the extreme values. Using the same values provided under "Measures of Central Tendency," we find that the lowest number is 1 and the highest is 17. So we subtract 1 from 17, and we can easily see that the spread or range is 16. The range does not, however, describe where most of the observations or numbers are clustered.

Standard Deviation
Standard deviation is a primary indicator of the extent to which our observations deviate from the mean. This measure is calculated by subtracting the mean from each observation, squaring the subtotals, adding them up, dividing them by the number of observations, and finally finding the square root. The formula for standard deviation is:*

$$\sqrt{\frac{\sum (X - \bar{x})^2}{N}}$$

where

x = mean

X = actual value of each observation

N = number of observations

* This formula pertains to application wherein all observations of the entire population are included. If, however, standard deviation is used with a random sample such that the observations in the sample are assumed to be representative of the population, then the denominator of the formula should be "$N - 1$" rather than "N."

Standard Deviation, Example 1

Using the sales department example described in the section, "Mean," we have a series of seven numbers to plug into the formula, as well as the mean itself.

			[X] [x]		[X − x]²		
Salesperson	1 sold	1 unit	1 − 11.28	=	10.28 squared	=	105.68
	2 sold	9 units	9 − 11.28	=	2.28 squared	=	5.20
	3 sold	10 units	10 − 11.28	=	1.28 squared	=	1.64
	4 sold	12 units	12 − 11.28	=	0.72 squared	=	0.52
	5 sold	13 units	13 − 11.28	=	1.72 squared	=	2.96
	6 sold	17 units	17 − 11.28	=	5.72 squared	=	32.72
	7 sold	17 units	17 − 11.28	=	5.72 squared	=	32.72
	N=7						**181.44**

$$\sqrt{\frac{\sum(X - \bar{x})^2}{N}} = \sqrt{\frac{181.44}{7}} = \sqrt{25.92} = 5.09$$

The standard deviation is 5.09.

Nobody I know regularly figures out standard deviation without a computer or calculator. And to put your mind totally at rest, each and every quantitative formula in this book and, for that matter, in any university-based MBA course of study is calculated by machine. You need only to punch in the raw numbers.

Central Limit Theorem
To appreciate the value of the standard deviation, we must first understand that it makes sense only within the context of what is known as the central limit theorem. For our immediate purposes, I ask that you accept on faith the following:

1. No matter what type of distribution you have (i.e., normal or otherwise), the mean of your sample will roughly approximate the mean of your entire population.
2. To be representative of the population, a sample size of at least 30 observations is required.
3. Of all observations (see Figure 4.4):
   34 percent will fall within the first "section" *above* the mean
   34 percent will fall within the first "section" *below* the mean
   13 percent will fall within the second "section" *above* the mean
   13 percent will fall within the second "section" *below* the mean
   3 percent will fall within the third "section" *above* the mean
   3 percent will fall within the third "section" *below* the mean
4. "Section" is, for the moment, synonymous with standard deviation.

Figure 4.4 Standard normal distribution

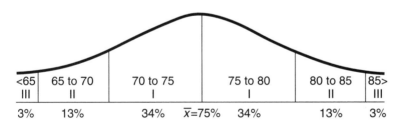

<65 III	65 to 70 II	70 to 75 I	75 to 80 I	80 to 85 II	85> III
3%	13%	34%	$\bar{x}$=75% 34%	13%	3%

So if you are the vice president of sales overseeing 100 salespeople and the mean annual sales are 75 units per salesperson and the standard deviation is 5 (rather than 5.09, to use a whole number for ease of math computation), you will find that:

34 (34 percent) of your salespeople sold between 75 and 80 units
34 (34 percent) of your salespeople sold between 70 and 75 units

13 (13 percent) of your salespeople sold between 80 and 85 units

13 (13 percent) of your salespeople sold between 65 and 70 units

3 (3 percent) of your salespeople sold more than 85 units

3 (3 percent) of your salespeople sold fewer than 65 units

Note that there is a range of 5 (the standard deviation) for each "section," except those at the extremes.

Since 94 salespeople (94 percent) fall within two standard deviations from the mean and sell more than 65 but fewer than 85 units, it may be said that there is not a great deal of dispersion, that is, there is not a great deal of variation in the data.

Standard Deviation, Example 2

Standard deviation is a very important indicator for portfolio managers and other investment counselors. Assume that the financial advisor is weighing two investment options that are likely to yield a similar mean dividend, yet one has a low standard deviation while the other has a high standard deviation. Given that high standard deviation (i.e., in the form of wide swings or fluctuations) in this context is indicative of exposure to risk, a senior citizen client living on a fixed and ostensibly limited income would probably be discouraged from investing in the option with the high standard deviation. Securities analysts find it useful to use the beta factor to reflect the degree of a stock's volatility relative to the market in general. If beta is 1.25, this means that the stock is 25 percent more volatile than the market viewed as a whole. The lower the beta, the better.[1]

The examples we have used for mean, median, and mode involve observations that comprise the entire population (i.e., seven observations) rather than a mere sample of the population. Therefore, due to the purely descriptive nature of our sample, it is okay to use the standard deviation even though we have fewer than 30 observations. Aside from this exception, we might elect to use the *standard error* for samples of fewer than 30 observations.

A Statistical Anecdote: What Is "Normal"?

I'd like to share a personal anecdote with you to underscore further the practical applications of statistics.

I was concerned about hair loss from my scalp so I visited my dermatologist. He asked approximately how many hairs I lose each day. Is it more than 25? My response was that I hadn't even thought of it in those terms, only in terms of perceived thinning. When pressed for an answer, I reluctantly suggested that it is possible. He then asked whether the figure is less than 100, to which I responded with somewhat greater confidence that it was. He then explained that this was "normal." Upon hearing this, I shared with him my sense of relief since I thought that I was going bald. My sense of well-being was instantly shattered by his comment, "Oh, you're going bald, but that's normal."

In retrospect, I find this episode sort of funny because the word "normal" meant something different to me from what it meant to my physician. To me, "normal" meant that "it's okay" or even "desirable." I viewed the term judgmentally, that bald is bad. To the dermatologist, "normal" meant nothing more than "common in occurrence." In statistical terms, he was saying that my mild case of male pattern (or genetically induced) baldness falls within one standard deviation of the mean, that some thinning of hair is very common among men in their late thirties.

This was not a value judgment on his part, merely an objective observation.

Stories behind the Statistics: Creative Interpretation

Scenario 1: Low Dispersion

Figure 4.5 depicts a symmetrical distribution with little dispersion. Let's assume that each of those little square boxes clustered near the mean represents the job evaluation of an employee in a given department of your company. Assume that you are the personnel director

Figure 4.5 Low-dispersion distribution scenario

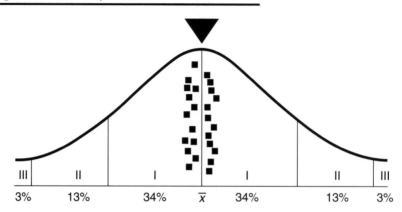

III	II	I	$\bar{x}$	I	II	III
3%	13%	34%		34%	13%	3%

and that you are routinely examining this diagram as an illustration of what's going on in this department. What do you suspect this distribution signifies? (*Remember*: Even the best of detectives have many suspects before they ultimately arrest the guilty party.)

One possibility is that all the employees in the department are producing at about the same level. If they work on an assembly line, it might indicate a union-encouraged work slowdown or perhaps merely a highly collegial and noncompetitive working environment having nothing whatsoever to do with a union, in which no employee wants to show up or outperform his or her peers. Another possibility is that the manager of this department is an indiscriminate and poor evaluator.

Scenario 2: High Dispersion

Figure 4.6 depicts a bimodal distribution with considerable dispersion. Let's assume that you are routinely examining this diagram as an illustration of what's going on in another department. What do you suspect might be going on here?

One possibility is that the evaluations are actually fair and accurate and, if so, that one grouping or segment of employees was poorly trained while the other segment was properly trained, or that one was not properly motivated and the other one was properly

Figure 4.6 High-dispersion distribution scenario

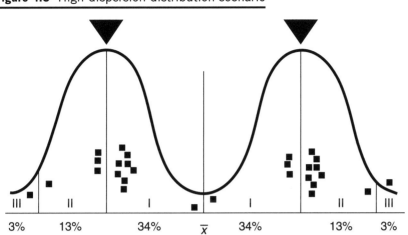

motivated. A more ominous possibility is that the manager of this department is a biased and unfair evaluator. This suspicion could be quickly supported or refuted by exploring further to see whether or not the grouping that has received the less favorable evaluations is composed primarily of minorities such as people of color or women, while the grouping that has received the more favorable evaluations is composed of middle-aged white males. Toward this end, you might want to examine *each* of the personnel files for this department and perhaps also interview a cross section of employees as well as the manager. (This scenario presumes, of course, that the manager of this department is white and perhaps male, as well.)

Regression Analysis

Regression analysis[2] is a statistical method that allows us to examine the relationship that exists between variables. It is commonly used in forecasting. It also explains why manufacturers of toys, for example, keep an eye on the divorce rate. They have found that, as the divorce rate goes up, the parents who are splitting up (as well as loving grandparents) will tend to shower the children with toys and such, either out of guilt or to vie for the children's affection.

It does not, however, suggest that one variable is caused by another, only that a relationship exists and that we can ascribe a magnitude of strength to the relationship. In fact, the issue of causation can become a particularly difficult one when we *confuse* which variable affects the other. For example, we may find a very high degree of correlation (let's say, 0.9) between children who have poor grades in school and the fact that they watch many hours of TV each week. One interpretation is that their grades suffer because children spend so much time watching TV that they don't study. Another interpretation (which may be closer to the truth) is that these children have learning disabilities and would have problems with grades whether or not they watched so much TV. One might reasonably assume that they rely on TV so heavily for entertainment because it is a medium that requires no active skills, so it is easy for them to participate, and they really can't fail at it. To quote Wallace Irwin, statistics show that of those who contract the habit of eating, very few survive.

The *correlation coefficient*, denoted by r, reflects the magnitude of the relationship. The closer the r value is to $+1.00$, the greater the positive relationship between the variables. Such is the case between the variables of sales and advertising in Figure 4.7. As advertising increases, sales increase, too. Conversely, if the r value is close to -1.00, there is a strong negative relationship. Such is the case between the variables of sales and interest rates (see Figure 4.8). As interest rates increase, sales decrease.

Figure 4.7 Example of positive correlation coefficient. R is positive

Figure 4.8 Example of negative correlation coefficient. *R* is negative

Sales

Interest rates

Regression analysis is almost always done by computer, requiring only that the raw numbers be inputted. The software does the rest. If you wanted to find the r value manually, it would be a time-consuming process.

The *coefficient of determination*, denoted by r^2 (i.e., the r value squared), reflects the degree to which other variables are related. If we arbitrarily assume that $r^2 = .25$, we can then say that only 25 percent of the variation in sales is related to the variation in interest rates (or advertising expenditures).

Time Series Analysis

Time series analysis[3] allows us to observe performance of a given behavior or variable over a period of time. Like regression analysis, it is commonly employed in forecasting and involves plotting a line. We refer to this as a *trend line*, and it appears with three other lines representing variations (see Figure 4.9) as follows:

1. Secular trend (general trend)
2. Seasonal variation (periodic or regular phenomenon)
3. Cyclical variation (economic cycle, one year plus)
4. Irregular variation (random or chance events)

Trend analysis can be more simple and primitive, of course. A single-line representation can easily be created by, for example,

Figure 4.9 Time series analysis

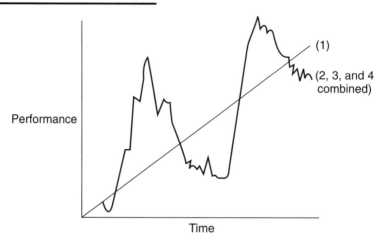

posting sales figures for each month in a one- or two-year time frame and connecting the dots to form a line.

There are other statistical methods that you are unlikely to use on a regular, hands-on basis. It is not necessary that you know how to perform these tests. However, you should understand that statistical tables can help you determine whether or not values or results yielded by the tests are significant and to what extent you can rely on them.

Exponential Smoothing

To forecast short range, one may wish to use this method. Exponential smoothing involves using a weighted average. Remember what we did back in Chapter 2, "Accounting and Finance," when we discussed an alternative to the LIFO and FIFO methods and earlier in this chapter? Well, in this case, we use a weighted average, too. However, the reliance or weight is disproportionately greatest in the most recent past. It is most appropriate to use this method when periodic demand manifests no particular pattern and in the absence of seasonal variations. *Caveat:* Exponential smoothing *does not* factor in economic considerations, including but not limited to changes in pricing or competitive events. The choice of a *smoothing constant*, which determines how much you will depend upon recent data, is subjective.

However, that decision may be reached by calculating the *mean square error (MSE)*, which is something akin to a standard deviation covering historical data and new forecast periods. Is this a little confusing? If so, don't be alarmed. Exponential smoothing is typically done by computer. A manager needs only to enter the raw information for historical data as well as to assign a value for the smoothing constant.[4]

Other Parametric Statistical Methods

The following methods[5] also require normal distributions, those with observations of 30 or more. However, the vast majority of managers and decision makers, unless they are in highly technical areas such as research or engineering, are not likely to be using these.

T-Test

The *t-test* (expressed as a *t* value) allows us to examine the means of two discrete groups and to compare the groups regarding some variable (e.g., gender).

Analysis of Variance (ANOVA)

Analysis of variance or *ANOVA* (expressed as an *F* value) is similar to the t-test, but it allows us to compare more than two groups or variables (e.g., gender, ethnicity, age).

Nonparametric Statistical Methods

The statistical tests discussed below[6] do not require normal distributions.

Chi Square Analysis

Chi square analysis allows us to examine a limited set of values (e.g., male or female) to help determine if a variable is related to behavior or a state of nature (e.g., gender re attendance).

Poisson Distribution

A *poisson distribution* allows us to estimate the probability of an occurrence (e.g., that a production line will suffer a bottleneck).

Statistics and the Renaissance Man (or Woman)

When we think of the application of statistics for business decision making, many of us have to restrain the impulse to tape our eyelids to our foreheads, so that it won't be so obvious that we've actually lost consciousness from boredom. However, as one of those students who used to carry a roll of Scotch tape to class, I can tell you that statistics can actually be fascinating when you apply it to "real life" situations rather than the dull examples found in many B-school stat textbooks.

For example, in sports, statistical methods have been employed to support or refute the contention that "Shoeless Joe" Jackson of the Chicago White Sox team of 1919 accepted a bribe to "throw" the World Series of baseball. Jackson claimed that, while his teammates may have taken such bribes, he did not. He explained that his poor performance during the World Series games was due to his experiencing a few "off days" and that could happen to anyone. Although this still remains a controversial topic, a group of statisticians who are baseball fans found that Jackson's lackluster performance during the World Series games was not *statistically significant* as a departure from his normal level of play, such that it was entirely possible (if not actually likely) that he really just had a few off days and did not take bribes.

In literature, it has long been suspected that some of the works of William Shakespeare were actually ghost-written by his contemporary, Francis Bacon. (Bacon was acknowledged to have been a brilliant man with writing ability, and it was commonly known that he was often strapped for cash.) When the private (i.e., unpublished) writings of Bacon were compared to some of the published works attributed to Shakespeare, it was found that the *correlation* between the two was greater than the *correlation* between Shakespeare's private (i.e., unpublished) writings and his own published works. (What did they measure? Such elements as *mean/median/standard deviation* regarding the number of words per sentence, sentences per paragraph, and paragraphs per chapter.)

I don't expect you to drop what you are doing to run out to buy books on statistics. Just keep your mind open to the possibilities.

A Cautionary Note

I'm sure that someone in your life who "wears sensible shoes" and is down to earth reminds you from time to time: "Don't believe everything you read." This can be especially so as it pertains to statistics. For example, some statisticians reported a high correlation between income and the likelihood of being accidentally injured in your home. If we were to scratch just slightly below the surface, we might realize that people from lower-income families are not likely to go to hospitals for treatment of all but the most serious of injuries. And since statistics are gathered from the records of hospitals and similar institutions, we can reasonably assume that many cases of accidental injury in the home are never reported and never documented at all. To this day, certain crimes that carry social stigma (such as incest, rape, and spousal abuse) often go unreported and are certainly underreported.

Therefore, it is important to find out *how* the statistical information was gathered and *how* it was analyzed. And, perhaps most significantly, it is important to find out who has an *"agenda"* and is likely to profit from your buying into the information.

A Reminder

Although there are additional statistical methods, the aforementioned ones represent those commonly used by management decision makers. Please keep in mind that these are generally calculated by computer and that software is widely available to allow inputting of raw numbers, yielding desired answers or information. In other words, you don't have to know the formulas.

The Statistics Checklist

1. Have I used the best research methods to serve my purpose and budget?
2. Have I gathered the necessary information randomly and without bias?
3. Do the tests or methods that are used yield valid and reliable results?
4. What do measures of central tendency and dispersion reveal about what I am studying?

5 ECONOMICS

Economics is widely regarded as the theoretical sister of finance, which, in contrast, may be regarded as a more practical discipline. To support this contention, George Bernard Shaw once said, "If all economists in the world were laid end to end, they still wouldn't reach a conclusion." Economics is occasionally referred to as "the dismal science." This is attributed to the pessimistic influence of Thomas Malthus (1766–1834), who prognosticated dire consequences because population increases geometrically while the means of subsistence increases only arithmetically.

Economics involves the study of human behavior as it relates to the consumption and utilization of resources to satisfy wants. The social sciences are often drawn upon, since so much of economic behavior and decision making is influenced by motives and incentives. Economics is also concerned with methods of organizing the production, distribution, and sharing of goods and services. In fact, the word is derived from two Greek words, *oikos*, "house," and *nemein*, "to manage." Apparently, the principles gleaned from the management of households may also be employed for substantially larger units, such as businesses, cities, countries, and groups of countries. *Macroeconomics* is the branch of economics that deals with analysis of broad and general aspects of an economy. In contrast, *microeconomics* is the branch of economics that deals with analysis of particular aspects of an economy.

Macroeconomics

Primary macroeconomic concerns include assessment of:

Aggregate income (as reflected by gross national product and gross domestic product)

Employment (as reflected by unemployment level)

Price (as reflected by the consumer price index and the producer price index)

GNP and GDP

Aggregate income is measured by *gross national product (GNP)*, the total amount of goods and services produced *by* a nation, or by *gross domestic product (GDP)*, the total amount of goods and services produced *within* a nation. The latter indicator has taken on increasingly greater significance in light of the trend of U.S. businesses to produce outside the nation's borders, with the intent of substantially reducing labor and other costs.

GNP and GDP each consist of consumer spending (i.e., individual/general public buying), investment spending (i.e., commercial buying), and government spending. Both indicators should be viewed in light of a positive net trade balance, such that exports exceed imports. The formula for GNP or GDP is:

$$GNP \text{ or } GDP = C + I + G$$

where

C = consumer spending

I = investment spending

G = government spending

Consider, if you will, the following: approximately 12 percent of U.S. GNP is generated by the medical and health-care segments of the economy. Is this good or bad? One view suggests that it is a good thing that a nation can afford to devote such a large slice of the pie to the health of its people, whereas a divergent position suggests that it should be a matter of great concern that the nation's people are so unhealthy as to require so much in the way of care. Moreover, medical and health care (and services, generally speaking) are not universally regarded as truly "productive" in the sense that the manufacture and delivery of tangible goods are. What do you think?

Employment

Actually, unemployment. The distinction is drawn between frictional, structural, and cyclical unemployment. *Frictional* refers to individuals who are out of work for relatively short periods of time due to such varied reasons as pregnancies and career transitions, as well as seasonal dislocations. *Structural* refers to individuals who are out of work for extended periods of time due to a lack of skills, such as the "hard-core" unemployed of the inner cities and those whose considerable skills have been rendered obsolete by automation and new technologies. "Full" employment suggests that the structural component is very low and that the frictional component is at a "normal" level. *Cyclical* refers to individuals who are out of work due to downturns in economic cycles.

Price

Changes in price are measured by the *consumer price index (CPI)*, the indicator of choice for retail prices of goods and services, and the *producer price index (PPI)*, the indicator of choice for wholesale prices of goods and not services at the manufacturer's door. These measures compare price levels against those associated with a base year. So, if current prices are assigned a value of 240, this means that prices increased by 140 percent over those of the base year, given that the base year bears a value of 100.

Money Supply and Its Velocity

The *money supply* is the total amount of a country's money that can be spent. This is composed of currency and all types of bank deposits. Prices will tend to rise when people are spending briskly and the money supply is constant. Conversely, prices will tend to fall when people are spending reluctantly and the money supply is constant. *Velocity* is the speed at which the money supply "turns over" or recirculates; the formula for velocity is:

$$\text{Velocity} = \frac{\text{Gross national product}}{\text{Money supply}}$$

Business Cycles

In Ecclesiastes, it is said that there is "a time to laugh and a time to cry," "a time to reap and a time to sow." In economics, we observe that business activity often occurs in cycles over time, from boom to bust periods.

Inflation

Inflation is the state in which prices go up and buying power of currency goes down. (This doesn't mean that personal buying power goes down, because income may be rising faster than prices.) To (jokingly) quote Senator Alan Cranston in 1984: "Inflation is not all bad. After all, it has allowed every American to live in a more expensive neighborhood without moving." Inflation may be observed in any of three types:

- *Demand pull:* Happens with high levels of employment. When demand exceeds supply, prices go up: a boom period or, if you will, "good" inflation.
- *Change in composition of output:* Happens when an economy shifts its emphasis to the creation and delivery of services rather than products. This is thought to be related to the notion that economies of scale for services are "exhausted" sooner than those for

products (see the section "Economies of Scale," in Chapter 3, "Human Resources and Operations Management").

- *Cost push:* Happens when supply diminishes relative to demand. This, in effect, increases demand and drives prices up. It is characterized by high unemployment and is especially dangerous when accompanied by *stagflation*, increases in price in the absence of economic growth.

Recession

Recession is a major downturn in the economy, a "bust" period. Although criteria are subjective and vary considerably among economists, a commonly accepted criterion is two consecutive quarters with a decrease in growth (as measured in gross national product). A domino effect of sorts takes place when the downturn causes employers to cut costs, including those associated with labor. Such downsizing, if anything, tends to fuel the recession further, in light of the understandable reluctance on the part of the unemployed to spend any more than is necessary.

Unfortunately, many businesses view economic downturns as periods in which they must cut costs and contract the range and magnitude of the activities in which they would normally be engaged. Actually, this perspective is shortsighted and usually not ultimately in the best interests of the organization. Recessions present a fine opportunity to address developmental areas, such as training. And although customers may be restrained relative to their normal buying behavior, marketers would be wise to "stay close" to the customer precisely at this critical point in time, for two important reasons. First, it may be possible to configure or reconfigure products and services to serve the particularly cost-conscious attitude of customers, such that business may be maintained to some degree or new market segments may emerge. Second (and figuratively speaking), the seeds that are planted today will produce fruit tomorrow. Of course, this is totally congruent with the orientation of customer focus, which should not cease simply because there is a hiatus or alteration in customer buying patterns.

In a similar vein, employers should be extremely reluctant to discharge skilled labor, even during economic downturns. It is often much harder to replace these individuals than is commonly anticipated. Incidentally, observers seeking an indicator for the end of a downturn typically keep an eye on the corrugated box industry. The shipping of boxes or cartons takes on a brisk pace is suggestive that recovery may be forthcoming.

Depression

A *depression* is a prolonged and extremely severe downturn in the economy. Usually precipitated by a stock market "crash," banks and other businesses fail. Production and investment are reduced to a very low level while unemployment soars.

Fiscal Policy versus Monetary Policy

Economists differ as to the type of policy that should be implemented to spur economic growth. Advocates of *fiscal policy* believe that the government should rely heavily upon taxation as well as its spending. Spending takes the form of transfer payments (for which no services or goods are actually given in return, such as unemployment benefits, social security, and Medicare/Medicaid coverage), infrastructure development projects (such as building of highways and hospitals), and investment in other programs.

In contrast, advocates of *monetary policy* believe that the government should effect desired change by means of altering the money supply and the interest rate. Yet these proponents find it disconcerting that they cannot forecast with any reliable degree of accuracy when actions taken by the Federal Reserve System will actually kick in. So they would be content simply to have the Fed foster economic growth at a modest albeit roughly fixed rate.

The Federal Reserve System (specifically, the Federal Reserve Board) has as its objective the nation's economic well-being and tries to accomplish this on three fronts. It is actually a rather complicated system. *The Federal Reserve Board (the "Fed"),* a group of individuals who serve as the governing body of the Federal Reserve System, performs the following functions:

1. *Purchases Treasury bills if it wishes to stimulate the economy and sells them if it wishes to slow down economic growth* that is either too extreme or that is accompanied by an unacceptably high rate of inflation.

2. *Requires that banks maintain reserves against the loans they grant.* The smaller the reserve requirement, the more money the banks are able to lend; the greater the reserve requirement, the less money the banks are able to lend. The more money banks are able to lend, the greater the likelihood of economic growth. (The irony here is that many banks have substantial reserves, but are reluctant to lend to any borrowers except the best credit risks. This helps to explain why recovery may be slow and incomplete.)

3. *Acts as a bank to other banks,* lending money to these entities at a preferred rate of interest, known as the *discount rate.* The lower the discount rate, the more money the banks are likely to borrow; and the more they borrow, the greater the likelihood of economic growth. When the discount rate is higher, banks tend to borrow less money, and there is less likelihood of economic growth.

The influence of the monetarists was most strongly felt when the Reagan administration's Nobel laureate Milton Friedman essentially defined the movement in his pleas for a free market economy (i.e., laissez-faire or minimal government intervention). In some important respects, he walks in the footsteps of Adam Smith who, about two centuries earlier in his book, *The Wealth of Nations* (1776), espoused the notion of the "invisible hand," wherein Smith took the position that a business enterprise pursuing its own self-interest nonetheless serves the interests of society as well. So government should not interfere. Of course, both Smith and Friedman assumed that free competition always exists. (Obviously, neither could easily justify this stance in view of the reign of the "robber baron" monopolists at the turn of the twentieth century.) Both would also seem to favor what may be regarded as supply-side economics. This policy is skewed toward stimulation of production (i.e., supply) by means of tax incentives.

In contrast, the influence of those who favor fiscal policy was most evident during the two decades immediately preceding the Reagan presidency. The preeminent proponent of fiscal policy was John Maynard Keynes. His influence was so great that those who advocate fiscal policy are commonly referred to as Keynesians. Keynes, in his book, *General Theory of Employment, Interest and Money* (1936), contended that economic downturns could be prolonged and extended. Therefore, government should intervene by "fine-tuning," stimulating economic growth via spending and reducing taxes.[1]

Deficit in the National Budget
Simply put, the government spends more than it receives. As a result, future generations will have to bear the tax burden. In the United States, the vast majority of political responses call for an austerity program of some kind as a solution to the problem.

Foreign Trade

Balance of Payments
The budget deficit is closely linked to the negative balance of payments in the United States. In other words, Americans buy more from foreign nations in the aggregate than foreign nations buy from the United States. Since deficits lead to devaluation of the dollar and lower currency exchange rates, the products that U.S. firms export become less expensive abroad, and the products that are imported to the United States become more expensive.

What causes a negative balance of payments? One explanation relates to the perception of the generally inferior quality of a nation's products within a certain product class or groups of product classes. For example, U.S. quality in the manufacture of automobiles is widely regarded as poor by Japanese standards (see TQM in the section "Systems Era (1980–Present)," in Chapter 3, "Human Resources and Operations Management") and Japanese demand for

U.S. cars is low. Others counter that the Japanese aren't buying U.S. vehicles not because of poor quality (as such), but because Japanese trade barriers close markets to foreign companies. Yet even those who might agree with this contention would have to admit that U.S. marketers have often been grossly insensitive to differences in cultural preferences. For example, the American Motors Jeep is the first American-made car with a steering wheel on the right side to be sold in Japan. Why did American manufacturers persist (until 1993!) in making cars with steering wheels on the left side for the Japanese market which clearly preferred steering wheels on the right side?

The International Monetary System
In 1941, the world's major economic players came together to foster international trade. Several years later, these nations established the World Bank and the International Monetary Fund (IMF), entities that grant credit to member countries and third world nations for relatively high-risk undertakings and to other nations suffering unfavorable balance of payments (i.e., more funds leaving or spent by a nation than come into it or received by it).

Microeconomics

Primary microeconomic concerns include analysis of

Supply and demand
Utility
Productivity
Nature of competition

Supply and Demand (Laws of)

The Supply Curve
The higher the price of a product or service, the greater the quantity of the item that producers will be willing to make available (i.e., supply), and conversely, the lower the price of a product or service, the smaller the quantity producers will be willing to make available (see Figure 5.1).

Figure 5.1 Supply curve

The Demand Curve

The lower the price of a product or service, the greater the quantity of the item that consumers will be willing to buy (i.e., demand), and conversely, the higher the price of a product or service, the smaller the quantity consumers will be willing to buy (see Figure 5.2).

Figure 5.2 Demand curve

Equilibrium

Equilibrium is the point at which supply meets demand. More often than not, it represents an ideal rather than a truly attainable goal (see Figure 5.3).

Figure 5.3 Equilibrium

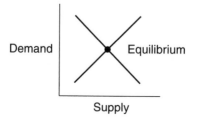

Ceilings and Floors

Economic markets may be characterized by artificially imposed maximum (i.e., ceiling) and/or minimum (i.e., floor) supply and/or demand levels that interfere with the free market. For example, certain municipalities have enacted rent control laws (i.e., price ceilings), wherein landlords are required to keep residential rental levels below what, in effect, would be the "fair" market rate (i.e., equilibrium). As a result, many of those dwelling units covered by rent control tend to be inhabited by individuals or families who would be forced to live elsewhere if they were required to pay the true market rate. Moreover, by taking rent-controlled units off the "regular" market (i.e., diminishing the supply of unprotected housing), the demand for unprotected housing is increased, and prices would reflect this.

Conversely, the federal government has enacted minimum wage laws (i.e., price floors), in which employers are required to compensate their workers at a certain minimum scale or at a higher level. By increasing the price of labor, demand for it diminishes and unemployment increases. Interestingly, during the first term of his presidency, Ronald Reagan proposed the creation of an "additional" and lower minimum wage level, to coexist with the incumbent minimum wage level. Reagan contended that application of this additional floor would be limited only to the "hard-core" unemployed, those who would not otherwise be able to find work. Employers, he reasoned, would have an incentive to hire these individuals, since the cost of labor would be perceived as "artificially" low, and they would have a greater incentive to hire more workers. Moreover, benefits in the form of new skills, along with a work ethic and a salary, would go to those hired. And, of course, unemployment would drop. (The plan was not adopted.)

Elasticity of Demand

The degree to which demand for a product or service can be altered by a change in price indicates the extent of the *elasticity* of that demand. For example, a person who seeks to purchase a particular brand and model of automobile may decide to shop competitively from dealer to dealer for the lowest price. This would characterize demand that is elastic. However, there are circumstances in which the level of demand is not altered by a change in price. For example, a person who is diabetic will probably be willing to pay as much money as he or she has to buy insulin, the medication that would sustain that individual's life. In this case, the demand is inelastic.

By the way, the insulin example has ominous implications as it pertains, for example, to the tobacco industry. The price of cigarettes has increased by about 5 percent every six months over the last few years. As long as the tobacco industry can get away with this while at the same time enhancing production efficiencies (and it does), it will be able continually to reap huge profits, even in the face of diminishing sales levels.

(In 1993, overnight and without advance notice, Philip Morris suddenly dropped the price of its Marlboro brand by approximately 30 percent. The rationale behind this move involved taking market share away from competing brands. The loss of revenues relating to the lowered price would, the company gambled, be more than offset by the increase in absolute revenue dollars relating to the increased market share and increased units sold.)

Cross-Elasticity of Demand

Cross-elasticity describes the effect that an alteration in the price of one item will have on the demand for another item. If the items are complements (such as peanut butter and jelly), a dramatic increase in the price of one item will be followed by a diminution in the price of the other. If, however, the items are substitutes (such as tea and coffee) and the price of one item goes up dramatically, consumers may switch to the lower-priced item.

Diminishing Marginal Utility (Law of)

The concept or economic *"law" of diminishing marginal utility* posits that the level of demand or "satisfaction" derived from a product or service diminishes with each additional unit consumed until no further benefit is perceived within a given time frame. This would help to explain the underlying marketing strategy of Schaefer beer, whose slogan, "Schaefer is the one beer to have when you're having more than one," implied that the rate at which marginal utility of this brand declines is slower than it would be with competing brands and this might be an ample selling point for heavy users. Therefore, marketers would be wise to conduct research to ascertain the quantity of a product that the consumer is likely to "be satisfied with" and buy within a given time frame. Having done so, the product can be packaged in a quantity or configuration designed to maximize the consumer's sense of utility.

Diminishing Returns (Law of)

Let us assume that you are renting a car for $300. If a friend joins you, you each pay $150. If two friends join you, the individual contribution goes down to $100. If five friends join you, each party kicks in $50.

However, the seventh friend who wants to join you will be declined because the car cannot safely seat seven passengers. So friend 7, barring other options, would have to hire his or her own car for $300. We have reached the point of diminishing return.

Comparative Advantage (Paradox of)

It is in the interest of a nation to import an item from another nation when it cannot produce the item as inexpensively. The concept of *comparative advantage* goes a step further, contending that it may be to a country's advantage to import goods from other nations even though it may be able to produce the goods less expensively at home. This is based upon the premise that not producing the item in favor of producing another item that offers better production efficiencies will ultimately benefit both countries (see the section "Economies of Scale," in Chapter 3).[3]

Creative Destruction (Paradigm of)

Early in the twentieth century, economist Joseph Schumpeter noted that new companies (i.e., those introducing new technologies) actually support the economic well-being of society by destroying the previously established competitors (who were relying on technologies or approaches now rendered inferior, if not obsolete). Contemporary examples include cellular telephone technology versus corded telephone technology, retail "superstore" chains such as Wal-Mart versus small and independent "mom-and-pop" stores in terms of efficiency and variety of goods, and video "on demand" (via the Internet or cable TV) versus videotape purchase or rental.

Intel, the world's largest producer of IC (integrated circuit) chips used in computers, is particularly interesting in this regard because it (in a sense) destroys or "cannibalizes" itself every time it introduces a new and faster generation of chips. And Schumpeter would applaud such a bold and aggressive policy in the interest of progress. In fact, he believed strongly that countries choosing to protect their incumbent industries were actually preventing creative destruction and, thereby, doing society a disservice.[4]

Zero-Sum Game (ZSG)

The concept of the zero-sum game (ZSG) was originally introduced by noted mathematician John von Neumann and popularized by economist Lester Thurow of MIT. Simply put, *zero-sum game* implies that for each economic player who gains a certain sum, another player must lose an equal sum (see "Decision Making Under Conflict: Game Theory," in Chapter 8, "Strategic Planning."). Enlightened managers may try to avoid zero-sum games, preferring instead the notion of win-win situations, in which one party need not lose for the other to gain. However, in a world in which economic players vie for their slices of a finite pie to increase market share in an industry in which growth is stagnant suggests that the gain in share comes at the expense of another entity's loss of that slice of the pie.

"Satisficing"

Herbert Simon, the Nobel laureate, is most closely associated with the term "satisficing." Essentially, Simon's contribution may be abstracted to suggest that the maximum or "the most" is not necessarily as good as "good enough."[5] For example, an organization that wins so much market share that it faces antitrust action and ultimately dissolution is clearly not as well off as another organization that claims a lesser market share but focuses more on profitability. In this light, we might opt to "satisfice."

International Commerce and Globalization

McDonald's serves as a useful point of reference in global commerce. By virtue of its size alone (if nothing else), McDonald's would seem to enjoy a considerable advantage in almost any host nations in which it chooses to operate. Yet the firm met serious competition in the Philippines, for example, where the much smaller and local Jollibee restaurant chain prevailed. This has been attributed to McDonald's having offered a burger that was not spicy enough to suit local tastes. Should the company have been more attentive to this difference in preferences? The term *glocalization* (or the blending of globalization with localization) suggests that perhaps the firm should have been. And this raises other questions. For example, if one of the "selling points" used in judging fast-food restaurant chains is uniformity of product (in other words, that a burger in New York should be prepared the same way as a burger in Hong Kong), then the firm is presented with conflicting criteria.

What does it take to become a world-class organization? Scenario planner Clem Sunter suggests the following criteria[6] (followed by examples in parentheses that I've chosen):

- *5 × 10 × 10 growth* in earnings of at least 5 percent per year over a 10-year period, with shareholders receiving a total real return of at least 10 percent per year over the same period.
- *Establish a niche* (Swatch)
- *Uniqueness* of the product in terms of product differentiation and branding (Nike, Mercedes-Benz).
- *Perpetual spirit of innovation* (3M).

- *Flexibility* or the ability of management to use its "radar" system to be alert to significant developments and act in a timely manner (General Electric).
- *Social and environmental awareness* (The Body Shop).
- Function as a *world player*, dealing internationally with global recognition.

The Economics Checklist

1. Can I be more proactive in anticipating changes in business cycles?
2. Does the pricing of my products adequately address supply and demand concerns, such as elasticity?
3. Does the configuration or packaging of my products maximize utility for my customers?
4. Which of my business activities are zero-sum games in nature and which are not? Can I change this? Do I want to? Is it in my interest to do so?
5. How do economic factors reframe the way I view competition?

6 TECHNOLOGY MANAGEMENT

The computer has revolutionized our culture and the way we do business. It has been posited that, if the aircraft industry had grown as rapidly as the computer industry has in the recent past, airplanes would carry as many as 10,000 passengers at more than 60 times the speed of sound—and the fare would cost far less than $10.00 per passenger.

Although computer technology has certainly proven to be extremely valuable and powerful in its own right, melding the computer with other technologies facilitates even more impressive synergies and exponential growth opportunities (see Figure 6.1). The following represents applications that are, for the most part, widely employed. However, the pace of change is so rapid that technological advances come, and in some cases, will have gone sooner than we expected.

Artificial Intelligence (AI)

Artificial Intelligence (AI) facilitates the analysis of problems and identification of their solutions. *Knowledge-based systems (KBS)* do so by searching for a historical match (i.e., a previous instance or case) and employing *case-based reasoning (CBR)*. *Expert systems (ES)* equal or exceed human intelligence. Artificial intelligence allows the computer to serve as an "advisor" of sorts to the user. It is this "human"

Figure 6.1 Combination of technologies to draw upon synergies

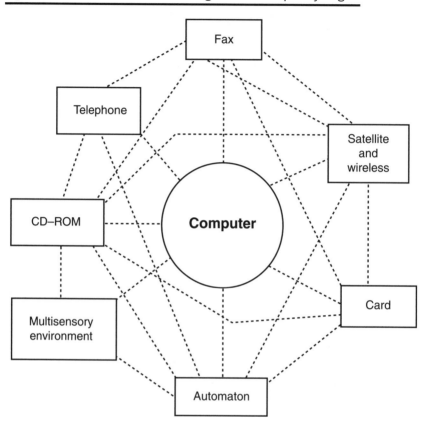

characteristic of AI that is so appealing and holds such great promise. AI can be used in the formulation of business strategies. It can, for example, evaluate macroenvironmental factors or market conditions as well as internal strengths and weaknesses, identify core problems, and suggest the appropriate remedies and plans of action. Some of the bigger securities firms use AI to forecast market patterns and the performance of stocks and bonds. The medical field was among the first to use successfully a version of AI (more specifically, ES). The physician is able to share the patient's family history and self-reported and empirically observed symptoms with the computer, which, in turn, identifies a probable diagnosis, a probable prognosis, and a suggested course of action (or choice of options) to treat the individual. An important human resources implication of ES is that less skilled personnel can be used to perform what would otherwise be regarded as more advanced and difficult tasks. For example, a nurse might be capable of performing the preliminary diagnosis, freeing the physician to perform emergency surgery.[1]

The "Laws" of Computer Technology

No, the laws of computer technology are not the kind of laws passed by some government legislative body or even the kind that you'd be likely to find in a text on the subject of computing. Nonetheless, they might serve to explain the collective mindset of those in the field.[2]

Moore's Law (1965, Gordon E. Moore)

In a nutshell: Smaller computers are better.

Moore, who was a founder of the Intel Corporation, correctly forecast that raw computing power would grow exponentially each year. (Since 1965, we have observed annual compounded doubling of chip density.) This supports the position that bigger is not better, at least in terms of computers. Moreover, prices will keep going down. So why not delay the purchase of a new computer if you can wait?

Metcalfe's Law (1980, Robert Metcalfe)

In a nutshell: Connected computers are better.

Metcalfe argued that the worth of a (computer) network can be gauged by the square of its number of users. His example: Having only a single telephone would be worthless, but value would increase with each additional telephone it can call or be called by.

Grove's Law (Andrew Grove)

In a nutshell: Competition is better.

As chairman of Intel, Grove refers to the slow technological progress of telephone companies over the past half-century as a prime example of underperformance. In contrast, he contends, look at the highly competitive computer field.

Brooks's Law (Frederick P. Brooks)

In a nutshell: Additional labor can actually delay results.

As a veteran IBM software executive, Brooks noted that supplementing manpower in order to complete an already-late assignment tends to delay completion even more so. To illustrate this point, it has been jokingly said that if IBM instructed its team of 100 programmers to jump across a 100-foot body of water, each of them would jump one foot.

Wirth's Law (Nicklaus Wirth)

In a nutshell: Machines may leap, but programs creep.

Essentially, Wirth stated that software generally does not fully utilize hardware. In other words, software gets slower faster than hardware gets faster. Or: "Grove (Intel) giveth and Gates (Microsoft) taketh away."

Database Management

Database management (DBM) allows the business enterprise to optimally organize and compile information for its operational and strategic purposes. DBM is the structured collection of information. It automatically maintains defined data relationships. "Infopreneurship," or the selling of specialized and proprietary information, is a particularly interesting and appealing phenomenon, since it is marked by rapid growth, and market entry is relatively easy.[3]

Basic DBM processes include the following:

- *Data refining:* Taking (seemingly) unrelated data and treating them so that they will heighten awareness and facilitate more critical and valuable analysis of the data. Raw material is (refined and) converted into integrated data, the end product.
- *Data refreshing:* Updating data on a regular schedule that serves business needs and is known to the client.
- *Data repository:* Organizing of data wherein different and multiple databases (e.g., one for revenues, another for expenses) are "housed" together, with specific applications in mind (e.g.,

accounts receivable and accounts payable, respectively, corresponding to the example provided above).

- *Data scrubbing:* Filtering, combining ("merging"), and translating data from its source.
- *Data warehousing:* Configuring and maintaining the data to support management decision making.

One of my favorite consulting clients is among the world's largest publishers of specialty newsletters and reference books. It is also probably the most successful in its segment of the industry. Although one cannot help but admire the firm's prowess at building up such an impressive subscriber base, it is interesting to note that a surprisingly large percentage of the company's profits derive from the rental of its mailing lists. In fact, each subscriber listed in the company's databases (yes, plural; because those who rent mailing lists may opt to buy "special selects" or subcategories of subscribers), may cost as much as a half-dollar each. Multiply a sizable portion of the couple of million names in the databases by that rate, and then multiply that total by the number of the firm's clients who rent their lists, and one might reasonably wonder whether the company isn't thought of as a giant direct response/mailing list provider rather than only as a respected publisher of specialty periodicals and books.

Electronic and Automated Information

- *Electronic mail (e-mail)* allows the user to send (and receive) written communications to other individuals with computers. It allows individuals to send or receive instantaneously a "broadcast letter," one that is capable of reaching many people.
- *Electronic data interchange (EDI)* enables disintermediation, which obsoletes third parties or intermediaries traditionally required for facilitation of transactions. EDI portends serious consequences for the banking industry as we know it, since financial institutions would no longer be necessary for check clearance. Moreover, transactions would be effected instantaneously. Procter & Gamble (P&G) has an EDI system in place with the Wal-Mart retail chain, allowing P&G to know when

inventory levels of the products it supplies to Wal-Mart stores are running low. Once this mechanism is "triggered," it then automatically reorders and simultaneously sets in motion the shipping and invoicing processes.

- *Automated voice response (AVR)* allows for automated and interactive communication (e.g., "press 1 for ..., press 2 for ..."). This can facilitate important tasks, including automated payroll processing and order taking. Voice mail systems are even more popular. However, a widespread criticism relates to customers calling an organization and often getting trapped in "voice jail" or a looped system that leads back to where the individual started or to a dead end wherein none of the options offered to the caller is applicable or desirable. Aside from taking greater care in the design of systems, the organization can minimize this problem simply by making a live, human voice available if the caller so desires (e.g., "press 0 for operator").

Free long-distance phone calls!! What a great idea!! Call China from New York for the same price as a local phone call. Advances in technology make the widespread use of free long-distance a reality—it's possible through technology like Skype.

As the cost of bandwidth (that is, the transmission lines, which may exist in wireless rather than cable form) progressively decreases while the information-holding capacity of bandwidth conversely continues to increase, near-Utopian visions of the future of humankind no longer seem far-fetched. For example, such notables as Freeman Dyson and George Gilder suggest that even the most primitive of peoples in developing (or nondeveloping) regions of the world that we live in will be able to meaningfully communicate with those of us who live in other very developed parts of that world.

Better wireless technologies such as short message service (SMS) and LEAP will facilitate oral conversation or e-mail between, let's say, a tribal chieftain living in some remote jungle and you or me (in the so-called "civilized" world) via language translation software.

Now, that scenario truly does illustrate the transformation of our entire planet into a "global village."

Wireless Technology

Over-the-air distribution allows us to receive services such as "canned" music (e.g., Muzak). The transition to over-the-air delivery greatly reduces or eliminates costs (i.e., duplication, shipping). The technology also exists to transmit feature motion pictures in this manner.

The Taco Bell fast-food chain employs wireless technology to speed up the taking and processing of orders when many people or cars are queued up and waiting to be served. An employee will fan out to the line, entering orders into a hand-held device that transmits them over the air to a screen above the food preparation area in the kitchen. *Wireless data communication* allows you to sit under a tree, create a document on your laptop computer, and send it wirelessly to a remote location. There, it can be printed in desktop quality and transmitted as a facsimile (if you wish) to other users and destinations.[4]

The Internet

Originally developed to minimize any disruption in communication in the event of nuclear war, the Internet has come to play an important role in many sociocultural areas, including education and entertainment, and, of course, in commerce, as well. Those who surf the Net can visit a Web site to learn about a company's products and services and place an order via credit card, PayPal, or other means. (Security problems regarding credit card fraud have been greatly reduced and will be even less of an issue in the future.)

The advent of "push" technology enables marketers to essentially edit—and thereby *personalize*—content that is sent to customers or prospective customers based upon their preferences. For example, the publisher of a newspaper could download just the sections that an individual is interested in or otherwise filter the content so that the person gets just what he or she is interested in. This goes a step beyond "on demand" such that we might call it "predemand."

Although the Internet is a medium that boasts "openness" and "access" to virtually all, there are aspects of it that are, in a sense exclusionary. For example, a company may share information internally, only among and between employees via its *intranet*, a "private" Internet of sorts. The company may selectively engage other groups outside the company via its *extranet*, such that distributors or retailers can give and/or get information quickly and place orders online.

An interesting series of "philosophical" questions come to mind regarding the commercial applications of Internet technology (and, for that matter, all other advanced modes of communication): Under which legal jurisdiction does a transaction take place and how are its laws enforced online? To which economic entity is a person or enterprise taxably liable? Davidson and Rees-Mogg have suggested that the mobility of e-commerce and related activity across national borders will cause nation-states to slash taxes and perhaps offer other inducements to lure economic activity and "domiciliary" to within its borders, much in the way that Switzerland has for many years negotiated tax treaties. Under this scenario, the "sovereign individual" will foster an opportunistic "expatriate" mindset, and the entrepreneur will reign supreme.[5]

Computer-Assisted Manufacturing (CAM) and Mass Customization

Computer-assisted manufacturing (CAM) allows manufacturers to avoid placing human lives in jeopardy, as with nuclear and other hazardous materials. Proponents of robotics would also be quick to tell you that robots do not make nearly as many errors as human beings, are capable of performing surprisingly delicate tasks, can work virtually 24 hours a day (minus maintenance time), and never complain.

A relatively new trend in computer-assisted manufacturing is that of *mass customization*. A hybrid of mass production and customization, the process allows the consumer to order an otherwise off-the-shelf product with made-to-order specifications. Levi's, the world's biggest clothing manufacturer, offered this in 1994, on its line of jeans for women. At its dozens of Original Levi's Stores in the United States, a "fit specialist" took the customer's measurements (waist, hips, rise, and inseam) and entered that information into a computer. Next, the data were transmitted to a manufacturing plant in Tennessee, where the jeans were assembled according to the customer's individual specifications. In anticipation of repeat orders, Levi's sewed a customer identification number inside the garment at the waist, and kept this record and related vital information on file. The jeans were generally ready in two weeks, and were priced at only about 25 percent more than the off-the-shelf version.[6]

Several years ago, I purchased a pair of *mass customized* shoes near my home at the Custom Foot in Westport, Connecticut. The shoes were well made, comfortable, and priced only a little higher than the mass-produced version. Nonetheless, the company is now out of business because (I believe) it did not truly *personalize* service by failing to attend to such small yet critical details as sewing the customer's monograms into the shoes and following up the purchase with a telephone call or note to minimize postpurchase dissonance—and perhaps to get an order for an *additional* pair of shoes or accessories.

Smart Card Technology

The *smart card* allows organizations to use credit card technology (i.e., card incorporating microchip technology) to automate transactions and record keeping.

While on a business trip to Dallas, a friend drove me to a meeting. As we approached a booth to pay the highway toll, I expected that she would gradually slow down to pay the attendant. Instead, she shot through the toll booth at about 50 miles per hour. I was shocked by the notion that she had "run" a toll and fully expected police cars with sirens blaring to follow in hot pursuit. My fears were calmed when my friend explained that she had a "toll tag" (i.e., smart card) on her windshield, which registered automatically each time she passed a toll checkpoint and that she received a monthly statement for all such toll charges.

Cards with internal memory would also enable physicians, for example, by processing a patient's card, to receive a detailed family history as well as a personal history of conditions, medications taken, and more.

Virtual Reality, Ubiquitous Computing, and Biometrics

- *Virtual reality (VR)* allows the individual to don a special apparatus to enter a "make-believe" multisensory environment. Can you imagine being "inside" or part of a video game in addition to just being a player at the controls? Or going on a scenic tour of Europe without leaving your hometown? Or displaying and demonstrating your entire product line for customers in a showroom that doesn't actually exist? Early inroads into VR were made by NASA in the form of simulations or "games" to train pilots.[7] The medical profession also pioneered use of the technology to simulate a wide variety of surgical situations. This would enable the med student to make an "incision" into the semblance of a human body and, if the "scalpel" motion were incorrect and nicked a "blood vessel," "blood" would actually spurt, a very realistic training method.

- *Ubiquitous computing (UC)* allows individuals to utilize and interface seemingly low-tech office tools such as notepads and blackboards that have computer intelligence built into them and are able to generate and send information. This is congruent with the vision of the "paperless office," wherein physical storage space of information is kept to a minimum and access to this information is quick. And the notion of Dick Tracy and his (then) high-tech wristwatch is no longer fiction, but truth in the various forms of the so-called "Wearable PC," apparatus that is quite literally worn on the body.

- Moreover, advances in *biometrics* will increasingly be used to "read" the iris of the human eye and fingerprints as well as the human voice, for identification as well as other purposes. And despite the dramatic results that can be attained by cosmetic plastic surgery, facial recognition scanning devices will not be "fooled" because, according to experts in the field of biometrics, the shape and other aspects of the human face are one-of-a-kind and cannot be altered sufficiently to avoid identification.

Personally, voice recognition technology holds a special place in my heart, since as an author and lecturer, I like to dictate an article that I'm writing while I lay down and rest my eyes at the end of a long day. Miniaturized digital cameras have been incorporated into cellular telephones and wireless palmtop computers, and in the near future, will be used instead of rear-view mirrors on automobiles. Perhaps most exciting are the advances in imaging technology that will enable the blind to see via surgical implantation of silicon chips.

Digitalization has also changed the world of print and the publishing of books. In contrast to the hardcover or softcover book with which you and I are well-acquainted, you may also be familiar with the "e-book," which can be purchased over the Internet and downloaded onto a device that serves as the surface upon which the printed word and image can actually be read. The size of the print can be adjusted to suit the reader's preference. But even the publishing of old-fashioned paper-based books has been transformed by digitalization. Consider if you will, that in the "old days," publishers were required to print books in a minimum "run" of (let's say) 2,000 copies at a time. In smaller lots, the cost per copy would not be economically feasible. However, today publishers can digitally publish in very small runs (let's say, a few dozen books at a time) and still be profitable. And this is a terrific development for authors, because it reduces the risk for publishers and, therefore, makes it more likely for authors to be published.

A Look into the Future

The possibilities of what might happen in the future stagger the imagination. If the research and advances of a *single* company are an indicator of what lies ahead over the next decade or so, consider if you will that Hitachi and others have been working on a "nanotechnology," which enables just one single component (an atom) to move and deliver goods rapidly through a computerized logistics system—even through crowded and gridlocked areas (via magnets that levitate the products), and even "biological" computers composed of "organic" components that will enable the machines to repair themselves. Buck Rogers, move over!

Management Information Systems

Management information systems (MIS) are designed to provide management with information for optimal decision making. This suggests the creation and maintenance of a wide variety of databases or bodies of information in virtually all functional categories, including but certainly not limited to marketing, finance, human resources, research and development, and strategic planning. And to the extent that "knowledge is power," MIS can be a powerful asset. Therefore, many organizations that make a serious commitment to the MIS function actually appoint a chief information officer (or CIO) to oversee its operation, just as a chief executive officer (or CEO) is ultimately responsible for the entire organization.

Knowledge Management

Knowledge management refers to the practice of identifying, creating, and distributing information within an organization. An integral part of the overall business strategy, many companies have substantial resources dedicated to their knowledge management efforts.

Intellectual Capital

Intangible assets may be grossly undervalued using the currently accepted and traditional methods of accounting. So much so, in fact, that some of the largest companies in the world, such as Coca-Cola, have between 50 and 70 percent of their net worth dependent upon these assets. This underscores the necessity of focusing on and maximizing the value of such *intellectual capital (IC)*. Increasingly, organizations are deploying their MIS or information technology (IT) resources to help decision makers *manage* intellectual capital.

Toward that end, intellectual capital must first be *identified*. I know that it may be hard for you to imagine, but many companies don't even have a very good idea of what intellectual capital they own. So, to help remedy this problem, an *audit* of intellectual capital assets would be performed by internal and perhaps external legal and accounting teams, much in the way that accountants audit financial records.

In addition to trademarks, copyrights, and patents that may terminate because of failure to file for renewals or because of abandonment, trade secrets in the form of "how we do things" often go undocumented. For example, many people learn their jobs on the job, via conversation with managers and coworkers. The creation and usage of an *operations manual* that explains tasks in a step-by-step and detailed manner would serve to *capture* this important knowledge. In fact, the Colgate-Palmolive Company created one so good that its "bundle book" is used by product managers throughout the company to provide step-by-step guidance on how to launch new products anywhere in the world. The practical side of this effort would become much clearer in the face of a key employee suddenly leaving the firm (whether it be due to death, resignation, or any other reason). Typically, the person who replaces the departed employee experiences a steeper learning curve than should be necessary because step-by-step guidance is not generally available. A worst case scenario involves work coming to a virtual standstill because nobody can figure out how the departed employee did the job.

By the way, writing an operations manual is not as easy to do as some people might think because it requires the ability to take what may appear to be straightforward information and make it simple and easy to understand. But few people realize that making something *appear* to be simple and easy to understand can be a deceptively difficult job. At one of my recent lectures, a participant disagreed on this point and said that he could easily create an operations manual. So, I invited him to do a "quickie" version of one right then and there, on a topic or task that seems ridiculously simple: how to open the door to the lecture room we were in. I asked him to face away from the door so that he could not observe it.

"Step 1?" I asked.

"Face the door," was his response, and I faced the door. (Not a bad start.)

"Step 2?"

"Walk toward the door and stop when you are within arm's reach of it." (I did so.)

"Step 3?"

"Put your hand on the door knob and turn it." I told him that I tried to do what he instructed me to do but it didn't work.

"Did you walk to the door, within arm's reach?" he asked. I nodded yes. "Did you put your hand on the door knob and turn it?" I explained that I couldn't.

When he asked why, I explained that the door slides open and closed on a track and that there was no knob on it.

He started to explain, "But I assumed that ..." and I interrupted to explain to him and the entire group that any of us could make this kind of mistake and that this is why it is not so easy to write an operations manual. We cannot merely *assume* and trust that to be adequate.

But what about the intellectual capital that is manifested at internal company meetings or in the course of telephone conversations or e-mail memos? Ideas, even ones that are shot down, may be regarded as potentially valuable intellectual property. We can capture or *archive* much of this material by using "group ware," and by keeping summaries, as much as possible, of meaningful dialogues involving the exchange of ideas, opinions—even "inklings" or "hunches." Not everything in business (or for that matter, in life) can be immediately quantified.

Next, valuation of IC assets would be wise, to help decide which ones are worth developing and which ones are not. This can be a difficult task, because much of it is based on subjective input (i.e., opinions). Factors include:

- Life span of the intellectual property (i.e., protection under the law regarding trademarks, copyrights, etc.).
- Projected future of the industry (i.e., growth).
- Projected future of markets (i.e., change in how the intellectual property can be used).
- Discounted cash flow (NPV) over the projected life of the intellectual property.

Once we have successfully identified, protected (more about that later), and valued our intellectual capital, our challenge is to *leverage* it. That means squeezing as much value from it as possible without diminishing its integrity and maintaining, if not actually enhancing, customer satisfaction. Examples of leveraging include:

- Licensing trademarks and patents.
- Distributing copyrighted material in new media (e.g., reissuing old hit vinyl records on CD or MP3s, or old movies on DVD or Blu-ray).
- Targeting of "new" or previously overlooked markets (e.g., selling consumer packaged goods in India).
- Promoting new applications of existing products (e.g., using Arm & Hammer baking soda to absorb unpleasant odors in refrigerators).
- Product line extension (e.g., taking a successful product such as Vaseline petroleum jelly and creating spin-off versions in the form of Vaseline Intensive Care lip balm, hand lotion, etc.).
- Selling proprietary information (e.g., renting internally generated mailing lists or primary research findings that might be of value to others).

It is particularly interesting that knowledge gleaned from even unsuccessful enterprises can be valuable. An example that comes to mind is that of SOCOG (Sydney Organizing Committee for the Olympic Games, 2000), which has made known that—for a fee—it will share its sensitive business information with other Olympic committees around the world (as well as with other event promoters and sponsors), so that others can learn from SOCOG's mistakes rather than learn themselves—the hard way.

Competitive Intelligence

Earlier in this book, we discuss the importance of internal control procedures in order to protect and minimize the loss of assets. What role should the IT team play in protecting the company's assets? And to take it a step further, what can the IT team do to gather valuable information about competitors that might appear to be a sort of "corporate espionage" but is actually legal and ethical?

This area of endeavor is known as *competitive intelligence (CI)*. It is conducted by various means, and it can garner valuable (in fact, very sensitive) information about companies that can be used to provide (at least) a competitive edge and in some cases, can facilitate the virtual destruction of a competitor. Viewed in this light, it should come as no shock to you that many consultants and senior executives in this field (particularly the more seasoned veterans) have solid backgrounds in military intelligence and/or with covert governmental agencies.

What can CI specialists find out?

- Simply by visiting the Web sites of competitors, trained professionals can "read between the lines" of product announcements (and more importantly, of product announcements *in advance of actual launch or formal introduction*) and, having gauged product strengths and weaknesses, beat the company to the punch by introducing a similar but even better version before the competitor introduces its own version.

- "Musical chairs" among top management and the emergence of a new leader may give a pretty good idea of the kinds of changes to come, based upon his or her background and business history.

- Openings and closings of facilities often signal expansion and contraction (respectively) and may indirectly reveal the volume of units that are being manufactured. Given that the selling price can be reasonably estimated, it's not much of a stretch to estimate a competitor's revenues for that period. After all, the number of units sold multiplied by the selling price equals *gross income*. And if you wanted to take this a step further, visit the Web sites of competitors' *suppliers* and *subcontractors* and, again, reading between the lines, you may be able to figure out what a competitor pays for parts or materials. As a percentage of total costs and factoring in industry averages, you can now take a shot at reasonably estimating the company's *net income* for that period.

- The seemingly innocuous listings of job openings in newspaper or magazine ads or elsewhere can signal changes in directions that may be very significant in terms of product modifications or shifts in market strategy.
- Most companies love to list "satisfied customers" in their ads and in their marketing efforts. What an easy way for a competitor to identify *new accounts* to target and "steal"!
- Filing of certain documents with government agencies is required of publicly held companies and is, therefore, available to the general public. Some documents (e.g., 10-K; www. edgar-online.com) may contain information about contracts that are in force with suppliers and customers. So, at a glance, an alert sleuth can get a pretty good idea (if not an exact and detailed picture) not only of what parts and materials a competitor buys from its suppliers and the price and terms of sale, but to make things worse (or better, depending upon whether you are the victim or the victor), the same information is available regarding contracts with *customers*. That's right! Now, the "enemy" knows not only who the firm's customers are but what they buy and what they pay for it! How long do you think it will take before they approach the firm's customers and offer better deals? It's a rhetorical question, of course.
- In our minds, we may subscribe to "unwritten laws," of sorts, regarding a right to privacy to which we believe a citizen should be entitled. Generally speaking, there are such laws in this country, and they tend to work quite well. However, there are some "loopholes" that permit businesses to legally exploit what might otherwise remain the private matters of individuals. For example, let's assume that a married couple is in the midst of divorce proceedings and negotiations get ugly and hostile. A spouse who suspects that his or her mate is concealing assets that might otherwise be split or shared in a settlement might contest the matter in court and, quite intentionally, reveal extremely sensitive information about that mate's financial dealings and the individual's corporate business. Keeping in

mind that divorce proceedings, once in the courts, become a matter of public knowledge (and access), many top executives choose to settle the matter privately via negotiation in order to avoid giving competitors "ammunition."

These are just a handful of examples. For more general information and some of the finer points, check out www.fuld.com, www.hoovers.com, and www.companysleuth.com.

Competitive Counterintelligence

But it is important to keep in mind that the same weapons that we use against competitors can be used successfully against us if we do not take precautions. And that brings us to the topic of *competitive counterintelligence* or, in other words, how to protect competitors from gathering valuable information about our organization.

What are some of the more common pitfalls and "windows of vulnerability"?

- You'd be surprised how easily a skilled questioner can interrogate a "dupe" without that party ever realizing that he surrendered valuable information. For example, imagine a vice president of sales with a major company attending a cocktail party reception sponsored by a trade association of which he is a member. A fellow member, a "friendly competitor" who used to work with him at another company, warmly greets him. She asks: "How've you been? How's your lovely wife and those terrific kids?" Great. Soon thereafter, the "friendly competitor" puts out some "bait," with a seemingly innocent remark, like: "So, I guess you're not doing much traveling these days. Huh?" The reply: "Sure I do. In fact, I just got back from a sales presentation to a big media company in Orlando." (The "friendly competitor" is wondering: Could that company be Disney? I'll probe deeper a little later.) "What would make you think I don't travel much anymore?" "Well, you guys haven't introduced any new products over the past year and ..." Taking the bait, the dupe's pride compels him to volunteer: "Actually, we are launching a brand new line of widgets next month that will revolutionize the industry, because they can _____ this without doing _____. It's all based on laser technology that has been used in the medical field." Now, the "friendly competitor" knows what kind of products will be launched, what makes those products appealing, the technology that it is based on, and when the product will be launched. Not bad for a few minutes work, and the night is young! I think you get the idea.

When I attend functions of this kind (where alcoholic beverages are served), I make it a point to avoid a case of "loose lips" by consuming no more than one cocktail (i.e., one ounce of liquor) per hour. And actually, this measure is probably not even necessary, because I instruct the bartender to put in lots of ice, and I wait for most of the ice to melt before I really drink, thereby diluting it further. When a business professional suspects that he is being "baited," he can choose any of several courses of action. He can:

1. Courteously but firmly decline to answer questions.
2. Simply change the subject.
3. Pretend that he's had a few too many drinks and "accidentally" let slip some "disinformation" (i.e., information that is false or misleading) in order to set his "friendly competitor" in the wrong direction, thereby causing a waste of her employer's resources and perhaps worse.

I don't generally recommend this approach for three good reasons.

First of all, in the process of planting disinformation, you risk losing your credibility. You may not think that it is an important thing to lose because it is in the eyes of a competitor whom you may not value, as such. However, life is a long road, my friend, and it is paved with surprises. And, for all you know, you may be working alongside this person for the same employer at some time in the future. With all the mergers and acquisitions going on, this is really not hard to imagine. Stranger things have been known to happen. Make the guarding of your reputation your cardinal priority.

Second, it takes a pretty good actor to convincingly play the role of someone who's had a few too many drinks, as manifested by slurred speech and balance problems. If you think you can really pull this off successfully, you are probably flattering yourself.

And finally, you *don't* want to get a reputation as a drinker who can't hold his liquor. As I said a moment ago: Make the guarding of your reputation a cardinal priority.

- Rank information in terms of its degree of sensitivity. Then make it available internally on a "need to know" basis.
- Whenever possible, include "noncompete" clauses in employment contracts, in order to prevent former employees from using your company's "proprietary" information on behalf of a competitor after they leave the company.
- Have your human resources specialists conduct "exit interviews" with employees who will be leaving the firm. Of course, it is a good idea to find out *why* people are leaving the company in order to prevent the further loss of valued people. But from a competitive counterintelligence standpoint, this may be your last opportunity to find out what valuable information these people actually possess, some of which may have eluded others in the organization and should be captured or somehow "archived." Of course, those employees who signed employment contracts with "noncompete" clauses should be asked who their next employer is. The answer should be noted and "tracked" over time, in order to explore the potential "drain" of talent (and knowledge) by a particular competitor and possible legal action that might result due to breach of "noncompete" clauses or other unfair business practices on the part of the new employer. Finally, just prior to ending the meeting, the departing employees should be gently reminded that they are bound by a "noncompete" clause and will be subject to legal action if they violate it.
- Immediately terminate or cancel the passwords that would otherwise allow departing employees to access the computers and even to merely enter the premises.

- Locks are installed on doors and file cabinets for a good reason. Use them.
- Be careful about using your computer in public places. Competitors can "shoulder surf" (i.e., read the monitor over your shoulder). In some cases, intelligence agents have zoomed in from a considerable distance using high-power telephoto magnifying lenses just like in James Bond movies. If possible, use a type size that is small and more difficult to read from a distance. (10 point or smaller is probably okay.)
- Secure your laptop computer (and handheld electronic organizer). If there is valuable information on the hard drive, download as much of it as possible as frequently as is practical to a secure computer and then delete as much information as you can from your portable machine.
- Be careful when discussing business in public. The person sitting well within earshot at the next table may be a competitor or someone who wishes to curry favor with a competitor by passing along some valuable information.
- Shred any documents that may contain sensitive information before you would normally discard them. It might be hard for you to imagine, but companies have been known to hire "investigators" to retrieve and sift through not only outdoor garbage bins at company facilities, but garbage cans outside the homes of top executives.
- Avoid sending and receiving faxes containing sensitive information while staying at hotels and at public facilities.

Perceptions about IT People

Though it may be unfair to make generalizations and draw stereotypes about groups of people (without even first getting to know them as individuals), there is a widespread bias against IT staff professionals, such that the line managers they serve are often heard to express the view that IT people "don't understand the business." In other words, they fail to help these managers and, in some cases, actually hold them back from meeting business objectives. Why? I believe there are two factors contributing to this perception:

- Technical people tend to see the world differently from the line managers they serve. For example, technical people often place a premium on testing software until it is perfect and free of any possible errors (and this, of course, takes time!), while the managers who will be using that software need to move quickly (due to competitive market pressure) and get increasingly irritated as they are waiting. Notwithstanding the merits of zero defects and quality assurance programs, it is sometimes appropriate to sacrifice a certain degree of quality in the interest of getting the product launched in a timely manner. The errors can be corrected later on, according to this mindset. A good example of this is Microsoft and its line of software products. Introduction was initially scheduled to correspond to the year mentioned in the product version (such as Windows '98, for the year 1998), but *actual* introduction took place between six months and one year later. (One can only imagine how much longer it would have taken if the IT people hadn't been prodded!) To minimize problems of this sort, it might help to jointly prioritize the various types of IT functions that need to be performed. Consider the following categories:

  Utility functions—those that absolutely "must" get done and done properly

  Enhancement functions—those that are important, but not absolutely essential

  Frontier functions—those that would be nice to have, but not necessary

- Technical people often lack key business concepts and skills. For example, how many IT people understand (and try to *meaningfully apply!*) financial terms such as NPV and IRR? If you don't speak the same language as that of the managers you serve, it makes it pretty tough to serve them well.

One of the unwritten rules of office politics is that, if you want to win points with your boss and your coworkers, do more than you are asked to do in anticipation of what these people want to achieve.

Let's say that the vice president of finance asks you to submit a list of all investments the firm has made over the past three years, including the sums of money involved. If you do that and nothing more, you won't get fired, but you're not likely to receive a standing ovation either. A response that would indicate you really "know the business" might include taking the liberty of calculating the NPV, IRR, estimated and actual payback, and more for each of these investments, and perhaps ranking them in descending order of performance for each of the criteria. Offer more than is required of you, with the other party's objectives in mind, and you will gain the respect of all (and maybe a promotion).

The High-Tech Challenge for Management

In light of the rapid change that characterizes high technology, there are numerous issues, opportunities, and obstacles that decision makers have been forced to address. These include the following.

Finance

Often, the pace of technological breakthroughs outstrips the schedule for recoupment of investments in a given technology (see the sections "Depreciation," "ROI," "NPV," "IRR," and "Payback," in Chapter 2, "Accounting and Finance"). So the organization must decide whether to upgrade to the state of the art even though the cost of the incumbent technology would not yet have been fully justified or to "stay the course" with the intention of meeting its original financial plans, although delay in embracing a new generation may render the company less competitive or otherwise cause it to forgo opportunities for substantial cost reduction or revenue generation that would more than offset the cost of upgrading.

There is a widely accepted rule that, in situations in which equipment is unexpectedly reduced to less than the state of the art before its cost has been recouped, hardware should probably be kept for up to two years while liberal expenditures on software to "soup up" the hardware would be acceptable (unless the need to upgrade is compelling). Another approach to dealing with obsolescence involves "cascading," wherein the organization's entire asset base of hardware is inventoried and *redistributed* internally, so that the most powerful equipment is allocated to areas where the needs are most critical while less powerful equipment is "cascaded" downward to less critical areas or functions (not unlike the way water cascades from high to low).

Marketing

We must weigh the trade-off of automation against personalization and the human touch (high tech versus high touch). Ultimately, customer focus is often the deciding factor. Early research indicated that approximately 33 percent of the entire universe of financial services customers resisted using *automated teller machines (ATM)* and presumably other high-tech equipment.[8] (Current anecdotal reports suggest that we adjust this figure to 20 percent.) These people fear or are simply uncomfortable with technology. They demand or require a "high-touch" or human approach. Service providers would prefer that customers use the ATMs rather than human tellers, since automated processing of transactions is less expensive. So, in the interest of satisfying these technophobic customers while trying to get them to accept and use ATMs, some imaginative service providers have equipped their ATMs with audio-video terminals that link the user to a specially trained human teller who can walk them through the procedure. This enables the hesitant user to "give it a try" and, once comfortable with the technology, continue using the machines without assistance.

Human Resources

Just as financial plans must be reappraised, the deployment of human capital must be adequate to introduce, operate, and maintain high-tech systems. Unfortunately, management and employees don't always understand how to use equipment efficiently. This may be attributed, to a large extent, to the lack of proper training. In addition, "techies" have long been criticized for failing to understand the user's actual needs and preferences; they simply "don't know the business." They must see the business through the eyes of their internal client or user, anticipate questions or concerns reflecting the users' particular orientation, and provide information before it is actually requested. In fact, they might even offer suggestions regarding ways that information can best be used. For example, a technology manager serving an internal client or user in the marketing department might anticipate her client's focus on segmentation and take the liberty of organizing databases toward that end. She might even include comments or recommendations as to which market segments are likely to be worth targeting. Serving a user in the finance department would, of course, shift the focus. In anticipation of investment analysis concerns, the technology manager might, for example, offer to provide information couched in terms of NPV, IRR, and payback—before it is specifically requested.

Another important human resources issue involves the contention that heavy utilization of technology may actually be explained as undue dependence on it. The late Calvin Pava, foremost expert on office design, warned against such overdependence. He stated that the effect of technology on human behavior can be to "engender passivity" and to stunt human potential.[9] If his theory is correct, the dilemma arises as to where exactly to draw the line between proper use and abuse.

Engineering/Security

The deployment of backup systems to avoid loss in the face of catastrophes is absolutely essential. Consider, if you will, the tremendous damage done in September 1991 when AT&T's long-distance telephone system "went down" due to equipment failure. In a similar vein, unauthorized access to computer systems by hackers and the introduction of viruses, which destroy or distort information, underscore the need for sophisticated security measures.

Ethics and the Law

See the sections "Privacy" and "Informed Consent" in Chapter 7, "Business Policy and Ethics."

Trivia question *du jour*: What is captology?

Answer: The study of computers as technologies and tools of persuasion. The field was originated by B. J. Fogg at Stanford University in the mid-1990s. Examples include business Web sites that design purchase transactions within the (enjoyable) framework of a game, as well as screen savers that reward your "virtual pet" with a "virtual toy" each time you print a document using the manufacturer's ink cartridge. The ethical issue hinges upon drawing the line between voluntary, beneficial persuasion, and the manipulative, coercive variety.

And that line is a fine one, indeed. Experts in the field suggest that it will take a tragic event or major catastrophe (such as a mass murder committed "because the computer *convinced* me to do it") before authorities step in to dictate limits.[10]

Strategic Planning

Because of the large capital outlays that may be necessary for high-technology research and development (as well as marketing), strategic partnerships or coventures with other organizations, perhaps even with those traditionally viewed as competitors, may make sense. For example, Apple Computer's strategic alliance with Sony is responsible for the great success of Apple's Powerbook and MacBook computers. The two organizations enjoy a powerful synergy, in that Apple is recognized for its strength in developing user-friendly or easy-to-understand computers, while Sony is acknowledged for its prowess at manufacturing miniaturized electronic products. Both entities operate globally.

Progress through Technology?

Is there progress through technology? Not necessarily. In fact, productivity may actually decline because of the following.

Poor Training

Users don't understand how to employ equipment efficiently.

Poor Procedures and Systems

"Techies" may not design systems intelligently because "they don't know the business" (see "Human Resources" in "The High-Tech Challenge for Management" section earlier in this chapter).

Poor Equipment

Hardware or software is often inherently flawed. This clearly indicates that the acquisition and nominal operation of high-ticket and high-tech equipment is just the tip of the iceberg, insofar as the technology manager is concerned. Now he or she must "manage" the technology as well as personnel. Responsibilities must include training, setting and maintaining procedural standards for operation, and ensuring the integrity of the equipment itself.

The Technology Management Checklist

1. What constitutes the state of the art in my field?
2. Am I making use of these technologies?
3. Can I combine technologies to enjoy synergies?
4. How can I minimize the potential pitfalls associated with the introduction or upgrading of technology?
5. How does technology influence the way I manage people?
6. Can I better balance "high-tech" and "high-touch" considerations?

7 BUSINESS POLICY AND ETHICS

E thics is the code of conduct or system of moral principles by which we lead our lives and carry out our business. In light of a proliferation of well-publicized, unethical behavior in the workplace and in the marketplace as well, business schools have slowly responded to the need to provide ethical guidance and education for students and executives. It is ironic and tragic that those who need to be educated in ethics the most are typically those who would claim that they don't need it at all, while those who actively seek guidance in this area are typically those who actually need it the least. For this reason, business schools are wise to offer ethics courses as mandatory core offerings rather than electives.

Although some take the position that the teaching of ethics should be conducted in Sunday school or houses of religious training, rather than the executive suite, they might do well to ponder that ethical business behavior is ultimately cost effective.[1]

Consider, if you will, the legal expenses and monetary damages that can arise from unethical behavior, not to mention lowered employee morale and, ultimately, the loss of customers.

Formulation of Ethical Standards

The formulation of ethical standards can be difficult. After all, ethics deals in terms of rights and obligations, and the perception of these is both subjective and qualitative. In contrast, analysis of investments in terms of their potential risks and rewards can be viewed rather more objectively and quantitatively.

And to whom is the ethical business manager responsible? Truly, the manager must serve numerous stakeholders (see Figure 7.1). These groups include employees (individually and collectively in the form of unions), customers, suppliers, competitors, stockholders, and various governmental and communal entities (local, national, and global). So what does the manager do when the interests of these stakeholders are at variance with one another (as is often the case)? For example, closing a marginally profitable manufacturing plant in a community that is heavily dependent upon the company for its employment must be weighed against the ability to cut costs to maximize returns for stockholders.

In describing the nature of management decision making, in general and (I would suggest) ethical decision making, in particular,

Figure 7.1 Stakeholder interests facing the manager

the dean of Oxford's business school put it rather well, saying that it is essentially a skill of balancing.

General Guidelines

There is no single correct or "cookie-cutter" solution. However, the decision maker has to weigh the five points listed here,[2] keeping in mind the trade-off of costs and benefits:

1. The nature of "good" or "bad" that is in question.
2. The urgency of the circumstances.
3. The certainty of a particular outcome.
4. The intensity of one's influence on the outcome.
5. The availability of alternative means.

When in doubt, trade and professional associations can be valuable resources in the formulation of ethical business codes. On a personal note and "off the record," I would like to suggest an unscientific method for helping to make difficult ethical decisions, which, I believe, can be valuable to all but those with sociopathic tendencies. After weighing decision options, the individual should ask himself or herself the following "litmus test" question: "Would I be ashamed (not just embarrassed) to read the news of my decision on the front page of my hometown newspaper, where all my family, friends, neighbors, and business associates will know about it?"

If the answer is no, the decision is probably okay. The value of this exercise points to the need for executives to keep in touch with their true selves, to trust their visceral responses, and to further develop their intuition. You might want to consider using a couple of other widely-accepted methods:[3]

The Rotarian Test (of the Things That We Think, Say, or Do)

1. Is it the truth?
2. Is it fair to all concerned?
3. Will it build goodwill and better relationships?
4. Will it be beneficial to all concerned?

The Texas Instruments Test

This quick little ethics test is provided to employees of Texas Instruments on a small, business-card-sized pamphlet to carry with them. For copies of the card or further information, contact the TI Ethics Office at 1–800–33-ETHIC.

1. Is the action legal?
2. Is it consistent with Texas Instruments' values?
3. If you do it, will you feel bad?
4. How will it look in the newspaper?
5. If you *know* it's wrong, don't do it.
6. If you are not sure, ask.
7. Keep asking until you get an answer.

How does law relate to ethics? In principle, the laws of a society reflect its ethical standards. In practice, however, ethical standards often supersede legal standards. For example, it is not against the law in many jurisdictions to terminate an employee "at will." In other words, an employer may do so "without cause" or, if you will, just because he or she feels like it. Ethical standards suggest that an employee may be terminated only for "just cause" (i.e., for a good reason, such as stealing or substance abuse on the job or if survival of the business enterprise is endangered).[4]

Ethical decisions may be further complicated by cross-cultural considerations. For example, under Islamic law, the concept of *profit-and-loss sharing* is the proper model, and suggests (in Western terms) something along the lines of, "As you go, I too shall go." In contrast, the concept of *mudarabah*, which would allow the businessperson to negotiate terms most favorable to himself, regardless of the consequences for the other party, would not be ethically proper in Islamic culture. Typically, Westerners, despite their claims of striving to structure win-win deals (and this would be roughly analogous to *profit-and-loss sharing*), when asked to justify the one-sided outcomes that favor themselves, all too often justify their position by saying to the other party, in effect, "Look, you are an adult and you agreed to these terms of your own free will. Tough luck."

Consider, if you will, that there are also *philosophical* perspectives that color ethical decisions. For example, those who subscribe to the *meta-ethical* approach tend to see the world in absolutes of black and white, no gray areas. Something is either totally right or it is totally wrong. The rules are the rules are the rules—with no mitigating circumstances. Other people, though, may see the world in a more normative light, as a rather more complex playground, where in order to ultimately do the "right thing," one may have to choose between the lesser of two perceived evils. Do you believe that it is okay to tell a white lie in the interest of, let's say, not hurting someone's feelings? Well, your answer to this question might reveal which of the two philosophical camps you are at home with.

Application to Specific Business Issues

The following business issues are among the most important and commonly encountered, but by no means represent a complete set of legal and ethical guidelines for management decision making and behavior.

I suggest that for definitive and authoritative legal guidelines, managers would be well advised to refer to their employer's "Officer's Manual" (i.e., formalized code of behavior) or consult with the organization's staff attorneys or legal counsel. Legal obligations may differ by jurisdiction and may change as a result of challenges in the courts. They should be viewed as generalizations and will be considered from comparative legal and ethical perspectives (in alphabetical order):

Advertising, Truth in

If an advertisement has the effect of being deceptive, it is unethical, regardless of its intent. Law supports this position, but enforcement may be lacking in stringency.

Bribery

Bribery is action on the part of an employee to permit a third party to gain unfair advantage in dealings with his or her firm in return for being enriched in some way (e.g., kickbacks). This is both unethical and illegal.

Confidentiality

It is unethical for organizations to release confidential information about their employees or customers to third parties without express permission. If such information was originally obtained by the firm with the understanding that it would be kept confidential, then disclosure to third parties might constitute breach of an implied contract and subject the company to payment of damages under civil law. Failure by professionals (e.g., lawyers, physicians, psychologists) to honor confidentiality is not only unethical and illegal (under civil law) but may also subject them to revocation of licensure or other sanctions.

Conflict of Interest

If an individual enriches himself or herself at the expense of his or her employer or client, it constitutes *conflict of interest*. For example, the manager who hires her husband's catering firm to handle her employer's Christmas party may be creating a conflict of interest. The rule of thumb in these matters involves the element of concealment. Legally, conflict of interest does not exist if the party makes full disclosure regarding the potential for conflicts. If, for example, the manager revealed in advance to her boss that the catering firm she planned to hire was owned by her husband, that would not constitute a conflict. It might, however, be regarded as poor judgment.

Denigration

To spread false and damaging information about a competitor is both unethical and illegal, subjecting the offender to damages under civil law. If the claims are true, however, such action would remain within the bounds of legal behavior while ethical status would be problematic. The consideration here hinges upon the contention that infliction of harm upon a competitor may harm the entire industry.[5]

Discrimination

Bias against individuals on the basis of race, ethnicity, creed, age, gender, or sexual orientation is unethical and illegal. Aside from being morally reprehensible, it is also irrational. For example, the manager who fails to promote an individual on the basis of prejudice is underutilizing the firm's human capital.

Firing Employees

From a legal standpoint, whether a termination is rightful may depend upon whether it is based upon "at will" (i.e., employer's discretion or whim) or "just cause" (i.e., employer's justification) considerations. Generally, discrimination cannot justify termination. From an ethical standpoint, however, employers may not fire "at will," and employees are entitled to due process, the opportunity to state their case and be judged fairly (i.e., overruling a biased or unfair immediate boss). If they are terminated, it is the employer's ethical if not legal obligation to obviate the damage inflicted (e.g., via severance or outplacement services).

Gifts

Since gifts are things of value, they can be used to obtain unfair advantage (see "Bribery" above). However, the normative standards for "stepping over the line" can vary dramatically. For example, many government agencies, as a matter of formal policy, do not permit their employees to accept even a cup of coffee free of charge from potential vendors, whereas executives in the entertainment industry are often wined and dined in fine restaurants at vendor expense. As a rule of thumb, many organizations have established the policy that allows managers to accept gifts of "nominal value" (widely regarded as under $25 in value) and requires them to return items of greater value tactfully or obtain permission to accept these from superiors or "integrity officers."

Ignorance of the Law

Simply put, ignorance of the law does not constitute a justification or defense from a legal or ethical standpoint.

Informed Consent

If a party to a business relationship is put at risk as a result of performance under the terms of this relationship, the party can reasonably expect to be informed in advance of the risks involved. For example, the buyer of a product is entitled to know the real or potential dangers involved in using that product (and these can be listed on the label and/or in an accompanying pamphlet). If the consumer then knowingly purchases the item, consent is implied. Failure to obtain informed consent is unethical and may subject the offender to damages under civil law.

Moonlighting

Generally, moonlighting (i.e., working at a part-time job, "on the side") is neither unethical nor illegal. It may become an issue where the employer specifically prohibits it and/or where the "other" job is with a competitor, supplier, or customer (i.e., where there is potential for conflict of interest).

Price Cutting

The deciding factor in price cutting is intent. Cutting price to dispose of inventory would not be unethical, whereas doing so to undercut the competition would be. Price cutting is not, in and of itself, illegal.

Price Fixing

Conspiracy by "competitors" to set prices is both unethical and illegal.[6]

Privacy

Privacy is a right, legally as well as ethically. If your actions will cause the violation of someone's privacy, you must inform the individual of your intent, explain the risks involved, and obtain the party's consent (see "Informed Consent" above).

Report, Obligation to

Employees who have *suspicion* of an unethical activity are not ethically obligated to report it. If there is *knowledge* of such an activity, ethical obligation to report it would be discretionary and would depend upon the individual's cost-benefit analysis. While suspicion of a crime does not legally obligate an employee to report it, knowledge of a crime (before or after the fact) does call for the individual to come forward. Failure to do so may cause the individual to be regarded under the law as an accomplice or accessory to the crime.[7]

Sexual Harassment

Unequivocally, unwelcome sexual advances or coercion is unethical and illegal.

Whistle Blowing

See "Report, Obligation to" above.

Contracts

While ethical codes help us to establish standards governing the rights and obligations that exist in business relationships, these standards can be translated into agreements known as contracts. Parties to a contract exchange promises. These may be expressed (i.e., communicated explicitly and clearly, either in oral or written form) or implied (i.e., deduced from actions or behavior). Proper contracts involve the following conditions:[8]

1. One party makes an offer that is accepted by the other party.
2. Each party must offer the other consideration (i.e., something of value) in return for what the party is to receive from the other party.
3. Both parties must act of their own free will, free of duress and undue influence.
4. The agreement cannot include fraudulent claims or representations.
5. The agreement cannot be in violation of the law.
6. Certain types of contracts must be in written form (e.g., those involving real estate).

Alternative Dispute Resolution (ADR)

What happens when disputes arise from contracts? Litigation (i.e., fighting it out in court) can be extremely time-consuming and expensive, often involving years of legal processes and millions of dollars spent and, arguably, wasted.

The following alternative dispute resolution (ADR) methods are increasing in popularity because they can be conducted in a matter of a few days and at a minute fraction of litigation cost.

Arbitration

The parties argue their case before impartial referees or judges (i.e., arbitrators) under the sponsorship of an organization such as the American Arbitration Association. They mutually agree to be bound by the decision of the arbitrators (i.e., binding arbitration). There is no right of appeal if things don't go your way.

Mediation

The parties argue their case before impartial referees or judges (i.e., mediators). However, they are not required to accept the decision.

Minitrial

The parties argue their case before a panel of "judges" gathered from both sides of the dispute (e.g., executives employed by each organization) and moderated by an impartial guide. These settlement proceedings are not formal and do not require adherence to rules of evidence. The judges typically arrive at a solution, with or without the participation of the impartial guide.[9]

Note: Strategically, litigation may be a preferred remedy when one litigant plans to win a legal "war of attrition." For example, a large corporation with vast financial and other resources might enjoy a decided advantage over a "little guy" who may not be able to afford a protracted court battle. On the other hand, a large but image-conscious corporation might prefer ADR, viewing it as a means of minimizing adverse publicity.

The Business Policy and Ethics Checklist

1. Am I able to articulate, formulate, and feel comfortable with a set of ethical standards?
2. Do I have a better understanding of how to deal with particular business and workplace issues from an ethical standpoint?
3. How do I feel about ethics as it relates to law?
4. How does a contract address ethical as well as legal concerns?
5. What alternatives do I have to resolution of disputes through the court system?

8 STRATEGIC PLANNING

Strategic planning is concerned with identification and actualization of long-term organizational objectives. This is distinguished from operational planning or the functioning of the organization on a day-to-day basis. In terms of time horizons, it might be helpful to consider that the typical short-range forecast is revised on a quarterly basis, and the typical medium-range forecast on an annual basis. Long-range forecasts, in contrast, can project five or more years into the future. In fact, some of the most sophisticated organizations such as AT&T, IBM, ITT, and Exxon purportedly work on something in the vicinity of 50-year time lines. But Japan's Matsushita Corporation outdoes these firms, planning strategically some 250 years into the future!

Interestingly, some companies may no longer resemble their former selves at the point of the outer limits of their forecasts. One petrochemical giant, for example, projected that its primary business activity 50 years hence would be space colonization (i.e., providing housing in space). It is easy to understand, therefore, that an inverse relationship exists between the elements of time and accuracy in forecasting. As shown in Figure 8.1, the further into the future we forecast, the less likely we are to obtain an accurate result.

Figure 8.1 The relationship of accuracy and time in forecasting

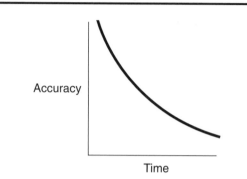

Objectives, Strategies, and Tactics

Business planning is not unlike military planning."[1,2] After all, business involves engaging in warfare, of sorts. And all wars have objectives. Armies fight to win terrain, kill or disable adversary combatants, and/or extract money from their victims. Companies fight to capture market share, generate sales revenues, enhance profits, and/or simply insulate themselves from competition (to the extent that this is possible) by finding a market niche. Both armies and business enterprises try to achieve their objectives through strategies. These "grand" plans are, in turn, transformed into more specific and perhaps more localized measures, commonly known as *tactics*. Generals and senior executives determine objectives and strategies, whereas field commanders and midlevel executives may have the discretion or authority to determine tactics (i.e., how the strategies are actualized).

A common pitfall in strategic planning pertains to the lack of proper follow-up. I believe that this phenomenon is to some degree justifiably associated with the negative stereotype of the yuppie MBA who is drawn to the perceived glamour of the planning process, yet disdains the formative evaluations and modification or "fine-tuning" of the plans. Clearly, strategic planning must be accompanied by strategic management.

In large organizations, strategic planning is a formalized process and ritual. It invariably leads to creation of a formal written document, the *strategic plan*. In my conversations with owners of small businesses, I often find that they do not have a formal written document. They typically explain that it's "all in my head." This is unfortunate for three important reasons:

1. *Continuity and succession planning:* If the entrepreneur becomes incapacitated or dies, his or her plans for the business die too.
2. *Quality of decisions:* Putting ideas to paper actually aids the thought process. In fact, psychologists who subscribe to the "cognitive" psychotherapeutic approach advise their patients to, for example, write down pro and con considerations concerning a difficult decision in which there may be internal conflict. (If the column of pro factors is longer than the column of con factors, this might rationally suggest the more appropriate option.)
3. *Commitment:* We live in a litigious society, one in which people might be well advised to avoid signing any document (i.e., contract) if it can be avoided. However, if an individual owns and operates a business enterprise, it is reasonable to assume that he or she should be committed to its success. It is in this light that the strategic plan should be viewed as a formal contract entered into with one's self. The written plan serves as a psychological tool to reaffirm this implicit commitment and to strengthen it.

As it would relate to objectives and strategies, growth may be accomplished by:

- Selling more of the organization's existing products to its current customers.
- Selling new products to existing customers.
- Selling new products to new customers.

The current trend toward globalization can be appreciated better when viewed in the context of growth for several reasons. First, domestic markets can become exhausted or saturated. Second, the resources required for a large-scale investment may suggest the participation of two or more international or multinational "players" to garner the necessary capital, human, and other resources as well as to share or pool the associated risks. And, of course, the increase in quantities bought, produced, and/or sold is often associated with enhanced economies of scale (except in situations involving markets that are too fragmented or too small to be profitable).

However, potential cross-cultural issues must be identified and addressed. A classic example of failure in this regard relates to General Motors's introduction of its popular domestic automobile, the Chevrolet Nova, to the Latin market in South America. The company launched the car there under the same name. Unfortunately for GM, the phrase *no va* in Spanish literally means "does not go." As you might imagine, the results were less than spectacular. A small oversight with serious consequences. *The lesson:* A little bit of sensitivity to cultural differences can go a long way.

Wouldn't it be nice to have a desk reference that could walk you through the strategic planning process? Well, you'll be pleased to know that Figures 8.2, 8.3, and 8.4 provide "boilerplates" for your convenience,[3] to help you establish your organization's goals, articulate the actions that must be taken to realize these goals, and to critique your plan. Explanatory text is provided.

Figure 8.2 Steps in establishing corporate objectives

1. a. What is the present condition of the market and our share of it?
   b. Who are our competitors and to what extent do they pose a risk?
   c. What are our company's strengths and weaknesses?

2. What will our future position be without change?

3. Is this satisfactory?

4. If our future position without change is not satisfactory, what can we do internally to improve things?

5. If our future position without change is not satisfactory, what can we do externally to improve things?

6. What will our future position be if we make these changes?

7. Compare step 2 to step 6.

8. Decide to maintain the status quo or make changes.

Figure 8.3 Steps in creating the strategic plan

1. Analyze the nature of the business.
2. Analyze the macroenvironment.
3. Identify obstacles.
4. Identify opportunities.
5. Determine and quantify goals.
6. Develop plans of action.
7. Determine allocation of finances and other resources.
8. Select methods to measure, review, and control procedures.
9. Submit the proposed written plan for review and approval.

Figure 8.4 Steps in evaluating the strategic plan

1. Does performance history provide adequate background, or do we need more information?
2. Has the macroenvironment been adequately appraised?
3. Have the capabilities of the organization been thoroughly examined?
4. Have the best opportunities been identified?
5. Have all opportunities and downside risks been identified?
6. Have all possible alternative strategies been considered?
7. Does the marketing mix flow logically from the chosen strategy?
8. Are recommended projects necessary and properly funded?
9. Are financial data clear and consistent?
10. Have benchmarks and controls been established?
11. Is the strategic plan compatible with prevailing attitudes, interests, and opinions (i.e., corporate culture, public image)?
12. Is the strategic plan defensible?

Establishing Organizational Objectives

Writing a strategic plan without clearly knowing the organization's objectives is similar to hailing a taxicab and when asked by the driver, "Where to?" answering, "I don't know, but take me somewhere."

Before an organization decides what it will strive to achieve in the arenas of industry and commerce, it might be a good idea to first identify its sets of values; in other words, what the organization stands for; its larger purpose beyond profit. Naturally, the business objectives should be an outgrowth of these values. An interesting contrast is that of Zenith and Motorola, two companies that manufactured TVs. Zenith confined its activities pretty much to TVs, while Motorola got involved in many other areas, including microprocessors and integrated circuits. "Zenith thought mainly in terms of what it was making, while Motorola thought mainly in terms of what it stood for. It defined its core purpose as 'applying technology to the benefit of the public.'"[4]

Toward this end, organizations articulate what they stand for in what is commonly known as *mission statements*. In order for these declarations to be meaningful, they should embody five key characteristics:

1. A mission statement should inspire people *inside* the company.
2. It must express a position that could be just as valid a century from now.
3. It should help people think broadly about what could be accomplished but is not yet being done.
4. It should help people determine what *not* to do.
5. It must be true to the organization and genuinely reflect what it is collectively about.

Some examples of mission statements (in summary form):[5]

Disney: To make people happy.

Marriott: To make people away from home feel that they are among friends and really wanted.

Mary Kay: To give unlimited opportunity to women.

Merck: To preserve and improve human life.

Nike: To experience the emotion of competition, winning, and crushing competitors.

Sony: To experience the sheer joy of advancing technology and applying it for the public's benefit.

3M: To solve unsolved problems innovatively.

Wal-Mart: To give ordinary folk the chance to buy the same things as rich people.

I am particularly impressed by word-of-mouth about "the card" that is distributed by Perot Systems to all its employees and to its "partners," as well. It states, essentially:

Our Values: WE SERVE OUR CUSTOMER
with innovative, responsive solutions to their needs.

WE TREASURE OUR PEOPLE
by attracting, developing, and recognizing outstanding people, and caring for them and their families.

WE OPERATE WITH INTEGRITY
by treating our customers, people, and suppliers in a fair and honest manner ... as we wish to be treated.

WE REWARD OUR STAKEHOLDERS
by providing strong financial performance from which everyone benefits.

WE CONTRIBUTE TO OUR COMMUNITY
by using our talents and resources to better the conditions in the diverse communities in which we live.

Do you know what your organization *claims to* stand for?

Does it *really*?

What makes your organization different from others?

What (who) is the customer base that you are dedicated to serve?

Why would someone want to work for you?

Why would someone want to do business with you?

Establishing Corporate Objectives

1. a. *What is the present condition of the market and our share of it?*
    We must assess the potential growth of the industry and our standing in it.

    b. *Who are the competition and to what extent do they pose a threat?*
    Too often, business strategists not only underestimate the competition, but they sometimes can't even identify who the competition really is. Showtime, the cable entertainment programming company, realized that it wasn't just competing against other premium cable services, such as HBO. In fact, it was competing against home video rental companies. Research discovered that many cable TV subscribers were discontinuing service because they perceived a relative advantage with video rentals. After all, videos enable the customer to view a movie of one's choice at a time convenient to the customer, whereas cable TV programs or movies are transmitted on a fixed schedule which may not be convenient. Moreover, cable TV programming schedules varied from day to day, complicated further by the perception that some published guides or schedule lists were difficult to read. How did Showtime respond? The company launched a campaign that involved showing a feature every evening at a fixed time, implicitly inviting subscribers to videotape the movies.

    Back in the "good old days," companies thought that they clearly knew who their competitors were and who their allies were, as well. It was all pretty much a black-and-white matter. But in the age of *co-opetition* (competition + cooperation, get it?), things are not necessarily so simple and often change dramatically and sometimes with little advance notice. For a business to survive in the current (and future) environment, it must understand its place in the business "ecosystem" or community, as an "ecological unit," of sorts. Microsoft, for example, flourishes within an ecosystem that encompasses a panoply of suppliers (such as Intel and Hewlett-Packard) and customers cutting across numerous market segments. In this sense, business ecosystems influenced and in turn, are influenced by other of its members, whether they are allies or opponents.[7]

The merger of Chrysler Corporation with Daimler-Benz A.G. (maker of the Mercedes Benz) was precipitated by a capacity glut brought on by a global economic downturn.[8]

AT&T entered into an agreement to buy the global data network division of IBM for $5 billion. Each of the companies agreed to provide each other with $9 billion in outsourcing business. This is a win-win deal in the sense that AT&T wanted to strengthen its position for gaining market share in the local communications market, to expand its global presence and to enhance its advanced data services, while IBM concluded that it no longer made economic sense to run a communications system all by itself.[9]

c. *What are our company's strengths and weaknesses?*
Simply put, this is the decision maker's moment of truth. This is the time to assess what is, not what he or she would like it to be. An accurate assessment here is absolutely necessary to set realistic objectives. There may be a natural tendency to focus on maximizing strengths while paying less attention to weaknesses. It is human nature to gravitate toward that which "feels good" rather than that which does not. Paradoxically, though, facing up to weaknesses and redoubling efforts to address them is, in our business lives as well as in our personal lives, a sign of strength.

Welcome to the ideological battle of the Harvard professors.

On the one hand, we are encouraged by Hamel and Prahalad to focus upon what is commonly referred to as the company's *core competencies* (i.e., its basic "historical" strengths) and divest or outsource the remaining activities (in the spirit of reengineering). Examples of core competencies might include Sony's expertise at miniaturization and portability in the electronics field and Chrysler's innovative design in the automotive field. Yet, some firms decide to shift to change their core competencies. For example, Unisys has shifted from manufacturing computers to providing services within the computer industry. General Electric (GE) receives over 40 percent of its revenues from financial services rather than the manufacture of electronic products. In fact, if GE decides that it cannot dominate an industry to become either the number 1 or number 2 player within it, the corporate "rule" is to divest or sell that division. This may be done in a manner that is not obvious to the general public or average consumer. In fact, GE's entire consumer electrical appliance business was sold to Thomson, although the GE name and trademark remained on those products during a transition period. And this move toward becoming a "lean" if not "mean" organization is such a widespread and significant phenomenon that the typical U.S. manufacturing firm has cut in half the number of SIC codes or industrial categories in which it operates.[10]

On the other hand, Michael Porter suggests in his *Competitive Strategy* that the firm focus its attention *externally* upon the opportunities that present themselves in the market.

2. *What will our future position be without change?*
See "Forecasting Methods" later in this chapter.

3. *Is this satisfactory?*
Change can be a very touchy subject. Too often, good decisions are rejected in favor of the status quo or those that are "comfortable." Clearly, comfortable is not necessarily best.

4. *If our future position without change is not satisfactory, what can we do internally to improve things?*
We might, for example, alter our modus operandi in the areas of marketing, research and development, human resources, facilities, and equipment.

5. *If we view our future position without change as unsatisfactory, what can we do externally to improve things?*

We might, for example, evaluate the feasibility of entering different, new industries or fields and perhaps even acquiring existing companies toward that end. In any event, we would establish criteria in terms of demonstrated or anticipated levels of sales, profitability, and rate of growth. We would also evaluate the extent to which the move allows us to take advantage of synergies. In other words, does the opportunity (or company to be acquired) "fit" and help to make the whole greater than the sum of its parts? And, of course, we must assess whether we have the managerial competence and financial resources to succeed.

6. *What will our future position be if we make these changes?*

7. *Compare step 2 to step 6.*

8. *Decide to stay the course or make changes.*

Creating the Strategic Plan

1. *Analyze the nature of the business.* (By the way, what business is the company really in?)

When we think of General Motors (GM), for example, we perceive that GM is primarily in the business of manufacturing automobiles. However, the company earns more from its financing division, General Motors Acceptance Corporation (GMAC), than it does from its manufacturing operations. So perhaps the more appropriate question should be: "What business *should* the company really be in"[11]

William Wrigley apparently knew the correct answer. A century ago, he was in the baking powder business. As an incentive to buy his product, Wrigley offered customers two free packs of chewing gum with each purchase. This gambit to "double their pleasure" proved so successful that he left the baking powder business entirely and built a chewing gum empire that nets approximately $2 billion a year.

Barnes & Noble, the world's largest retailer of books, apparently decided that being the "biggest retailer" wasn't good enough. So the company decided to *integrate forward* by trying (unsuccessfully) to acquire the Ingram Company, the world's biggest book distributor, which would have given B&N not only better access to its own supply, but also more *control* over supply to its competitors. In addition, Barnes & Noble *publishes* books, too, thereby *integrating even further forward.* (What next? Yes! E-books, electronic "print" books are in store for the future.)

Too often, there is a tendency to narrow rather than broaden an organization's self-image—and this has the effect of limiting its potential opportunities. So, if an organization views itself as being in the motion picture business (i.e., narrow), it might be healthier to view itself as being in the entertainment business or, better yet, the communications business.

In any event, the organization must have a clearly defined *raison d'etre* or purpose. This should be conveyed in a brief *mission statement* that expresses the company's ultimate goal. It generally emerges from discussions and exercises geared toward corporate soul-searching or introspection and reflects the organization's values. The mission statement also addresses the company's ability to differentiate itself from the competition; to be unique and special. Antonio Stradivari, the craftsman of what is widely regarded as the world's finest violin (the Stradivarius), expressed his philosophy and sense of purpose 300 years ago in his version of a mission statement: "God needs violins to send His music into the world, and if any violins are defective God's music will be spoiled. Other men will make other violins, but no man shall make a better one."

2. *Analyze the macroenvironment.*

Factor the exogenous or uncontrollable variables that impact on your business. These include sociocultural, politicolegal, technoscientific, economic, and competitive factors (see "The Macroenvironment" in Chapter 1).

3. *Identify opportunities.* SWOT Analysis

SWOT Analysis
(strengths, weaknesses, opportunities, threats)

(Internal)

	Strengths	Weaknesses
Opportunities (External)	I	II
Threats	III	IV

a. What Strengths do we enjoy that allow us to exploit the Opportunities?

b. What Weaknesses do we have that hinder or prevent us from exploiting the Opportunities?

c. What Strengths do we enjoy that help us to overcome the Threats?

d. What Weaknesses do we have that hinder or prevent us from overcoming the Threats?

4. *Identify obstacles.*

Sometimes decision makers can't see the forest for the trees. They are too close to a decision area to be objective or simply imaginative. For this reason, it might be wise to bring in an "outsider," an external consultant or merely a peer, who does not have a vested interest or preconceived notion.

Early in the 1980s, Time, Incorporated, launched *TV-Cable Week* magazine. Senior managers purportedly assumed that since the corporation owned American Television and Communications (ATC), the second-largest cable system operator, as well as Home Box Office (HBO), the largest program supplier, a cable TV guide would be a great success. So they thought: "Why bother to conduct a market test?" (It should be noted that Time's decision makers chose this course of action even though ATC management had reservations about the project early on.) Moreover, the two Harvard MBAs employed by Time and assigned to forecast the future performance of the prospective new publication tempered their optimistic projections with the recommendation that testing would be prudent and appropriate. The result: The vast majority of cable system operators (including Time's own ATC) had no interest in *TV-Cable Week*, and the magazine soon folded its operation. This episode is widely regarded as one of the most expensive and fascinating debacles in the history of print media. It illustrates how the arrogance of senior management can cause an organization to suffer substantial cash losses and far greater losses in the market value of its stock.[12]

5. *Determine and quantify goals.*

There are, of course, different types of goals. Some organizations want to be the leaders in their industries as measured in sales revenues, while others focus on profitability as measured in return on investment. Other firms strive primarily to insulate themselves from competition under the premise that their market niche will ensure their survival if not their growth and prosperity. In fact, there are even a few companies that place a premium on organizational "quality of life," such that growth is actually unwelcome. Yvon Chouinard, the iconoclastic owner of Patagonia, which manufactures high-ticket outdoor apparel, has actually said, "I just don't want to get any bigger."[13]

All objectives must be quantifiable, expressed in magnitude: market share as a percentage, sales volume in absolute dollars, and so on. Time frames or benchmarks for realizing objectives (and each stage thereof) must also be stated specifically. Naturally, it is necessary that the implementing team responsible for reaching the objectives be identified as well, with each member's role being clearly defined.

And, of course, none of these goals exists in a vacuum. To address this issue, Robert Kaplan and David Norton created a method known as the "balanced scoreboard," which links *all* objectives and involves *all* organizational players. The focus is on "outcome measures" (such as revenue, profit, rate of growth) and "performance drivers" (such as cycle time and defect rate). Kaplan and Norton contend that to seek goals without linking them to each other is analogous to a pilot of an aircraft who is concerned only with reading a single dashboard gauge, while ignoring others. Speed? Fine. Altitude? Not concerned about that now (crash!)[14]

Well, how do we know how well we actually did?

A popular method to measure performance is variance analysis. If you have never before heard the term, it might sound like some kind of complicated statistical method. But it is actually very simple to understand and use. Just measure the *variance* or difference between your goal and the actual result. In the following example, we observe that the company exceeded all goals, and that is good. However, the firm's management decision makers might want to examine why they weren't more optimistic about a gain in market share, given that they underestimated it by more than 50 percent. Perhaps if they were more venturesome or willing to assume more risk in investment, market share might have increased even more so.

Variance Analysis

	(Goal)	(Result)	(Variance)
Sales volume (in $)	30MM	35MM	+ 5MM ($)
Profit (in %)	17	20	+ 3 (%)
Market share (in %)	9	14	+ 5 (%)

6. *Develop plans of action.*
   Create the strategies and tactics that will be employed to realize the objectives. It is essential that these plans be logical and achievable (i.e., realistic). They must also be congruent with organizational culture. For example, the Disney organization assessed its future and realized that its prospects for growth were limited by its exclusive commitment to wholesome,

family-oriented entertainment. Research indicated that motion pictures with adult themes (i.e., those likely to receive "R" ratings), which might involve nudity and objectionable language, would fare well at the box office and for Disney, too. But this new direction would hardly be "congruent" with the Disney image and culture. So, what did the company do? Disney formed Touchstone, a subsidiary, to make motion pictures for the adult audience, and the Disney reputation was not the least bit sullied.

7. *Determine allocation of finances and other resources.*
   The name of the game is "budget." In terms of organizational finance, it is better to control more money than you need than not enough. In some organizations, you would be permitted to use the excess money for purposes other than those that were originally approved, whereas in other organizations, internal accounting rules would require you to give back money that is not used for the purposes specifically intended. In terms of corporate politics, the more budget or money you control, the greater your potential for power within the organization.

8. *Select methods to measure, review, and control procedures.*
   The term *variance analysis* pertains to the difference between what we plan or anticipate and what actually occurs. If we are pleased with the result, we may stay the course or step up our activities. If we are not pleased, we may make adjustments in the plan or the way the plan is executed.

9. *Submit the proposed written plan for review and approval.*
   In business as well as in military organizations, the best of strategic plans are substantively influenced by the divisional or departmental reports submitted by subordinates to those more senior decision makers who actually formulate and sign off on the plans. In other words, a manager may have more influence than he or she may realize. Management theory as well as practice tend to support the contention that the most well-run and profitable organizations are those in which influence can flow upward through the organizational hierarchy, such that the entity can be said to be managed from the bottom up.

Evaluating the Strategic Plan

Given the importance of the document, it would be wise to give the strategic plan the benefit of a sober critique. A checklist is provided in Figure 8.4. In addition, it wouldn't hurt to have a third party (such as impartial colleagues or even external consultants) play devil's advocate and try to poke holes in the plan. If they can pierce the armor of your document, then clearly there is more work ahead of you. If they cannot, then you can proceed with confidence. Either way, you win.

Forecasting Methods

We discuss quantitative methods in Chapter 4. Let us now address qualitative methods. These deal with what people do and what people say and are viewed as "soft," subjective, and vulnerable to challenge.

When I was studying for my MBA, one assignment that I will always remember involved the study of forecasting methods within a major corporation of my choice. A requirement of the assignment was that I personally interview a senior executive involved in the planning function. As it happened, I chose Clairol and found myself sitting with a senior vice president. He lit a cigar, leaned back in his chair in anticipation of my questions, and said, "Shoot, kid." In my first question, I asked him to identify the quantitative forecasting methods he relied upon. He asked what I meant by "quantitative." I suggested regression analysis and some other number-crunching methods to kick things off. "I don't use 'em," he responded. "What, then, do you use?" I asked. He leaned forward, savoring the moment with this "green" student, and said with a smile, "I ask my sales managers what they think." (See "Sales Force Estimates" below.)

Based upon my own empirical information and the anecdotes of my fellow management consultants, I can only say that most people would be very surprised to know just how many "sophisticated" organizations rely so heavily on "soft" or qualitative methods.

Qualitative Methods

The following methods are among the most commonly used.

Executive Judgment
Based on the input of top management, this method relies on the team's experience, talents, and instincts. While it can be valuable if management's track record is good, it sometimes reflects an "ivory tower" perspective when these individuals insulate themselves from what is really going on among rank-and-file employees and customers. The less time that management spends in the executive suites and the more time that it devotes to keeping current and close to employees and customers, the less danger this approach poses.

Expert Opinion
Based on the expertise of external consultants, this method can bring highly specialized and valuable assistance to the table. However, management may retain such consultants to provide a "rubber stamp" or approval for actions that had already been taken and may go bad.

Sales Force Estimates
Sales force estimates as a source of input can be of great value, since the salesperson is generally closest to the customer. This is of particular importance within technologically volatile industries. The primary danger lies in the potential for bias, since salespeople may believe that their estimates will be used to establish quotas to which they will have to adhere.

Consumer Surveys and Market Tests
Consumer surveys involve gathering information directly from the consumer, using market research techniques. An example that comes to mind is the Pepsi "taste test," which involved asking consumers to sample Pepsi-Cola and Coca-Cola and to indicate their preference. However, findings can be very inaccurate if sampling is not representative (see Chapter 4, "Statistics") or if questionnaire design is flawed. Supposedly, Coca-Cola's decision to withdraw the "old Coke" from distribution is attributable in part to imprecise phrasing of a survey

question. The question did not specifically ask how the consumer would feel about the prospect of Coke being taken off the market.

Market tests involve promotion and distribution of a brand on a limited basis. Generally, new brands are tested in "bellwether" markets, those key cities or towns that are representative of the consumer universe. Ostensibly, if the brand does well in these markets, it may launch or "roll out" on a national basis. However, if product weaknesses are detected, the brand may need to be improved or perhaps even abandoned. A risk inherent in conducting market tests is that they can be monitored by competitors. Remember that these corporate "spies" can gain valuable information from your efforts.

Group Discussion

Group discussions are decisions by committee or consensus. All members of the group must agree on a single decision (i.e., come up with "a number they can live with"). When it works, the method is usually indicative of group cohesiveness. However, a "bully" may exert undue influence on the other members of the group to get them to agree with him or her.

The motion picture *Twelve Angry Men* illustrates this point rather well. The story involves a jury brought together to decide the guilt or innocence of a young man charged with manslaughter. A juror initially succeeds in pressuring all but one of his fellow jurors into agreeing with his guilty vote. The single "holdout" juror stands up to the bully and, ultimately, the entire jury votes to acquit the defendant.

Nominal group technique is a type of group discussion in which individual inputs are submitted but not immediately discussed. A moderator then distributes to participants a listing of all the others' inputs. The participants can then discuss the various positions, rank the various alternatives, and, having carefully reviewed them, ultimately come to a decision and consensus. These steps may be repeated for additional "rounds" until consensus (or something close to it) is reached.

Pooled Individual

Individual estimates are merged, and an average is derived. Each person's estimate has equal weight. Therefore, this method may be regarded as "democratic."

Delphi

Delphi is a variant of pooled individual. Here participants submit their individual estimates and then review those of other participants. They may then discuss and revise their original figures. In this sense, it may be regarded as a hybrid version of group discussion and pooled individual, drawing upon the strengths of each approach.

Quali-Quant Methods

As you can see, much decision making is based upon unknown factors and often upon subjective estimates. It is only natural, therefore, to seek out and apply some sort of "scientific method" in these "soft" situations, to make the process as objective as possible. Toward that end, we may elect to use Bayesian methods to provide us with the semblance of a quantitative formula to make qualitative and subjective (i.e., "soft") inputs "harder."

Index of Attractiveness

The *index of attractiveness* enables us to rank projects or products in order of their projected profitability. If funds are limited, the index can be used to help determine which ones to drop from consideration.

To calculate the index of attractiveness, we multiply the value representing its probability of successful development (T, expressed as a percentage) by the value representing its probability of commercial success if it is actually brought to market (C, expressed as a percentage). The resulting figure is multiplied by the value representing the amount of profit that is expected to be generated in the event of commercial success (P, expressed in absolute dollars). The total is then divided by the value representing the cost of development (D, expressed in absolute dollars).

The formula for the index of attractiveness is presented in Figure 8.5.

Decision Making under Uncertainty: The Payoff Matrix

The formula for *the payoff matrix* enables us to estimate the payoffs associated with various scenarios and strategies and ultimately to choose the strategy that is likely to give us the best payoff.[15] (The

Figure 8.5 Calculating the index of attractiveness

The formula for the index of attractiveness is:

$$\frac{T \times C \times P}{D} = \text{index of attractiveness rating}$$

where

T = probability of successful development

C = probability of commercial success

P = profit, if successful

D = cost of development

Using this formula, we compute ratings for the four projects as follows:

Project	T (%)	× C (%)	×	P ($)	/	D ($)	=	Rating
A	0.8	0.6		5,000,000		200,000	=	12.00
B	0.6	0.9		1,000,000		500,000	=	1.08
C	0.6	0.8		10,000,000		700,000	=	8.00
D	0.9	0.7		11,000,000		3,000,000	=	2.31

The higher the rating, the more attractive the option is likely to be. Therefore, we would rank the projects as follows:

1. Project A (12.00)
2. Project C (8.00)
3. Project D (2.31)
4. Project B (1.08)

Note: The values for the variables T, C, P, and D are subjective estimates (e.g., derived by any of the qualitative forecasting methods. Index of attractiveness is a "quali-quant" method because those subjective estimates (qualitative input) are manipulated by a formula (quantitative framework).

implication here is that we may have to commit to a particular single strategy before we can determine which scenario will actually occur.) To identify the best strategy, we multiply each scenario's chance of occurring by the payoff (e.g., profit) associated with each strategy option for each of the scenarios. We then add up the subtotals for each strategy option and select the strategy option with highest payoff (see Figure 8.6).

Figure 8.6 Decision making under uncertainty: The Payoff Matrix

Note: The values or numbers depicted here represent subjective estimates and were chosen arbitrarily for illustrative purposes only.

The formula for ranking strategy options using decision making under uncertainty is:

$$CP \text{ for } A = (PSN \times IP) + (PSN \times IP) + (PSN \times IP) + \cdots$$

where

A = each strategy option

SN = each scenario

IP = payoff for each strategy under each scenario set

CP = payoff for each strategy under all scenario sets

We are asked to assume that scenario 1 (SN_1) has a 40 percent chance of occurring, scenario 2 (SN_2) has a 20 percent chance of occurring, scenario 3 (SN_3) has a 15 percent chance of occurring, and scenario 4 (SN_4) has a 25 percent chance of occurring. We may choose any one of three alternative strategies (A_1, A_2, or A_3). The numbers inside the accompanying matrix represent the payoff associated with each strategy for each scenario. Figures in brackets show how payoffs are computed (i.e., estimated payoff times the likelihood of scenario).

	SN_1 (0.40)	SN_2 (0.20)	SN_3 (0.15)	SN_4 (0.25)	= Payoff
A_1	9	3	5	6	= 6.45
	$[(0.40 \times 9)$ + (0.20×3) + (0.15×5) + $(0.25 \times 6)]$				
A_2	6	5	7	4	= 5.45
	$[(0.40 \times 6)$ + (0.20×5) + (0.15×7) + $(0.25 \times 4)]$				
A_3	4	8	4	8	= 5.80
	$[(0.40 \times 4)$ + (0.20×8) + (0.15×4) + $(0.25 \times 8)]$				

(Continued)

Figure 8.6 *(Continued)*

Let's assume further, in terms of the weather, that

SN_1 = it will rain

SN_2 = it will snow

SN_3 = it will be warm and humid

SN_4 = it will be clear and dry

and that

A_1 = carry an umbrella

A_2 = wear a winter coat

A_3 = wear a T-shirt and shorts

So, given that strategy A_1 offers the highest payoff, we would carry an umbrella in anticipation of rain.

Note: In the "real world," planning exists on more than a single plane and is multidimensional and often very complex. To consider dozens or even hundreds of alternative strategies in the face of a similar number of scenarios would not be unrealistic.

Decision Making under Conflict: Game Theory

Developed by legendary mathematician John von Neumann, *game theory* is similar to decision making under uncertainty. However, it explicitly factors in the notion that our adversaries make rational decisions and take actions in response to our own actions.[16] In other words, decision making and business game playing don't exist in a vacuum; your adversaries are plotting their chess moves against you just as you move against them.

Decision Tree

The *decision tree* allows us to depict visually possible scenarios (i.e., branches on the tree) that may spawn even more scenarios (i.e., subsequent scenarios or smaller branches on the tree).[17]

Figure 8.7 depicts the four "primary" scenarios corresponding to Figure 8.6. It goes on to suggest secondary or subsequent scenarios. For example, SN_1 branches off into two resulting scenarios, each of

Figure 8.7 Decision tree

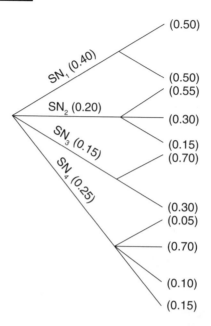

which has a 50 percent chance of occurring. The probability of either occurring would be 20 percent ($0.40 \times 0.50 = 0.20$).

The Aggregate or Merged Forecast

If you are using more than one forecasting method, how do you come up with a single bottom-line forecast? This is accomplished by multiplying the forecast amount or input for each method by a weighting percentage reflecting the degree to which we are willing to rely upon that method. We then add the subtotals to derive a single forecast figure.

Figure 8.8 shows the merging of four different forecasting methods we discussed earlier. (Of course, you could decide to use other or additional methods, including quantitative approaches such as regression analysis; see Chapter 4, "Statistics.") In this example, the results of executive judgment, expert opinion, sales force estimates, and customer surveys are multiplied by the *weighting percentage* (an expression of how reliable we think each forecast is likely to be). This

Figure 8.8 Aggregate or merged forecast

Combine or merge the results of various forecasting methods so that each can be "weighted" and be a component of the overall projection.

Method	Forecast amount (millions)	Input weighting	(millions)
Executive judgment	$10	0.30	$ 3
Expert opinion	8	0.25	2
Sales force estimates	20	0.20	4
Customer survey	4	0.25	1
		1.00	

Aggregate projection: $10 million

percentage may reflect how reliable a method has been in the past or how reliable we believe it will be based upon a new development.

In any case, the percentages for all methods that are used must add up to 100 percent. By adding together these four subtotals, we get the aggregate projection.

Let us assume that we find, at the end of the year, that the forecast in this example was pretty much right on the money and that sales revenues were actually very close to the $10-million figure. We would then assign greater weighting to executive judgment in next year's forecast, perhaps allowing it a weighting of 50 or so percent and adjusting the weightings for the other methods accordingly.

As you can see, strategic planning is a very broad functional area spanning the range of business disciplines. It involves the identification of organizational objectives and the translation of these into strategies that, in turn, are implemented as tactical or "action" plans, for day-to-day operational activities. More than any other area, strategic planning calls for the integration of countervailing qualities and considerations: creative and analytical; long term and short term; strengths and weaknesses; opportunities and threats.

The Strategic Planning Checklist

1. Are my corporate objectives realistic and appropriate?
2. Is the strategic plan likely to help realize these objectives?
3. How can I critique and refine it?
4. Have I been completely honest with myself in assessing the organization's strengths and weaknesses?
5. In what ways can I improve my forecasting?
6. Who in my organization will be involved in these functions?

EPILOGUE: REFLECTION, INTROSPECTION, AND ENLIGHTENMENT

Management Decision Making: Art or Science?

As we near completion of *MBA in a Nutshell*, you might be wondering: Is management decision making an art or a science?

Algorithms and Heuristics

Clearly, there are scientific methods and bodies of knowledge that can be of great value to managers. Yet, especially in today's complex business environment, many situations do not easily lend themselves to problem solving by means of *algorithms*, the formulas or equations used to solve problems with assured accuracy. Instead, managers are often forced to rely on their sets of *heuristics*, their value-laden assumptions or rules of thumb.

I remember that when I rented my first apartment, the widely accepted heuristic of the day dictated that individuals should not spend more than one quarter of their monthly take-home pay on rent. As the cost of housing has risen over the years, very few people in my city find that they can abide by this heuristic. So the problem with heuristics is that they can become obsolete with the passage of time—and managers may not realize that the heuristics that may have served them well in the past have become obsolete.

Can you identify or characterize some of the heuristics that you depend upon?

Might other heuristics, upon reflection, serve you better?

The illustration in Figure E.1 depicts the face of a telephone. This is what you see when you use the instrument. You will notice that the 12 buttons you would press to dial a telephone number are left blank. Fill them in, with the correct numbers, letters, and/or special characters and symbols. (Do not read further until you have completed this exercise.)

Figure E.1 Memory exercise

Change: The Cognitive and the Affective

Management decision making involves not only how we think (i.e., the cognitive), but also how we feel (i.e., the affective). And one of the most pressing issues in business today is how we feel about change. Change is inevitable and unavoidable. So do we anticipate it and embrace it, or do we fight it? Too often, we fight it. This may be attributed to any of the following:

- We may not understand the nature of a particular change. For example, an individual who does not understand computer technology might reasonably resist it.
- We may fear that introduction of a particular change will cause us to lose power within the organization.
- We may have "plateaued" and no longer wish to assume a new challenge.
  To what extent do you resist change?
  How do you feel about that?
  How do you feel about how you feel?

Referring to the exercise you completed a few moments ago, the vast majority of people who attempt it fail to fill in the missing numbers, letters, and characters/symbols accurately (see Figure E.2). It is interesting that we use the telephone so often and have done so for many years. Shouldn't we know it better? Maybe we thought that we knew it a lot better than we actually do. If such is the case, that might reflect the "arrogance" of management and portends unfortunate consequences. Truly, "Pride goeth before destruction, and a haughty spirit before a fall."

Enlightened executives examine and continually reexamine their assumptions and standard operating procedures. Self-appraisal and improvement should, therefore, be regarded as ongoing processes. The enhanced sense of self-awareness that usually comes to those who deliberately work toward this end is closely related to self-actualization, not only in terms of professional growth, but in terms of personal growth, as well.

Now That You Have Finished the Book ...

Congratulations! You have completed the academic curriculum of this program! At the end of just about every *MBA in a Nutshell* class that I teach, I notice an interesting and widespread phenomenon: Students feel exhausted by the intensity of the experience yet exhilarated by the realization that they have absorbed so much valuable information in such a short period of time. Invariably, some student poses the following question to me as we prepare to conclude:

"Is that all there is to an MBA?"

The answer is both yes and no.

Yes—you have been introduced to key concepts and methods that MBAs commonly use, but you've done it in only a matter of hours. And, I trust, it wasn't painful and might have been enjoyable.

No—you may wish to learn more about some or many of the subjects covered in *MBA in a Nutshell*. At the end of this book, a bibliography is provided to suggest supplemental readings. Organizations to support your development in each functional area are also listed there. If your interest in the content of this book is strong enough, you may actually decide to pursue an MBA degree. In that case, you will be able to enjoy the camaraderie of other students and the rich experience of group learning. You also stand to gain a great deal from private and informal conversations with some of your professors.

In any event, your education will still not be complete—not because the MBA curriculum is lacking, but because education is a continuous and ongoing process. I have earned a doctorate as well as an MBA.

Yet I feel the strong desire, if not the need, to read journal articles and thought-provoking books as well as attend seminars as my schedule permits. (Keep in mind that professionals, such as physicians, lawyers, and accountants, are required to be recertified periodically and must study to keep up with professional standards.) I believe that the best of students are eventually struck by the fact that there is always so much more to learn.

Figure E.2 Solution to memory exercise

POSTSCRIPT: EDUCATION AND CAREER PATHING

You Are a Product!

In planning your career objectives and the educational means likely to help you actualize them, you might find it helpful to employ a multidisciplinary approach similar to the one that MBAs use in making business decisions (given a little creative license, of course). Toward that end, ponder the points that follow.

Marketing

In seeking a job, the blunt truth is that *you are a product*. It is important that you differentiate your brand (i.e., yourself) from other brands competing against you in the marketplace (i.e., other job seekers). So it is important that you identify and evaluate the sets of skills and educational accomplishments that will best help you differentiate and position your product. For example, you might choose to enter a joint JD/MBA program, garnering a law degree as well as a business degree. Or you might pursue a major in digital communications, a very hot area of expertise. Or you might learn a foreign language or two (conversationally, if not fluently).

When I taught the course, *MBA in a Nutshell*, a student asked my advice regarding how he, a computer systems analyst who speaks five European languages fluently, might find a job. Before I could answer, another student (who just happened to manage international operations in her organization) addressed her peer with two sweet-sounding words: "You're hired."

In addition to (spoken) language skills, nominal computer language skills are an unspoken requisite. However, truly mastering the use of software programs such as Excel would be a good selling point. Also, an aspect of your personal background that you may take for granted may be a big plus with certain companies. For example, General Electric, EDS, and Perot Systems were known to consider service in the military as implicit indicators of proven leadership ability. (On the other hand, less than five years of business experience on the part of an applicant to an MBA program straight out of a bachelor's program—even with excellent grades and GMAT scores—is a negative, insofar as most of the top graduate business schools are concerned.)

I was often approached by a good number of students who tell me that they really want to find a job with an online company, but they feel that their current job working for a "brick-and-mortar" or traditional manufacturing- or service-based company would make it unlikely for them to get hired. This is a *totally false* assumption, in most instances; the exception being a highly technical position, for example: a Webmaster. And, even then, an individual who "oversees" the Web site for his or her "brick-and-mortar" company stands a pretty decent chance of making the transition to a dot-com. But if, for example, you are experienced and successful in "soft skills" categories (such as human resources, sales, and marketing), you may actually be very much *in demand*, especially if your current (or past) brick-and-mortar employer is a "blue chip," respected company and (believe it or not) you are 35 to 45 years old!

If you are wondering about the "age thing," consider that a lot of dot-com start-ups are conceived and run by upstarts in their twenties who would benefit from some maturity. They often acknowledge this point and are willing to "rent" the maturity.

Accounting and Finance

Assess your net worth (in the career universe), identifying and ascribing values of magnitude to your assets and weaknesses. Weigh educational options not only in terms of their potential to increase your net worth, but also in terms of their net present value, internal rate of return, and return on investment. In other words, you would want to estimate the probable payoff or value of the time and money that you may invest in your development.

Economics

In terms of diminishing marginal utility, ascertain just "how much (education) is enough." Also, consider what the demand for your product is now and is likely to be in the future.

Statistics

Get your hands on a lot of research (the secondary or preexisting kind will do just fine). Get the information to support your preliminary decisions. Look for relationships and trends.

Human Resources Management

Use a Myers-Briggs Type Inventory or some other tool to help you reach valuable insights about your personality characteristics and the implications these have in terms of the nature of job tasks, work settings, and types of learning that would suit you the best. Also, create something akin to management by objectives to help you commit to actualizing specific educational and/or career goals within particular time frames.

Off the record, I can't begin to tell you how many "successful" people I meet who are very unhappy in their careers. One who immediately comes to mind: the highly paid corporate executive who started out as a schoolteacher but was pressured to study for an MBA and get on the fast track because his family told him that he "should" earn more money. He confided in me that the financial rewards he receives in the business world pale when compared to the gratification he got from helping kids develop in their formative years. To live your life according to the expectations of others rather than realizing your *raison d'etre* is a tragic waste. In the words of Joseph Campbell, "Follow your bliss. The money will come." And I say that if it doesn't come, that's not so bad. You're still better off.

Strategic Planning

Weigh all the aforementioned points and integrate your assessments in a strategic plan. Chart your course. The self-diagnostic tool in Figure PS.1 may be helpful toward that end.

Do You Really Need an MBA?

If you're wondering whether you really need an MBA, the answer is that depends upon the considerations that follow.

Career Stage and Aspirations

Where are you now in the hierarchy of your organization? How well do you know your industry? Are you a seasoned veteran or a relative newcomer? Generally, the MBA credential can at best only allow you access to the so-called "fast track." It does not guarantee that you will ascend to the dizzying heights of the executive suite. On balance, if you are a "shirt-sleeves" manager who has received promotions at regular intervals and are otherwise pleased with your progress, pursuit of the MBA would probably not offer much utility, unless you are on a periphery of senior management or already within its ranks. In that case, having or not having the degree might make the difference between being considered for a particular slot or not.

Corporate Culture and Personal Orientation

Does your employer (or the norms of your industry or specific job function) implicitly or explicitly require the credential? In many instances, employers would prefer to hire bright and eager individuals with baccalaureates in any number of academic areas and train them in the company's own ways. As a matter of fact, none other than the respected Procter & Gamble operates in this manner, to the extent that even MBAs who are hired out of business schools purportedly must put in time stocking supermarket shelves and performing some of the less glamorous tasks not usually associated with the patina of

Figure PS.1 Career self-examination

Directions: Place a square around a number to indicate how important you feel that item is to your career position. Place a circle around a number to indicate what you perceive your present situation to be.

Scale: High/Excellent — 5 — 4 — 3 — 2 — 1 — Low/Poor

Items:

1. Making as much money as is normal for your job in other organizations.   5 4 3 2 1

2. Making as much money as you need.   5 4 3 2 1

3. Making as much money as you want.   5 4 3 2 1

4. Having the opportunity to increase your income significantly while in this firm.   5 4 3 2 1

5. Having vertical growth opportunities in the organization (upward in management).   5 4 3 2 1

6. Having lateral growth opportunities in the organization (other jobs or career paths).   5 4 3 2 1

7. Living in the part of the country where you want to live.   5 4 3 2 1

8. Living locally where you want to live.   5 4 3 2 1

9. Having satisfactory time/energy balance between job and personal life.   5 4 3 2 1

10. Having job security.   5 4 3 2 1

11. Having your family/significant others satisfied with your career path choice.   5 4 3 2 1

12. Having your family/significant others satisfied with your present job.   5 4 3 2 1

13. Being generally satisfied with this organization.   5 4 3 2 1

14. Having the opportunity to be creative in this organization.   5 4 3 2 1

15. Having a reasonable work schedule.   5 4 3 2 1

16. Having a satisfactory work environment.   5 4 3 2 1

Figure PS.1 *(Continued)*

17.	Having opportunities to update/learn new skills.	5 4 3 2 1
18.	Taking pride in your job.	5 4 3 2 1
19.	Having opportunities for career path counseling.	5 4 3 2 1
20.	Taking pride in the organization.	5 4 3 2 1
21.	Being satisfied with your coworkers.	5 4 3 2 1
22.	Being satisfied with your supervisor/manager.	5 4 3 2 1
23.	Being satisfied with upper management.	5 4 3 2 1
24.	Avoiding excessive job stress and burnout.	5 4 3 2 1
25.	Making a positive contribution to the organization.	5 4 3 2 1

Your present overall career satisfaction:

Scale: (circle one)

Very High—10—9—8—7—6—5—4—3—2—1—Very Low

Taking into account your present career situation—age, experience, skills, talents, contacts, and so forth—what do you think your job satisfaction could be?

10 9 8 7 6 5 4 3 2 1

If there is a significant difference between your present career satisfaction and what you think it could be, what might you need to narrow the gap?

_____

_____

What might you need to do to lessen any significant differences between the squares and the circles, the importance and the current position, in your self-assessment?

_____

_____

Source: John Douglas Stewart, *The Power of People Skills* (John Wiley and Sons, Copyrighted 1986) pp. 208–209. Reprinted in 1993 by University Press of America.

the MBA. Clearly, the emphasis in such an environment, at least at the beginning of one's career, is learning the business from the bottom up. And that may cause some dirt to accumulate under the fingernails.

Of course, if you are an entrepreneur and career track as such is not an issue, the credential may hold little value. The value of the body of knowledge associated with the credential is, of course, considerable. Yet it is possible to acquire it (or the components of it that you actually need) through other courses of action. (By the way, many entrepreneurs already do on a daily basis and take for granted what MBA candidates learn about in their lessons and case studies. In fact, I have even met a number of successful entrepreneurs who intuitively know what MBAs strive to learn.)

Time Constraints

Do your job schedule and personal commitments allow you to devote time to class attendance, homework assignments, and study? Keep in mind that the typical full-time (i.e., daytime) MBA program requires two years, while the degree may be attained in three to five years of part-time (i.e., evening) study or three consecutive full-time (i.e., daytime) summer sessions over three years.

Some universities have established "executive MBA" programs specially suited to fast-track corporate executives and successful entrepreneurs. Admission (for other than entrepreneurs) often requires employer sponsorship, and for this reason, candidates tend to be the "fair-haired boys and girls" rather than rank-and-file aspiring executives. To accommodate the student's business obligations, the course of study may involve one full day per week of class attendance during the academic year, along with a three-week intensive summer session over a two-year period.

Some organizations make only a lip service commitment to learning opportunities and development of its employees, while other companies make a very serious commitment. For some companies, executive new hires are purportedly required to attend several weeks of training before they even report to the office. There is a distinction, however, between "training" on the company's time and "education" on or off the company's time.

Cost

Are you prepared to spend $60,000 or more? Weigh this against median pay of $82,000 per year for graduates of the Top 25 B-schools and it may seem like a pretty good cost-benefit trade-off. But, keep in mind that not everyone can get into a top school and that pay for grads from schools with lesser reputations may command a far more modest compensation package. Also, consider that all this is seen through an American lens. Corporate recruiters in Europe tend to prefer hiring grads of their own continental INSEAD over Harvard and other top U.S. B-schools.

Choosing an MBA Program

Visit mba.com or mbaprograms.org. If you have decided that getting an MBA will empower you to achieve your career goals, the following considerations should be weighed in selecting the program best suited to your needs:

The Institution

Is the school properly accredited? This is generally an important criterion. To what extent is the school's curriculum geared to a specific industry? If you are committed to a career in the insurance field, for example, an MBA granted by the College of Insurance might make a lot of sense, whereas it might not if you are contemplating a career in a field other than insurance.

The Department

What percentage of the faculty is retained on a full-time rather than part-time (i.e., adjunct) basis? What percentage has earned doctorates? What percentage publishes scholarly articles and is involved in formal research projects? The answers to these questions tend to illustrate the extent to which the department is geared toward scholarship.

The Learning Environment

Are classes small and individualized, or are students "warehoused" in huge lecture halls? Perhaps a particular blend of the two settings would best accommodate your particular learning style. Are the library and computer facilities extensive and state of the art? They should be.

"Distance learning" via an online MBA course may be a viable option, given time and/or geographical constraints that may make it difficult or impossible to attend an MBA program. "On-demand" or "asynchronous" programs allow you to start and stop and start again as many times as you like within a given timeframe, or what I call a "cyber semester^{SM}" in the convenience of your own home or at your office. ("Synchronous" programs, however, would require you to "be there" at fixed times.) But, please, realize that the vast majority of these accredited MBA programs cost just as much (!) as their traditional counterparts.

Employment Search Support

Does the job placement office have a strong track record in arranging interviews with better firms, or is it pretty much a waste of time? Does the alumni club function as an "old boys/girls network," helping to place graduates by drawing upon its membership resources? Clearly, the greater the support, the better (assuming, of course, that you place a premium on having it).

Alternatives to the MBA

In the wake of the 2008 economic collapse and on the heels of a subsequent recession, the value of the MBA credential has been called into question by some human resources executives, educators, and graduate business school students and their "would-be" counterparts who wonder whether the course of study is still worth the effort. Taking into consideration the limitations of the aspiring learner, the following options are offered as viable alternatives to the traditional MBA course of study:

Other Graduate Programs and Degrees

As the saying goes, there is more than one way to skin a cat. Study in the fields of natural science and technology as well as behavioral science also presents significant potential springboards.

Applications in Science and Technology

MSTM	Master of Science in Technology Management
MSEE	Master of Science in Electrical Engineering
MSChE	Master of Science in Chemical Engineering
MSIE	Master of Science in Industrial Engineering
MSME	Master of Science in Mechanical Engineering

Applications in Human Resources Management

MSILR	Master of Science in Industrial Labor Relations
MSEd	Master of Science in Education

Applications in International/Cross-Cultural Spheres

MSIA	Master of Science in International Affairs

Certificate Programs

Universities offer education modules of short duration and of a specialized nature. In a mere four to ten days, an individual may participate in a certificate-granting program specializing in advanced sales management, corporate finance, human resources management, operations research, telecommunications management, strategic planning, or any of hundreds of other offerings that may deal in areas of subspecialization (i.e., compensation or industrial labor relations rather than the general discipline of human resources management). I am a big fan of certificate programs, and I have found that job interviewers often tend to value a certificate granted by a prestigious school over the MBA degree granted by anything less than a top business school. This is especially true when interviewing seasoned managers rather than those at or near entry level. Moreover, the opportunity to network with peers during and after these programs can be rich. Depending on the certification program, the price tag varies. For more information, visit worldwidelearn.com.

Synoptic or MBA Overview Programs

Private management consulting firms and corporate training organizations may offer overviews of the MBA curriculum. The seminar is of a highly intensive nature, ranging from two to five full days in duration, designed to present the essence of the MBA body of knowledge in just a few days. The range of quality within this category is broad. One program may be delivered by a university professor who, despite respectable academic credentials, refers primarily to "textbook" points of reference and views the business community from an ivory tower of sorts. Another program delivered by an educator with a background in management consulting or corporate training and similarly impressive credentials (i.e., a doctorate and professional recognition) may focus to a greater extent on the real-world perspective of business.

To the extent that we regard the MBA curriculum (if not the credential) as a legitimate vehicle for professional and perhaps personal growth, it is my contention that we are living in times that warrant considerable optimism. The elitist stigma of the MBA and the "yuppie" image with which it is sometimes associated are things of the past. I suggest that virtually anyone who wants to learn what an MBA is expected to know can do so, inexpensively and within a relatively short amount of time. This is the era of "everyman's MBA." Find the version that feels right for your purposes. It's out there. Study.

APPENDIX 1: RECOMMENDED READING

Chapter 1: Marketing and Product Management

Kerin, Roger A., et. al., *Marketing*, 9th ed. (McGraw-Hill, 2008).

Kotler, Philip, *Marketing Management* (Prentice Hall, 2008).

Levinson, Jay Conrad, *Guerrilla Marketing* (Houghton Mifflin, 2007).

Scott, David Meerman, *The New Rules of Marketing and PR* (John Wiley & Sons, 2007).

Chapter 2: Accounting and Finance

Atrill, Peter, and Eddie McLaney, *Accounting and Finance for Non-Specialists* (FT Press, 2008).

Brealey, Richard, *Principles of Corporate Finance* (McGraw-Hill, 2007).

Cooke, Robert, *36-Hour Course in Finance for Non-Financial Managers*, 2nd ed. (McGraw-Hill, 2004).

Downes, John, and J. E. Goodman, *Dictionary of Finance and Investment Terms* (Barron's, 2006).

Chapter 3: Human Resources and Operations Management

Borlander, George, and Scott Snell, *Managing Human Resources* (Cengage Learning, 2006).

Dessler, Gary, *Human Resource Management* (Prentice Hall, 2007).

Renckly, Richard, *Human Resources* (McGraw-Hill, 2007).

Smith, Shawn A., *The HR Answer Book* (AMACOM, 2008).

Chapter 4: Statistics

Berenson, Mark L., *Basic Business Statistics* (Prentice Hall, 2008).

Freedman, David, et al., *Statistics*, 4th ed. (W. W. Norton & Company, 2007).

Fung, Kaiser, *Numbers Rule Your World* (McGraw-Hill, 2010).

Gibilisco, Stan, *Statistics DeMYSTified* (McGraw-Hill, 2004).

Chapter 5: Economics

Freedman, David, et al., *Statistics*, 4th ed. (W. W. Norton & Company, 2007).

Fung, Kaiser, *Numbers Rule Your World* (McGraw-Hill, 2010).

Gibilisco, Stan, *Statistics DeMYSTified* (McGraw-Hill, 2004).

McConnell, Campbell, Stanley Brue, and Sean Flynn, *Economics* (McGraw-Hill, 2008).

Sowell, Thomas, *Economic Fact and Fallacies* (Basic Books, 2007).

Wessels, Walter J., *Economics* (Barron's, 2006).

Wheelan, Charles, *Naked Economics* (W. W. Norton & Company, 2003).

Chapter 6: Technology Management

Baltzman, Paige, Steven Haag, and Amy Phillips, *Business-Driven Technology* (McGraw-Hill, 2008).

Collins, Jim, *Good to Great* (HarperCollins, 2000).

Morgan, Lames, *The Toyota Product Development System* (Taylor & Francis, 2006).

Wooten, Simon, *Strategic Thinking* (Kogan Page, 2006).

Chapter 7: Business Policy and Ethics

Bogle, John, *Enough* (John Wiley & Sons, 2008).

Ferrell, O. C., *Business Ethics* (Cengage Learning, 2006).

Maxwell, John C., *Ethics* (Center Street, 2005).

Maxwell, John C., *There's No Such Thing as Business Ethics* (FaithHouse, 2007).

Chapter 8: Strategic Planning

Bradford, Robert W., *Simplified Strategic Planning* (Chandler House Press, 2000).

Bryson, John M., and Farnum K. Alston, *Creating and Implementing Your Strategic Plan* (John Wiley & Sons, 2003).

Nolan, Timothy N., and Leonard Goodstein, *Applied Strategic Planning: An Introduction* (Pfeiffer, 2008).

Wooten, Simon, *Strategic Thinking* (Kogan Page, 2002).

Epilogue: Reflection, Introspection, and Enlightenment

Kuhn, Thomas, *The Structure of Scientific Revolutions* (University of Chicago, 1996).

Minsky, Marvin, *The Emotion Machine* (Simon & Schuster, 2007).

APPENDIX 2: ORGANIZATIONS AND RESOURCES

Chapter 1: Marketing and Product Management

American Marketing Association (www.marketingpower.com)

Association for Integrated Marketing (www.pmalink.org)

Direct Marketing Association (www.the-dma.org)

International Customer Service Association (www.icsatoday.com)

Kauffman Foundation (www.kauffman.org)

National Association of Sales Professionals, 800–489–3435
(www.nasp.com)

Product Development and Management Association (www. pdma.org)

Sales and Marketing Executives International (www.smei.org)

U.S. Patent and Trademark Office (www.uspto.gov)
(http://patft.uspto.gov)

Chapter 2: Accounting and Finance

American Institute of Certified Public Accountants (www. aicpa.com)

Active Captive Management (risk management) (www.activecaptive.com)

Association for Financial Professionals (www.afponline.org)

Financial Executives International (www.financialexecutives.org)

Institute of Finance & Banking (www.ibf.org.sg/)

Risk & Insurance Management Society Inc. (www.rims.org)

Virtual Financial Library (www.fisher.osu.edu/fin/overview.htm)

Chapter 3: Human Resources and Operations Management

American National Standards Institute (www.ansi.org)

American Society for Quality (www.asq.org)

American Society for Training & Development (www.astd.org)

Association for Operations Management (www.apics.org)

Council of Supply Chain Management Professionals (www. cscmp.org)

Global Business Council (www.imaps.org/gbc/index.htm/)

International Quality & Productivity Center (www.iqpc.com)

International Society of Logistics (www.sole.org)

International Warehouse Logistics Association (www.iwla.com)

Outsourcing Center (www.outsourcing-center.com)

Outsourcing Institute (www.outsourcing.com)

Society for Human Resource Management (www.shrm.org)

Chapter 4: Statistics

American Statistical Association (www.amstat.org)

Chapter 5: Economics

The Dismal Scientist (www.economy.com/dismal/)

The Financial Times (www.ft.com)

South China Morning Post (www.scmp.com)

Chapter 6: Technology Management

Association of Information Technology Professionals (www. aitp.org)

Bitpipe (www.bitpipe.com)

E-Commerce Guide (www.ecommerce-guide.com)

Electronic Frontier Foundation (www.eff.org)

Information Technology Association of America (www.itaa.org)

Omicron (www.omicron.com)

Society for Information Management (www.simnet.org)

Chapter 7: Business Policy and Ethics

Business Ethics from an Islamic Perspective (http://www.islamist.org/
images/ethicshm.pdf)

Cornell University Law School Legal Information Institute
(www.law.cornell.edu/topical.html)

Council for Ethical Leadership (www.businessethics.org)

CyberEthics (cyberethics.cbi.msstate.edu)

Ethics Resource Center (www.ethics.org)

Institute for Business & Professional Ethics (www.depaul. edu/ethics)

International Business Ethics Institute (www.business-ethics.org)

Josephson Institute of Ethics (www.josephsoninstitute.org)

Social Venture Network (www.svn.org)

The W. Maurice Young Centre for Applied Ethics (www.ethics. ubc.ca)

Chapter 8: Strategic Planning

Strategic Performance Institute (www.strategicplanning.com)

Epilogue: Reflection, Introspection, and Enlightenment

Aspen Institute (www.aspeninstitute.org)

Center for Creative Leadership (www.ccl.org)

Esalen Institute (www.esalen.org)

The NTL Institute (www.ntl.org)

Dr. Milo Sobel. *MBA in a Nutshell* (mbainanutshell.com)

Dr. Sobel can be contacted via iam@milosobel.com or drsobel@
optonline.net. His website is www.milosobel.com.

Postscript: Education and Career Pathing

America's Job Bank (www.jobbankinfo.org)

Business Women's Network (www.businesswomensnetwork.org)

Career.com (www.career.com)

CareerBuilder (www.careerbuilder.com)

CareerMosaic (www.careermosaic.com)

CareerPath (www.careerpath.com)

Contract Employee's Handbook (www.cehandbook.com)

Dice.com (www.dice.com)

Exec-U-Net (www.execunet.com)

Financial Job Network (www.fjn.com)

Future Step (www.futurestep.com)

HotJobs (www.hotjobs.yahoo.com)

Indeed.com (www.indeed.com)

Job Circle (www.jobcircle.com)

Jobs Online (www.jobsonline.com)

Just Tech Jobs (www.justtechjobs.com)

MBA Forums (www.mba.com)

Monster (www.monster.com)

NationJob (www.nationjob.com)

Professional & Technical Consultants Association (www.patca.org)

Top Jobs (www.topjobs.net)

APPENDIX 3:   ENDNOTES

Chapter 1: Marketing and Product Management

1. Nancy Yoshihara, "Chain Sets Itself Apart with an Old-Fashioned Service Policy," *Los Angeles Times*, September 30, 1984, part V. pp. 1, 17.

2. David H. Hargreaves, *Interpersonal Relations and Education* (London: Routledge & Kegan Paul, 1972).

3. Robert Fulghum, *All I Really Needed to Know I Learned in Kindergarten* (New York: Villard Books, 1988).

4. L. Berey and R. Pollay, "The Influencing Role of the Child in Family Decision Making," *Journal of Marketing Research*, vol. 5, February 1968, pp. 70–72.

5. Leon Festinger, *A Theory of Cognitive Dissonance* (Evanston, IL: Row Peterson, 1957).

6. U.S. Trademark Association, *U.S. Trademark Source* (New York: U.S. Trademark Association, 1992).

7. Courtesy: International Trademark Association.

8. Julie Monahan, "Identity Crisis," *Income Opportunities*, October 1996, p. 56.

9. M. William Krasilovsky, personal communication, February 1993.

10. Robert B. Downs, *Books That Changed the World* (New York: New American Library, 1983), p. 317.

11. David A. Aaker, *Developing Business Strategies* (New York: John Wiley and Sons, 1984).

12. "Why New Products Fly or Fail," *Your Company*, October/November 1997, p. 59.

13. Dylan McClain, "Duplicate Efforts," *New York Times*, November 30, 1998, p. C4.

14. Yumiko Ono, "Wobblers and Sidekicks," *Wall Street Journal*, September 8, 1998, p. B1.

15. David A. Aaker, *Pocket Guide to Media Terms and Media Math* (New York: Media Resources and Research, J. Walter Thompson USA, Spring 1984).

16. www.admedia.org/internet; www.doubleclick.net.

17. Gary Hennerberg, "17 Marketing Measurements," *Targeting Marketing*, October 1996, pp. 86–92.

Chapter 2: Accounting and Finance

1. *Source:* Microsoft.

2. *Source:* Banker's Trust.

3. Adapted from "The Acronymic A-List," *CFO*, October 1996, p. 46.

4. Arvind Singh, "Know When to Hold 'Em," *CFO*, November 1997, pp. 99–100.

5. All ratios except ROI are from Michael R. Tyran, *The Vest-Pocket Guide to Business Ratios* (Englewood Cliffs, NJ: Prentice Hall, 1992).

6. Roger Cohen, "The Creator of Time Warner, Steven J. Ross, Is Dead at 65," *New York Times*, December 21, 1992, pp. Dl and D12.

7. W. W. Cooper and Yuri Ijiri (eds.), *Kohler's Dictionary for Accountants* (Englewood Cliffs, NJ: Prentice Hall, 1983).

8. Kerry Hannon, "Going Public to the Public," *U.S. News and World Report*, June 17, 1996, p. 74.

9. "Heard on the Street," *New York Observer*, April 27, 1998.

10. Debra Sparks, "A $2.5 Trillion Market You Hardly Know," *BusinessWeek*, October 26, 1998, p. 124.

11. Interview with Fred Adler, *Inc.* magazine, June 1980.

Chapter 3: Human Resources and Operations Management

1. Lee G. Bolman and Terrence Deal, *Modern Approaches to Understanding and Managing Organizations* (San Francisco: Jossey-Bass, 1984).

2. Abraham Maslow, *Motivation and Personality*, 2nd ed. (New York: Harper & Row, 1970).

3. J. F. Evered, *Shirt-Sleeves Management* (New York: AMACOM, 1981).

4. Douglas McGregor, *The Human Side of Enterprise* (New York: McGraw-Hill, 1960).

5. Michael Miller, "80 Years Ago in Success," *Success*, March 1998, p. 12.

6. Bolman and Deal, *Modern Approaches to Understanding and Managing Organizations.*

7. Jean M. Kummerow, *Verifying Your Type Preferences* (Gainesville, FL: Center for Applications of Psychological Type, 1992).

8. Bolman and Deal, *Modern Approaches to Understanding and Managing Organizations.*

9. Bruce Tulgan and Jean Casison, "Ten Ways to Make Your Feedback More Frequent" and "Giving Feedback to Your Employees," *People Performance*, November 1998, pp. 24 and 27.

10. W. Edwards Deming, *Quality, Productivity, and Competitive Position* (Cambridge, MA: Massachusetts Institute of Technology, 1982).

11. Philip Crosby, *Let's Talk Quality* (New York: McGraw-Hill, 1989).

12. Joseph M. Juran, *Juran's Quality Control Handbook*, 4th ed. (New York: McGraw-Hill, 1988).

13. Adapted from Joseph Conlin, "Secrets of Their Success," *Successful Meetings*, December 1990, p. 44.

14. Tom Peters, *Liberation Management* (New York: Alfred A. Knopf, 1992).

15. Richard Ensman, Jr., "Morale Audit," *Incentive*, October 1998, pp. 177–178.

16. E. Hunninger (ed.), *The Arthur Young Manager's Handbook* (New York: Crown, 1986).

17. "3M Meeting Effectiveness Study," *Corporate Travel Quarterly*, Fall 1990, and "Survey Reveals Profile of the Typical Meeting," *Meeting Management News*, vol. 1, no. 5.

18. E. Hunninger, op. cit.

19. Milo Sobel, *The Secrets of Professionalism* (New York: The Coronet Consulting Group, 1986).

20. Ibid.

21. David Ogilvy, *Ogilvy on Advertising* (London: Prion Publications, 1983, p. 50).

22. Leonard Nadler, *Designing Training Programs* (Reading, MA: Addison-Wesley, 1982).

23. Compiled by Elizabeth A. McDaniel, assistant vice president and professor for academic affairs and professor of special education, University of Hartford. Most of these suggestions are excerpted and paraphrased from a book by Raymond J. Wlodkowski, *Enhancing Adult Motivation to Learn* (San Francisco: Jossey-Bass, 1985).

24. Hamdy A. Taha, *Operations Research* (New York: Macmillan, 1976).

25. Ibid.

26. Richard Saltus, "Waiting—Scientists Have a Name for It: Queue Management," *Orange County Register*, November 1, 1992.

27. Malcolm W. Browne, "Coin-Tossing Computers Found to Show Subtle Bias," *New York Times*, January 12, 1993.

28. Shigeo Shingo, *A Study of the Toyota Production System* (Cambridge, MA: Productivity Press, 1989).
29. Christine Ammer and Dean S. Ammer, *Dictionary of Business and Economics* (New York: The Free Press, 1984).

Chapter 4: Statistics

1. Christine Ammer and Dean S. Ammer, *Dictionary of Business and Economics* (New York: The Free Press, 1984).
2. Robert Parket, personal correspondence, 1993.
3. Robert Parket, *Statistics for Business Decision Making* (New York: Random House, 1974).
4. Jae K. Shim, et. al., *Vest-Pocket MBA*, (Englewood Cliffs, NJ: Prentice Hall, 1986), p.223.
5. George J. Brabb, *Introduction to Quantitative Management* (New York: Holt, Rinehart and Winston, 1968).
6. Hamdy A. Taha, *Operations Research: An Introduction* (New York: Macmillan, 1976).

Chapter 5: Economics

1. Susan Lee, *Susan Lee's ABZs of Economics* (New York: Pocket Books, 1987).
2. Stephen D. Casler, *Introduction to Economics* (New York: Harper-Collins, 1992).
3. William J. Baumol and Alan S. Blinder, *Economics: Principles and Policy* (New York: Harcourt Brace Jovanovich, 1991).
4. Gary Becker, "Making the World Safe," *BusinessWeek*, February 23, 1998, p. 20.
5. Susan Lee, op. cit.
6. Clem Sunter, "What It Takes to Be World-Class," *F&T Weekly*, October 31, 1997, p. 71.

Chapter 6: Technology Management

1. Bob Metcalfe, "There Oughta Be a Law," *New York Times*, July 15, 1996.
2. Ibid.
3. Rachel McLaughlin, "Database Marketing," *Target Marketing*, November 1998.
4. Robert E. Calem, "Look, No Wires! But the Pages Fly!" *New York Times*, November 8, 1992.
5. Duncan Anderson, "Astonishing Future" (review), *Success*, March 1997, p. 66.
6. J. A. Cooke, Store Front: "Fit to Be Tried and True," *New York Times Magazine*, April 6, 1997.
7. Steve Ditlea, "Virtual Reality Virtually Here," *Hemispheres*, October 1992.
8. Rod F. Monger, *Mastering Technology* (New York: The Free Press, 1988).
9. Calvin Pava, *Managing New Office Technology: An Organizational Strategy* (New York: The Free Press, 1983).
10. Gary Anthes, "Persuasive Technologies," *Computerworld*, June 28, 1999, p. 76.

Chapter 7: Business Policy and Ethics

1. Robert C. Solomon and Kristine Hanson, *It's Good Business* (New York: Atheneum, 1985).
2. Thomas M. Garrett and Richard J. Klonoski, *Business Ethics*, 2nd ed. (Englewood Cliffs, NJ: Prentice Hall, 1986).
3. Stanley Fish, "A Question of Ethics," *My Business Success*, September 1997, p. 37.
4. "Manager's Toolbox," *World Executive Digest* (originally *Management Quality & Competitiveness*), May 1998, p. 10.

5. Thomas M. Garrett and Richard J. Klonoski, op. cit.

6. Thomas M. Garrett and Richard J. Klonoski, op. cit.

7. Thomas M. Garrett and Richard J. Klonoski, op. cit.

8. Donald A. Wiesner and Nicholas A. Glaskowsky, *Schaum's Outline of Theory and Problems of Business Law* (New York: McGraw-Hill, 1985).

9. Tamar Lewin, "An Alternative to Litigation," *New York Times*, March 4, 1986.

Chapter 8: Strategic Planning

1. David J. Rogers, *Waging Business Warfare* (New York: Kensington, 1987).

2. John McDonald, *Strategy in Poker, Business & War* (New York: W. W. Norton and Company, 1989).

3. Format suggested by I. Robert Parket.

4. Jim Collins, "What Comes Next," *Inc.*, October 1997, p. 42.

5. Ibid., pp. 45–46.

6. Ibid.

7. Melanie Berger, "Imagine: No More Competition," *Sales & Marketing Management*, June 1996, p. 90.

8. Keith Bradsher, "Capacity Glut Likely to Spur More Auto Mergers," *New York Times*, November 14, 1998, p. C1.

9. Seth Schiesel, "AT&T Buying IBM Network," *New York Times*, December 9, 1998, p. C1.

10. Robert Talbot-Stern, "Core Competency v. Self Sufficiency," *Company Director*, February 1999, pp. 38–39.

11. Stan Davis and Bill Davidson, *2020 Vision* (New York: Simon & Schuster, 1991).

12. Christopher M. Byron, *The Fanciest Dive* (New York: W. W. Norton and Company, 1983)

13. Andrew E. Serwer, "Patagonia CEO Reels Company In," *Fortune*, December 14, 1992.

14. Robert Kaplan and David Norton, *The Balanced Scoreboard* (Cambridge, MA: Harvard Business School Press, 1998.)

15. Hamdy A. Taha, *Operations Research* (New York: Macmillan, 1976).

16. Stephen D. Casler, *Introduction to Economics* (New York: Harper-Collins, 1992).

17. Taha, *Operations Research*.

APPENDIX 4: BIBLIOGRAPHY

Aaker, David. *Developing Business Strategies*. New York: John Wiley and Sons, 1984.

Ammer, Christine, and Dean S. Ammer. *Dictionary of Business and Economics*. New York: The Free Press, 1984.

Baumol, William J., and Alan S. Blinder. *Economics: Principles and Policy*. New York: Harcourt Brace Jovanovich, 1991.

Berey, L., and R. Pollay. "The Influencing Role of the Child in Family Decision Making," *Journal of Marketing Research*, February 1986.

Bolman, L. G., and T. E. Deal. *Modern Approaches to Understanding and Managing Organizations*. San Francisco: Jossey-Bass, 1984.

Brabb, George J. *Introduction to Quantitative Management*. New York: Holt Rinehart and Winston, 1968.

Browne, Malcolm W. "Coin-Tossing Computers Found to Show Subtle Bias," *New York Times*, January 12, 1993.

Byron, Christopher M. *The Fanciest Dive*. New York: W. W. Norton and Company, 1983.

Carbonneau, Thomas. *Alternative Dispute Resolution*. Urbana: University of Illinois Press, 1985.

Casler, Stephen D. *Introduction to Economics*. New York: Harper-Collins, 1992.

Cook, Thomas M., and Robert A. Russell. *Introduction to Management Science*. Englewood Cliffs, NJ: Prentice Hall, 1977.

Cooper, W. W., and Yuri Ijiri (eds.). *Kohler's Dictionary for Accountants*. Englewood Cliffs, NJ: Prentice Hall, 1983.

Crosby, Philip. *Let's Talk Quality*. New York: McGraw-Hill, 1989.

Davis, Stan, and Bill Davidson. *2020 Vision*. New York: Simon & Schuster, 1991.

Deming, W. Edwards. *Quality, Productivity, and Competitive Position*. Cambridge, MA: Massachusetts Institute of Technology, 1982.

Downs, Robert B. *Books That Changed the World*. New York: New American Library, 1983.

Evered, James F. *Shirt-Sleeves Management*. New York: AMACOM, 1981.

Festinger, Leon. *A Theory of Cognitive Dissonance*. Evanston, IL: Row Peterson, 1957.

Fulghum, Robert. *All I Really Need to Know I Learned in Kindergarten*. New York: Villard Books, 1988.

Garrett, Thomas M., and Richard J. Klonoski. *Business Ethics*, 2nd ed. Englewood Cliffs, NJ: Prentice Hall, 1986.

Hunninger, E. (ed.). *The Arthur Young Manager's Handbook*. New York: Crown, 1986.

Juran, Joseph M. *Juran's Quality Control Handbook*, 4th ed. New York: McGraw-Hill, 1988.

Kotler, Philip. *Marketing Management*. Englewood Cliffs, NJ: Prentice Hall, 1984.

Lawrence, P., and J. Lorsch. *Organization and Environment*. Cambridge, MA: Harvard Business School, Division of Research, 1967.

Lee, Susan. *Susan Lee's ABZs of Economics*. New York: Pocket Books, 1987.

Maslow, Abraham. *Motivation and Personality*, 2nd ed. New York: Harper & Row, 1970.

McDonald, John. *Strategy in Poker, Business & War*. New York: W. W. Norton and Company, 1989.

McGregor, D. *The Human Side of Enterprise*. New York: McGraw-Hill, 1960.

Monger, Rod F. *Mastering Technology*. New York: The Free Press, 1988.

Nadler, Leonard. *Designing Training Programs*. Reading, MA: Addison-Wesley, 1982.

Pava, Calvin. *Managing New Office Technology: An Organizational Strategy*. New York: The Free Press, 1983.

Peters, Tom. *Liberation Management*. New York: Alfred A. Knopf, 1992.

Rogers, David J. *Waging Business Warfare*. New York: Kensington, 1987.

Saltus, Richard. "Waiting—Scientists Have a Name for It: Queue Management," *Orange County Register*, November 1, 1992.

Serwer, Andrew. "Patagonia CEO Reels Company In," *Fortune*, December 14, 1992.

Shingo, Shideo. *A Study of the Toyota Production System*. Cambridge, MA: Productivity Press, 1989.

Sobel, Milo. *The Secrets of Professionalism*. New York: The Coronet Consulting Group, 1986.

Stewart, J. D. *The Power of People Skills*. New York: John Wiley and Sons, 1986.

Taha, Hamdy A. *Operations Research*. New York: Macmillan, 1976.

Tyran, Michael R. *The Vest-Pocket Guide to Business Ratios*. Englewood Cliffs, NJ: Prentice Hall, 1992.

Wiesner, D., and N. Glaskowsky. *Schaum's Outline of Theory and Problems of Business Law*. New York: McGraw-Hill, 1985.

INDEX

ABOUT THE AUTHOR

Dr. Milo Sobel earned his doctorate from Columbia University and his MBA from the City University of New York. He has served as manager of training for Citibank and is a member of the Academy of Management. He lives in Fairfield County, Connecticut.